MIRACLES, FAITH,
AND UNANSWERED PRAYER

To order additional copies of *Miracles, Faith, and Unanswered Prayer*, by Richard Jensen, call 1-800-765-6955.

Visit us at www.reviewandherald.com for information on other Review and Herald® products.

MIRACLES, FAITH, AND UNANSWERED PRAYER

RICHARD JENSEN

REVIEW AND HERALD® PUBLISHING ASSOCIATION

Since 1861 | www.reviewandherald.com

Review and Herald® titles may be purchased in bulk for educational, business, fund-raising, or sales promotional use. For information, e-mail SpecialMarkets@reviewandherald.com.

Review and Herald® Publishing publishes biblically based materials for spiritual, physical, and mental growth and Christian discipleship.

The author assumes full responsibility for the accuracy of all facts and quotations as cited in this book.

Scripture quotations marked NASB are from the *New American Standard Bible,* copyright © 1960, 1962, 1963, 1968, 1971, 1972, 1973, 1975, 1977, 1994 by The Lockman Foundation. Used by permission.

Texts credited to NIV are from the *Holy Bible, New International Version.* Copyright © 1973, 1978, 1984, International Bible Society. Used by permission of Zondervan Bible Publishers.

Texts credited to NKJV are from the New King James Version. Copyright © 1979, 1980, 1982 by Thomas Nelson, Inc. Used by permission. All rights reserved.

This book was
Edited by Gerald Wheeler
Copyedited by James Cavil
Designed by Trent Truman
Cover photo by: © jamirae/istockphoto.com
Typeset: Bembo 12/15

PRINTED IN U.S.A.
12 11 10 09 08   5 4 3 2 1

Library of Congress Cataloging-in-Publication Data
Jensen, Richard, 1959-
   Miracles, faith, and unanswered prayer: Is your faith built on a miracle-dispensing God? / Richard Jensen.
       p. cm.
   1. Miracles. 2. Prayer—Christianity. 3. Storytelling—Religious aspects—Christianity. I. Title.
BT97.3.J46 2008
231.7'3—dc22
                            2007022720
ISBN 978-0-8280-2015-2

ACKNOWLEDGMENTS

My wife, Dana, has been profoundly supportive and encouraging throughout this project. She has been amazingly patient with me as I have devoted many late nights (and early mornings) to this manuscript. Even though she has read and heard version after version, she has always had fresh insights and wisdom to offer. I will always remember with profound affection and joy seeing her poring over yet another draft, writing notes in the columns, catching yet another round of typos, and often massaging my way of wording things into something more graceful and appealing. She is my soul mate, my prayer partner, my fellow warrior, and the delight and love of my life!

One of my former students, Dustin Wolfsen, read both an early and a later draft and produced an article-length batch of superb insights and suggestions of his own. His careful and thoughtful reading and suggestions have greatly improved the current version, although, as is the case with all the people I acknowledge here, any responsibility for remaining problems must be mine rather than his.

Stan and Ellen Schrader read various drafts, and they both shared many, many comments and suggestions that improved the readability of this book. I am sometimes amazingly unaware of the multiple ways that people can interpret something. Ellen in particular called my attention to numerous passages that had unintended implications and alternative readings, and she also suggested smoother and cleaner ways of wording things in some places. Both Stan's and Ellen's efforts have strengthened the book.

Others I have subjected to earlier forms of this manuscript, and who have improved the resulting book by their insights and suggestions, include (in no particular order): Kate and Roger Gotch, Sylvia and Jose Acosta, and Jason Schrader.

A number of reviewers on the acquisitions committee at the Review and Herald Publishing Association offered comments that helped to sharpen and direct the final version I submitted for publication. I am profoundly grateful for the comments of one reviewer in particular (he knows who he is), and his carefully thought out comments have very much improved this final version.

As always, Jeannette Johnson at the Review and Herald is a joy to work with. Her ever-ready expressions of enthusiasm and encouragement are personally uplifting to me, as I'm sure they are to all authors. A project with Jeannette is always much better than one without her.

The final responsibility for this book rests with me, and I have made the final decision to accept or reject the suggestions of my readers; but it is indeed the product of the efforts of many people. I thank you all for your friendship, support, and efforts. How great heaven will be, considering that it can be this good working together on this dismal planet!

CONTENTS

Chapter 1

A GENUINE HEALING

When I was about 9 years old, I attended a family gathering at my grandma's house. My cousins, my sisters, and I were all playing a game of tag outside in the front yard. All of us were racing around and laughing like typically energetic kids. My sister Cathy, who was about 6 years old at the time, was running, and one cousin who was "it" chased after her. Hurtling along with her mouth open, laughing and looking back over her shoulder, she headed straight toward one of the yucca plants in the yard. Just as she turned to see where she was going she plowed face-first into the long, stiff, pointed leaves of the yucca plant. One of them stabbed completely through her tongue and pierced the back of her throat. Cathy stood screaming, impaled on the spine, until my cousin, Eddie, and I ran to her and pulled her backward to free her.

Immediately her mouth began gushing blood. We leaned her forward a bit and helped her inside. Cathy sobbed wildly with her tongue extended from her mouth, and it appeared to me as if the front half of her tongue had been almost completely severed from the back half. The amount of blood pouring from Cathy's mouth was appalling as she staggered into the front room, and it dripped all over the carpet. The entire family was gathered playing pinochle, drinking, and smoking. My mom, who was the solitary Christian in the family, rose from the table in a panic and darted to Cathy. Instantly the entire family gathered around.

A quick examination revealed that only the edges of her tongue still held the front and back halves of her tongue together. The yucca leaf had sliced it almost in two. Even leaning forward as she was, Cathy was swallowing some blood because the wound in the back of her throat had stimulated her swallow reflex.

Although her eyes were wide with fear, Mom somehow maintained a calm and soothing exterior as she helped Cathy into the bathroom. There she ran a washcloth under cold water and then pressed it against my sister's tongue to try to stop the bleeding. Mom realized that we would have to take the girl to the hospital, where the emergency room physicians would undoubtedly have to perform an extremely traumatic procedure. But the most important thing for the moment was to calm the girl down and get the bleeding slowed or stopped. The rest of the family gathered in the hallway around the bathroom, offered words of advice, and talked among themselves in horrified tones. Still pressing the washcloth firmly on Cathy's tongue, and in front of the whole family, Mom began to pray for her.

Mom's prayer was quite simple. She just asked God to be with Cathy, to help her, and to give her what she would need to get through the trying time that was ahead. After the prayer Mom gently pulled the washcloth away from Cathy's tongue to see if the bleeding had slowed at all.

The wound was completely gone. We saw no evidence that any damage had ever occurred. Brightening, Cathy said, "It doesn't hurt anymore."

The entire family was flabbergasted. Some of my aunts dropped to their knees, and everybody was speechless. Most of them had caught at least glimpses of the horrific damage to Cathy's tongue, and that it was now healed in answer to prayer was beyond their capacity to immediately grasp.

Standing next to Cathy when Mom pulled the washcloth away, I vividly remember the wave of awe that washed over me. I think that everybody in the house had an overwhelming sense for that brief time that we were standing on holy ground.

To be certain that Cathy was fully checked out, particularly since she had swallowed and lost so much blood, Mom took her to the emergency room. When they returned, Mom reported that the doctor who had examined Cathy had said that he saw no evidence that my sister's tongue had ever sustained the sort of damage that Mom had described to him. He had, however, found a small, round scar in the back of Cathy's throat that he had said looked to him like an "old piercing injury" consistent with the story. (Cathy retained that small scar into adulthood.) Apart from that small scar, the doctor had said that he could find nothing wrong with her.

Because the family was engaged in cleaning up the many and large bloodstains on the carpet, the doctor's report was powerful confirmation that God had indeed drawn very near to our family.

The First Grand Lie

Almost from the beginning of human history people have believed a lie. Satan began his involvement with the human race by telling us a lie, and we have believed it ever since. The lie had two intimately related parts: (1) God is withholding some great good from us, and (2) what He says (His word) isn't really true. Put these parts together, and the lie states that God withholds the truth from us *because* He withholds (at least some of) the good from us. Thus Satan asserts that he is the great liberator because he alone wants us to have *all* the good, even that good that God supposedly withholds. Since the first time that humanity began believing Satan's grand lie, the human race has brought upon itself all the woeful results of sin and bondage that are the necessary implications of accepting the satanic lie. But God seeks to build in us faith so that we will not believe such a deception. We are to "know the truth," and the truth is to "set us free" (see John 8:32).

But genuine faith is a very hard thing to come by, and many counterfeits exist. Faith is a function of believing, but I cannot believe just any old thing. I cannot, for example, right here and now just make *myself* believe that I have a million dollars in my pocket.

Faith has something to do with *evidence*. Yet what often passes for "faith" is nothing more than a gullible worldview. So the problem of getting and having *genuine* faith is at its core a problem of *properly* obtaining and evaluating evidence. We need to get very clear about the nature of the proper evidence that can ground genuine faith.

Satan's first grand lie has proved so successful through the ages that he has never abandoned it. Indeed, it acts as the foundation of his most subtle and creative attacks and temptations even today. To sustain the lie, he employs a vast array of devices designed to make it appear that the evidence is on the side of his lie. These devices range from the enticing "goodness" that appears embedded in temptations, to the crimes he perpetrates or induces us to commit, the long-term effects of which he then blames on a "bad" or "uncaring" or "unjust" God. To those disinclined to believe in God at all (or those entertaining doubts), Satan's lie takes the form of contrasting the "goodness" in his temptations against the emptiness of the uncaring, disinterested void, and thus he encourages secularists to invent their own ethics and seek for the "goodness" that they can find in the "now." In all cases, however, Satan continues his age-old strategy of substituting what God called good and true with his own versions. Thus Satan attacks in a multitude of ways, all based upon the first grand lie and all designed to thwart God's plan to develop faith in us.

Miracles and Their Stories

To thwart these attacks, we "believers" crave ongoing evidence that God is not just "real" but that He is really *near* to us, that He intervenes in our lives, that He *does* have our best good at heart, and that His word *is* true. The drive to find ongoing evidence of God's nearness and goodness is so strong that many of us unconsciously scour our everyday experiences for examples of it. When we detect possible incidents, we then recount them to others, because the stories are faith-building for both the teller and the listener. Usually our evidences of God's interaction with us are small and not subject to close examination: an impression we had, something that turned out right, or an event that seemed almost designed by providence for our personal benefit. Such things provide the everyday evidences of God's interactions in our lives. Occasionally, though, we experience or hear about an event that is more dramatic, one that we call a miracle. A good miracle story trumps a bushelful of doubt, so it is almost a truism that miracle stories build faith. They are the *big guns* that we wheel out to blast holes in Satan's grand lie.

But miracle stories have problems. For example, are the stories we typically recount really of miracles? I mean, in the strong sense of the word? What is a genuine miracle, anyway?

The philosopher and intellectual in me[1] often cringes (mildly) during church testimony sessions as I hear the familiar litany of "miracle stories" supposed to "build our faith." They include the "lost-and-found keys (document, pet, etc.—you fill in the blank)," the "saved from an accident because of a delay in plans," the "saved from an accident because of speeded up plans," the "impression that gave me a witnessing opportunity," etc. The philosopher in me (cringing a little along with the other closet intellectuals in the groups) says (internally), *Yes, I have no doubt that such an experience seemed very faith-building for you, but numerous entirely naturalistic explanations can also account for the phenomenon you just described. I want to hear a story without any apparent naturalistic explanations. I want to hear a story from a truly credible person about an event in which the best explanation[2] is that God must have intervened.*

The philosopher in me is asking a lot, I know, and, unfortunately such stories are few and far between. The teller has to be credible, and actually that's not an easy bar to get over. And the incident has to be a fairly dramatic intervention in which a supernatural explanation is obviously the best fit.

The Christian that I am, however, recognizes that God's everyday active involvements are usually not dramatically supernatural enough to qualify as clear-cut miracles, although our awareness of even such "everyday" involvements is crucial to our spiritual well-being. So this book is certainly not an exercise in "miracle one-upmanship" or a snide "My miracles are better than your miracles." I am not denigrating the less-dramatic experiences of God's involvement, as, indeed, the most profound experiences I have had with God have been very private and internal and thus not suitable for public scrutiny as miracles. Despite the miracle stories I tell in this book, the most amazing interventions in my life are the ones in which God changes me *inside,* alters my perspectives, transforms my heart, and enables me to see a situation differently and thereby respond to it in harmony with His perspectives. Such experiences would certainly not pass muster when scrutinized by an external "best account" or "best evidence"-seeking philosopher or scientist. But when God changes me inside, subjectively I know that there is nothing in me that could account for the transformation, and I know that the result is God working in me.

But the philosopher in me—in us—must be satisfied too if our "faith" is to be something more than mere gullibility. The philosophical side of all of us, for we are all acting philosophers,[3] whether we have received training in it or not, yearns for dramatic and objectively compelling evidence that the event that we have just experienced could have resulted *only* from God's supernatural intervention. We pray and cry out for Him to heal us and our loved ones from cancer, feed the 5,000 needy people that we know about, and fulfill a myriad of other interventions that we are convinced that we must have. The affirmative answers to such prayers would not only satisfy those immediate needs, but somehow vindicate and validate our relationship with God. And as Christians we deeply crave confirmation of God's reality and His active involvement in our lives. Both the subjective evidences and the more objective ones are important to us.

The very craving for objective evidence, however, can cause us to "lower the bar," so to speak, so that events with easy and apparent naturalistic explanations qualify in our own minds as *miracles.* Then we become credulous, gullible, and, as I will discuss, a host of new problems arise.

So I ask again: What is a genuine miracle, anyway? What does truly objective evidence consist of?

I have already alluded to what I mean by the term, but now I will make it clear. By a genuine miracle I mean an event that either defies a naturalistic explanation or one for which a naturalistic interpretation would be strained and clearly not the best one. An example is Jesus' walking on water. Sure, we could conjure up a naturalistic explanation, given enough imagination. Unknown to us, perhaps, Jesus actually was wearing small pontoons on His feet that kept Him afloat just enough so that His feet appeared to rest on the surface of the water (or the recent theory that made national news, that the Sea of Galilee partially froze over so that Jesus was actually floating on a small iceberg). But the story, taken just as it is told, begs for a supernaturalistic explanation. And given its context, the divinity of Jesus is certainly a reasonable interpretation.

Blind people receiving their sight, lame individuals raised up to walk, the dead resurrected—a sister's cleaved tongue instantly healed—these are genuine miracles, and we see precious few of them today. Even the couple cases of "cures" of cancer I have heard of ended up, in both cases, with fairly rapid "reappearance" of the disease soon after the requisite testimony sessions. Perhaps the scans supporting the pronouncement of the cure were in error, or perhaps charts got mixed up at the hospitals. I don't know how the people were declared "cured," but their cancer returned pretty quickly after the testimony sessions, and it seems very odd to me that God would genuinely remove cancer from people so that they can testify for Him, and then let it kill them within months of that "miracle." God's ways are often inscrutable, but it is difficult for me to accept as a miracle a "cure" for something that shortly thereafter *kills the person!* I tend to think that a person freed of cancer by divine intervention should ultimately die of some utterly unrelated cause, or perhaps live forever.

So what is the crisis of faith that most threatens Christians? What do miracle stories and other evidences of God's involvement shield us from?

If we look into the deepest pit inside us, honestly confronting our most withering doubts, we find that we are actually, really, and profoundly scared. We are terrified that, in fact, God does not exist . . . or that He is aloof, we are insignificant to Him, and He has no concern for us as individuals. Perhaps we worry that we have distanced ourselves from Him, and that He cannot or will not bridge the gap we have created. But our deepest fear is fundamentally the same: we shrink from the idea that we are really and terribly alone and that we are immersed in a meaningless void.[4]

Another way of expressing this point is that our deepest, darkest terror is that our religion is all a charade, that, as the existentialists[5] tell us, religion really is a crutch to keep us relatively sane and nonsuicidal in a universe that cares nothing for us and provides no objective values to guide us. In the face of such a fear, a good miracle story will build up our faith again. So we find ourselves settling for the many personal testimonies that pass for miracles, and we accept as true the secondhand or thirdhand accounts that we sense have become embellished with repeated retelling. The genuine miracle stories, ones that will stand up to some serious scrutiny, are actually few and far between.

Another problem with miracle stories surfaces as soon as we are willing to think critically about them. Even assuming that they might be true, we must then question why God seems to utterly ignore the impassioned pleas of some while He lavishes others with seemingly constant affirmative answers to their most trivial requests. We assume that God would not play favorites, so why does He not provide a miracle to me when I really must have one? Where is His intervention when I believe that I most need it? What good for *my* faith are stories that portray an active God, yet when I require His help most I find myself alone?

In this book I tell a number of miracle stories, some more dramatic and compelling than others, but all from my own firsthand personal observation and experience. All of them are true and un-embellished, and all of them either defy naturalistic explanation (as does my sister's healing) or strain such explanations, thus favoring the obvious and immediately apparent (to the unbiased mind) response "That was a miracle."[6] I will use these stories to explore some of the background and "subtext" of God's dealings with us, and I hope that they will not only be genuinely and *legitimately* faith-building for you (although not in the way you probably initially think), but that the surrounding discussion might better help you understand why God acts toward you as He does.

However, the even bigger issue is this: I am convinced that God's primary goal with each of us is to develop in us a deep, abiding, genuine, and mature faith. Such a faith is God's ultimate weapon against the grand lie of Satan. However, the faith-building relationship with Him is a process, and we must emphasize the word "building." Faith in a new believer starts out small and simple—immature, if you will. That faith does not yet permeate every facet and experience of life, and the new believer still doubts and questions God in many circumstances. But as faith grows, the Lord not only makes it deeper and wiser, but infuses it into increasing aspects of the believer's life—faith shapes more and more fundamental perspectives of the individual's existence. In time, and with experience, a more mature faith develops. A faith able to withstand stronger and more varied assaults from the enemy gradually emerges. Ultimately God wants each of us to know Him so well, to have such utter and total faith in Him, that we can respond to any situation as did Jesus: "The prince of this world cometh and hath nothing in me" (John 14:30). Only then will our victory over the first grand lie be complete.

I choose my miracle stories to tell, rather than others that I have heard (and believe), because I know firsthand that mine are true. They are not secondhand or thirdhand embellished tales. I was there. I saw and experienced the events, and they burned indelible impressions upon me. I have experienced so many of

God's interventions during the years of my life that I have found myself forced to think about the nature of genuine miracles and the principles of God's involvement in our lives.

Most important, I have spent years studying and contemplating the nature of mature faith and the role that God's interventions play in its development. In this book I do indeed tell you some genuine miracle stories. Much more than that, however, I discuss the principles of genuine faith. So I pray that these stories will indeed teach you about faith, but far more important, that they, and the surrounding discussion, will also develop your understanding, which is, ultimately, the most fundamental and unassailable basis for all faith.

Some Limitations of Miracle Stories

After the healing of Cathy's tongue, my extended family for a brief time stopped looking down on my immediate family's Christianity. My grandma and a couple of the aunts even attended church with us for a while. Sadly, however, the uncles remained unmoved, and my grandma and the aunts soon found more important things to occupy their time than going to church. The old lifestyle, never fully abandoned, swallowed up the impressions made that day, and those who were present that miracle day as non-Christians have either died as non-Christians or live today as non-Christians. Tragically, the profound impression that God sought to make on my family that day has, except for me, apparently vanished.

My mom died a few years ago, and as I write, Cathy herself only vaguely remembers the incident, so I alone retain the force of conviction it aroused. God heard Mom's prayer and answered it in most dramatic fashion to try to reach a lost family. Yet even the force of such an obvious and provocative miracle like this cannot reach those who choose to harden their hearts in sin and skepticism.

This leads to the first significant point about miracles as faith-building events. They will confirm the faith of those already open to believe, but will not sway the skeptical.

After Christ's first miracle, turning the water to wine, the Bible records that "his disciples believed on him" (John 2:11). It was the very beginning of His making good on His promise to Nathanael: "Thou shalt see greater things than these" (John 1:50). I can well imagine the smile on Jesus' face as He said those words to His new follower. His disciples were babes in the faith at that early point. Although convicted that He was special, and eventually that He was the Son of God, the Messiah, they still clung to each supernatural evidence of His power. Such evidences, as they saw the power of His word, gradually built their faith in Him.

For the disciples and a relatively few others, the miracles of Jesus strengthened the inclination to believe that they already had. I will discuss in a moment the initial formation of faith. But we see again and again in the story of Jesus that His miracles could not produce faith in those disinclined to believe in Him for other reasons. The leaders and the crowds that surrounded Him had, as Jesus often put it, hardened hearts. Hear His indictment of them: "You do not have His word abiding in you, for you do not believe Him whom He sent. You search the Scriptures because you think that in them you have eternal life; it is these that bear witness of Me" (John 5:38, 39, NASB).

The Word of God testified of Jesus, and He says that its witness alone should have been sufficient for the leaders and the crowd to believe in Him. But instead of believing in the Word of God, the leaders and people continually demanded more signs and wonders: "Unless you people see signs and wonders, you simply will not believe" (John 4:48, NASB). Then, as we see, even additional signs and wonders failed to produce faith. The leaders acknowledged the signs, but still saw them only as a threat to their entrenched perspectives: "What are we doing? For this man is performing many signs. If we let Him go on like this, all men will believe in Him, and the Romans will come and take away both our place and our nation" (John 11:47, 48, NASB). Jesus' miracles were the very basis of the leaders deciding to murder Him!

Worse, it turned out that the leaders were wrong about the effect that Jesus' miracles would have on the crowds. All His mighty miracles were insufficient to convince either the leaders or the crowds of the true nature and purpose of His mission to earth: " 'I showed you many good works from the Father; for which of them are you stoning Me?' . . . 'If I do not do the works of My Father, do not believe Me; but if I do them, though you do not believe Me, believe the works, so that you may know and understand that the Father is in Me, and I in the Father.' Therefore they were seeking again to seize Him, and He eluded their grasp" (John 10:32-38, NASB).

Contrast the desire for more signs and wonders with the basis of faith demonstrated by the Samaritans in John 4. After Jesus had spoken to the woman at the well, she went and told all her friends and neighbors of her conversation with Jesus. The only "sign" He performed during His stay in Samaria was that He initially told her certain things about her life that He had no normal way of knowing. Beyond that, there were no miracles. Yet notice the basis for the Samaritans' belief in Jesus: "So when the Samaritans came to Jesus, they were asking Him to stay with them; and He stayed there two days. Many more believed because of His word; and they were saying to the woman, 'It is no longer because of what you said that we believe, for we have heard for ourselves and know that this One is indeed the Savior of the world' " (John 4:40-42, NASB).

Some of the people "beyond the Jordan" that we read about in John 10:41, 42 (just after the leaders and crowd had tried to stone Jesus) echoed similar belief: "Many came to Him and were saying, 'While John performed no sign, yet everything John said about this man was true.' Many believed in Him there" (NASB).

Both the Samaritans who heard the word of Jesus and the group "beyond the Jordan" who heard the word of John on that basis alone—the Word of God—became convinced that Jesus was their Savior.

When we contrast the role of miracles and the role of the Word of God, I believe that the most profound principle of faith is this:

"So faith comes from hearing, and hearing by the word of Christ" (Rom. 10:17, NASB). This principle is so significant and fundamental that I will refer to it again and again and develop its implications throughout this book. Genuine, unassailable, mature faith has no need of "signs and wonders." It is the abiding belief in God's Word alone: it has in itself the very power to perform that which it says.[7] I will have much more to say about this as we proceed, because this principle, properly understood, is the key to the sort of faith that God wants to develop and mature in each of us.

You would think that in the face of the dramatic way that God healed Cathy my entire extended family would have become converted. But sadly, their cases mirror the experience of most of the people of Christ's day (and of today). Apart from an uncle on my father's side (he had no knowledge of or part in my life story), of my entire family today I am the only practicing Christian. Yet I must stress that I am not a Christian today because of the miracles in my life. In the following chapters we will explore the relationship between faith and evidence, and we will discover the foundation and implications of genuine, mature faith.

Where We Will Go

As you have probably already detected, this book will not be light reading, despite the stories. I *will* tell some good miracle experiences, and you will undoubtedly enjoy reading them. But I believe that such narratives are worse than useless in the absence of genuine understanding. My goal is to describe an overarching perspective about God and His dealings with us, hardly a simple matter. Furthermore, I realize that most of the points I make in this book counter well-established and widespread perspectives. It is not trivial to expect people to honestly stop a moment and really reassess the reasoning behind their thinking, particularly when their salvation is at stake. So I must carefully develop my points, rather than to presume that they will be acceptable at face value.

At times reading this book will get downright heavy, and you might have to reread and think about some sections multiple times. I have done my best to keep technical or philosophical jargon to a bare minimum, but you will find some of it. I explain briefly in footnotes (and a glossary of terms in the back), but you might find some outside reading to be helpful as you go along. I provide some suggestions for your aid. Also, unlike many books that have footnotes, the footnotes in this book are not just "asides" or citations. I have treated many of the footnotes in this book as sort of "hyperlinks" to important information that I didn't want in the main body text where it would disrupt the thought flow.

One presupposition that I carry into this book is that human beings have and are able to exercise free will. By this I mean that I believe that God is entirely sovereign because He has the power to make everything in the universe act according to His will, but I also believe that He voluntarily limits the exercise of that power in order to allow His creatures' freedom of choice. I realize that a long and honorable Calvinist tradition finds my presumption unacceptable in various ways. So what entitles me to presume free will throughout this book?

I might try to devote a chapter or two to the free will issue, but I honestly recognize that it would be a feeble effort to those who hold to various forms of Calvinism. It would be as though I was saying, "Look, free will is so obvious that in a chapter or two, including trotting out a few Bible texts, I will prove wrong countless books and centuries of smart people thinking about the issue." Since I cannot devote anything approaching the space or effort to handle the free will issue properly, I will not insult Calvinism with such a pathetic attempt. Instead, I will simply acknowledge the difficulty of the issue and presume radical free will in this book.

Because I will say so much about knowledge and evidence in the context of faith, I felt it only fair to outline the model of knowledge I am presupposing in this book. You will find it at the very back of the book: "Lockean Model of Knowledge." As with chapters 9 and

10, if you want to avoid some of the more rigorous philosophizing you can simply skip it. I have tried to keep the more intense philosophizing to those three sections. Although you will benefit from reading the material, this book is not crippled without them.

Above all, I have not prepared this book for you to close at the end of your first read-through with a satisfied smile and think, "Wow! Great stories. I enjoyed it, and it made me feel good." Instead, I wrote this book knowing you might think such things as "H'mm . . . I found some of that to be really tough. I don't think I fully understand or agree." And I hope you will then also reason something like "Chapter 8 helped, but I think I'll take a break and then reread some of those sections again. I'll get more out of them on another pass and with some more thinking." I know that we don't tend to read that way anymore. We expect authors just to give it to us, but for this subject, you will have to work a bit more.

At first glance my book will likely appear to be a shotgun blast of new ideas, and I certainly don't expect to bestow a sweeping perspective change on the first pass. Instead I assume that most people will catch and apply some of the ideas I present, which will have a small effect, and then later they will grasp more. Most people will find the benefit in this book after several readings and with ongoing thinking about its ideas.

Will it be worth it? I believe so, which is why I devoted the effort to write the book. But it is only fair to warn you not to be misled by the narratives into thinking that this is a story book. My goal is to show you a deep faith, a mature faith. Such a faith is explicitly not a light, story book faith. The narratives I will present illustrate principles of faith, and some of these principles are not easily grasped. "Narrow is the way, . . . and few there be that find it" (Matt. 7:14).

Already you might be thinking, "Wait just a minute! God didn't intentionally make salvation and faith *intellectually* difficult. His love and mercy are easily accessible to all, even those who can't pore through 'heavy' manuscripts." Perhaps you might conclude that I am already misapplying a text.

The reason that the way is narrow and hard to find is that it is diametrically opposed to our natural inclinations on many, many levels. Different people with different capacities and backgrounds will experience different difficulties in finding the way. Satan raises specific sorts of misunderstandings for various sorts of people. But he always, without exception, attacks faith.

Some people will never have particularly sophisticated attacks made upon them. For them, simple principles of faith will be all they ever need. They will find simple principles in this book.

Others, though, ask heavy questions or confront challenging situations, and those people need more sophisticated answers. Such answers are not trivial, and they require more effort to grasp.

We are promised that nothing will tempt us beyond what we can bear, but people will find that they are tempted just as much as they can endure. Satan will always attack us right up to the line that God draws. So whatever way the devil assaults your faith right now, I am confident that he is using your every weakness and attacking you at whatever intellectual level he can. Yes, the way is narrow and difficult to find in different ways for different people, and the principles of genuine faith have to meet your needs, whatever they may be. Some of those principles are not easy to grasp, and if you are at the point of needing heavy-hitting answers, then the "narrow way" for you just might include the fact that you have to struggle to understand God at a deeper level than most.

Light reading? No. Principles of genuine, mature faith? Yes. May the Lord employ this book to grant you whatever level of understanding you need right now.

---

[1] The author has a Ph.D. in philosophy from the University of California at Santa Barbara and has taught philosophy at the university level for a number of years.

[2] The very notion of a "best explanation" is contentious. So many factors can be emphasized or deemphasized in defining "best," and even what counts as an "explanation" is so subject to raging debate that it seems I am precluded from using this phrase. Rather than to turn this one phrase into a book in its own right, let me simply say that what I'm after

in a "best explanation" is a comprehensive and coherent assessment of the available facts in the context of a reasonably comprehensive and coherent worldview.

[3] A "philosopher" is strictly just a "wisdom-lover," but the term has come to mean a "truth-seeker." We are all truth-seekers to one extent or another, even though we do not always have the purest motives or employ the most reliable methods.

[4] I don't mean "alone" in a solipsistic sense here. Rather, I mean "alone" in the existential sense: "We come into this world alone, and we leave it alone. Along the way we try to convince ourselves that we are not alone, but, ultimately, we are. Our only sensible course is to invent ourselves by choosing our values and our priorities, so that we can at least be 'true to ourselves' in our actions."

[5] Existentialism, in its many variants, has one central tenet, which is "radical freedom." This freedom gets cashed out in various ways, depending upon the version of existentialism. However, the most widely known and popular form of existentialism emerged as a sort of nihilism, which is (at minimum) a denial of objective values. The primary proponents of this strand of existentialism were Nietzsche, Sartre, and Camus. Although nonnihilistic forms of existentialism do exist, we can properly group them under other philosophical rubrics, while "existentialism" has come to have widespread nihilistic connotations. So in this book I will refer to nihilistic existentialism when I use the word "existentialism." It is worth noting that on the face of it existentialism dovetails nicely with the worldview of modern science: the universe is devoid of objective value and is not "about us" at all. In such a model of reality, the existentialistic doctrine that we invent ourselves by choosing our values, priorities, and behaviors provides the only hopeful course. The only problem is that science's deterministic universe disallows such "radical freedom." "Choosing" is an illusion in such a model. Those who hold a "scientific worldview" along with an ever-popular pseudointellectual existentialism are fundamentally confused. I say pseudointellectual because most armchair philosophers that I have met, who consider themselves as intellectually sophisticated, like to think of themselves as existentialists as they expound on their highly superficial understanding of the concept.

[6] Of course, a miracle does not imply the work of the Judeo/Christian God. The Judeo/Christian supernaturalistic worldview is just one of many. But it is far beyond the scope of this book to outline the many inferences needed to elevate the Judeo/Christian God theory as "best explanation" above its competitors.

[7] The concept of the intrinsic power of the Word of God is not original with me. I first encountered it in a book by A.T. Jones and E. J. Waggoner: *Lessons on Faith: A Selection of Articles and Sermons*. Jones says that faith "is the depending upon the Word of God only, and expecting that word only to do what the word says."

Chapter 2

STRANDED

Not long after the healing of my sister's tongue, my immediate family moved from southern California to Alberta, Canada. The plan was that my stepdad would go on ahead to secure housing for us and register at a ministerial college he would attend there. My mom, my two sisters, and I would follow in an old pickup truck and trailer containing our worldly goods.

One morning we kids piled into the camper shell in the bed of the pickup and nestled down into whatever spaces we could find, and Mom pulled out onto the highway. My aunt had decided to come along to help with the driving, which meant that her two kids, my favorite cousins (well, at least the male one, Eddie, was my favorite) would be with us on the trip. It made the prospect of the long journey much more appealing, as Eddie and I made a much more potent force against the three girls than I did by myself.

As we traveled northward we made a vacation of the trip. We stopped at the "mystery places" that, through a clever arrangement of angles, seemed to defy the law of gravity. At night we camped on gorgeous beaches and beautiful mountain campgrounds. In short, we kids were having a grand time of it, despite the long sections of riding.

To make the driving as efficient as possible, my mom and aunt switched off and often drove through the night as we kids slept. Eventually we moved inland from the coastal highways, working our way into northern Idaho on the way to crossing into Canada at the (we kids gleefully shouted it again and again) Kingsgate border crossing. We loved that we would be crossing into a new land by the *King's* gate!

One night we were on a long, flat stretch of highway in northern Idaho when a terrible lurching and shuddering of the pickup, accompanied by a thump, thump, thump, awakened us kids. The driver's side rear tire on the pickup had literally come apart.

My mom managed to keep the pickup and trailer both heading the same way and in the direction of our intended travel, and slowly pulled our rig onto a gravel shoulder of the road.

I don't remember the exact time at this point, but it was in the wee hours of the morning. Everybody got out to survey the situation. My mom, ever the efficient organizer, quickly formed up a chain gang to shift things around in the back of the pickup truck, find the spare tire and assorted tools, and move the needed items out to the roadside. This process took many minutes, as the tire, jack, and tools were not together in the same place, and all were buried under boxes and blankets. Finally everything was ready for the tire-transplant operation to begin.

Jacking up the back of the pickup took more time, since none of us had ever assembled the jack before, but eventually we had most of the weight off of the destroyed tire, leaving just enough pressure on it so that the wheel would not turn when we applied the four-way lug wrench to the lug nuts.

I say "we" although "we" kids offered primarily moral support through most of the proceedings. It took the form of such comments as "Wow, it sure is cold! You can really see your breath. It will sure be nice to be rolling along again!"

Amid glares in our general direction, my mom and aunt figured out which of the four spokes of the wrench fit our lug nuts, and then proceeded to exert impressive efforts to loosen said nuts. But to no avail.

The last time that wheel had been put on, dinosaurs had roamed the earth, and the moisture of that primordial time surely accounted for the rust that bonded the lug nuts to the wheel even more effectively than the apparently massive amount of torque that had been applied by the mechanic's air-driven impact wrench.

At that time my mom weighed more than 300 pounds, so it was an inspiring sight to see her standing and bouncing on one spoke of the lug wrench, while my aunt pulled up on the opposite spoke. We had to put a piece of wood under the end of the lug wrench opposite the lug-nut end to support the wrench as the bouncing went on and on. About an hour passed as the women tried each of the lug nuts in turn. Not one would budge.

I should note at this point that during the entire incident thus far, not a single vehicle had passed us going either direction. As we stood there in the road, Mom wryly observed that she had not seen another car on the road all night, so our prospects of getting help from a passing driver seemed as remote as that stretch of highway.

When we had exhausted (in every sense of that term) every combination of people on various parts of the lug wrench, we finally concluded that we were well and truly stuck.

At this point Mom gathered us around and announced, "OK, it's time to pray." My aunt, who had witnessed Cathy's healing and consequently was a believer at the time, suggested that maybe we should have tried that earlier. Anyway, we all knelt down right in the road to pray.

We knew that we were in no danger, kneeling there in the road, because you could see for something like five miles in each direction, and the air was so crisp and soundless that it seemed you would be able to hear the snap of a single twig, much less an approaching car. Furthermore, we had not heard or seen any evidence of other vehicles anywhere in the entire northern part of the state!

Mom prayed for us, and it was pretty simple, something like "Lord we are really stuck. I guess we could just sleep through the night, but we don't know how long into tomorrow it will be before someone happens along. We're cold and tired, and we need help from somebody, because we cannot get that wheel off, as You have seen. Please help us, Lord. Amen."

As we opened our eyes to stand up, we were shocked to see a car slowing to pull onto the shoulder behind our trailer. A man got out and cheerily said, "Looks like you folks could use some help."

Now, I don't remember the details of what he looked like, but I do remember thinking, *He's not very big. If my mom bouncing on that wrench couldn't budge it, this guy's not getting anywhere with it!*

But he ambled over to the wrench with an air of confidence, knelt down by the wheel, and then proceeded simply to whip those lug nuts off effortlessly! In minutes he had the old wheel off and the new one on. As we stood gaping at him, he said, "Well, that should get you on your way," and turned back to his car. We waved and called out our thanks as he drove past us on down the highway. For a minute we watched his taillights, and then Mom reminded us that we should thank God for helping us.

Mom said another very quick prayer of thanks, because we were still freezing, and we rose to return to the interior of the pickup. Suddenly we noticed that the guy's taillights had vanished. We could see for many miles down the road. It had no dips or hollows or rises in either direction. Suddenly it struck us for the first time that we had not actually seen the guy either come or go. He had both appeared and disappeared while we were praying.

Day had dawned before we encountered any other traffic, and that only as we neared one of the small towns. Mom verified that the road was indeed totally flat for many miles from the spot we had pulled over. Where had the man come from, and where had he gone? More amazing, what account could we give for his superhuman strength, as he effortlessly accomplished what literally hundreds of foot-pounds of torque could not?

Of course, one could generate various convoluted and strained naturalistic explanations. However, I believe to this day that the Lord sent us an angel, who appeared and disappeared as we prayed.

God Our "Father"

To me, the interesting questions surface once we have already granted God's supernatural intervention in our situation—such as:

Why doesn't He intervene miraculously each and every time people pray for help in bad situations? (After all, ours wasn't even a really bad situation. At worst we would have been uncomfortable and delayed for a while.) Why does God appear to find the time to address relatively trivial matters, such as our being stranded, while He seems to ignore genuine crises? Why do some people seem to experience God's closeness all or most of the time, while others receive no apparent response at all?

The questions revolve around the sovereignty of God and the nature of our expectations of Him.

Before we can really grasp how He relates to us in our various life situations, we must first clearly understand how to think about and approach Him. The Bible states that we should approach Him as a "Father," but there is obviously a good deal of confusion about what that means.

For example, a church I once attended asked a man to offer the general prayer for the congregation. Before he prayed, he said that he had something he wanted to explain to the assembled congregation. He had recently attended another church and had been quite impressed with its "lively" worship style. The congregation had had, as he put it, a "beboppin'" approach to God, one that he believed was entirely correct, and that we should go beboppin' into the divine presence, because "God loves us so much that He wants to see us come with that sort of confidence into His presence." Then the man proceeded to do a sort of dance and shuffle, waving his arms and displaying various histrionics to demonstrate the attitude we should have as we go beboppin' into His presence to "ask Him for whatever we want."

Now, I have no way of knowing exactly what sort of worship style the man referred to, or if he even had correctly assessed what he saw. What concerns me here is the frivolous attitude he suggested that we adopt when approaching God. When viewing Him as our Father and "coming with confidence" into His presence gets reduced to "beboppin'," I am convinced that something has gone wildly wrong.

Have we so stressed the "Friend" and "Father" aspects of our relationship with God that we have lost the sense of reverence that should properly infuse our every dealing with Him? I believe so, and I want to emphasize instead the balanced, biblical way we should come to God with our prayers and requests.

Consider that the God we pray to dwells in pure light. The Creator and Sustainer of everything, His power is beyond comprehension or expression. Every scene we have of Him in the Bible (including, notably, Ezekiel and the book of Revelation) shows that perfectly holy and vastly powerful beings veil their faces and bow before Him constantly while in His presence. And sinful people cannot behold Him and live. Just look at the scene pictured in Revelation 4 and try to inject the "beboppin'" notion into it. No, our God is utterly sovereign and amazing beyond our wildest imaginations. And we see the appropriate reverence displayed in each and every one of the prayers of Jesus.

So there is a proper way to approach God, and the Bible clarifies repeatedly that frivolity and pride are deeply offensive to Him. We are not to live in fear of Him, but neither are we to regard Him lightly.

Yet many people treat God as though He is little more than a glorified bubble-gum machine. They go beboppin' into the presence of the Almighty, quickly lay out their concerns and requests, and then bounce out to live their lives as they see fit. They assume that because God is their "Father" He will give them only good things all the days of their lives (including everything they ask for), and then find themselves shocked and dismayed when He does not cater to them as demanded. They quote Matthew 7:7-11 as though God has a contractual obligation to give them whatever "good thing" they ask for, and if they think of how they live their lives at all, they view their "good works" as if they were the money they drop into the bubble-gum machine.

But what is it to be a "Father" in the biblical sense? Notice the words of Jesus in the Lord's prayer immediately following "Our

Father": "Hallowed be thy name" (Matt. 6:9). In Bible times a father was a lord. True, the general sense of the term implied benevolence, but it also implied rulership. A father was properly master of his household, and the family and others accorded him a significant measure of respect just in virtue of that position. As a father he was responsible for the discipline of the children and for passing along blessings and inheritance to the children as appropriate. When children approached a father, it was first and foremost with respect. In the context of that respect (which the Bible says is the responsibility of the father to command), children could enjoy many other attributes of their relationship (see 1 Tim. 3:1-7): "He must be one who manages his own household well, keeping his children under control with all dignity" (verse 4, NASB). Can we really imagine that the same God who inspired the attributes to be properly held by a church elder (bishop), such as control and dignity, is also one pleased to have His children come beboppin' into His presence? Ridiculous!

Thus the first thing we must understand about our relationship with God is that He is Lord, King, and Ruler of His universe. When we approach Him as a "Father," that very term implies profound dignity and respect. As we go to the Lord with our requests, we do so on bended knee in recognition of His unfathomable dignity and power, and we dare to come at all only because He Himself has encouraged us that He is a benevolent Father.

Whatever our requests, we must, as did Jesus, bring them with an attitude of respect and of submission. We do not demand of God. Instead we make our desires known and then submit to His will.

The point I am making here is that a partial answer to the question of why God seems to deal with people in different ways is that He is sovereign. He rules according to His unerring knowledge of how each person fits into His grand plan. I will have much more to say about the divine plan as we proceed, but for now let us at least be crystal clear that God is sovereign, and we must seek Him in respect and submission. No "beboppin'" or "bubble-gum machine" approach to God treats Him with due dignity. If we have such a distorted picture of whom God is and what His role is in the universe, then we will find ourselves often out of harmony with His plans, which will lead to continual misunderstanding and disappointment. Thus one of the most critical things that the Word of God makes clear is how to view and deal with Him, because a proper view of the Lord is foundational to genuine faith.

MFAUP-2

Chapter 3

OPEN YOUR MOUTH WIDE

During the three years we lived in Canada I considered it a childhood paradise most of the time. We had sledding and impromptu ice rinks for skating everywhere in the winter, and the rolling hills of long grass gave opportunity for wonderful sliding on cardboard boxes the rest of the year. However, we were grindingly poor the entire time my stepdad was in school.

Of course, I didn't understand the family finances at my age. I just remember that we were in an almost constant state of low-level anxiety about finances.

One time Mom gathered all of us together to pray. For whatever reason, we were totally broke, and there would be no food or money for weeks. It was a genuine crisis, as we lived hand to mouth.

We prayed fervently, as Mom had always taught us to do, and her own intensity certainly inspired us. We sensed that things were desperate, even though Mom had kept the impending situation from us until the crisis was genuinely upon us.

I remember in particular that her prayer seemed almost hostile, as if she were accusing God for not taking better care of us. She quoted Matthew 10:31 *at* God, asking Him, "Aren't we worth more than many sparrows?" I guess that Mom had been praying about the situation for some time, and now she had grown impatient with His apparent lack of concern.

Suddenly she stopped and said, "I just got the strongest impression, like words in my head, saying, 'Open your mouth wide, and I will fill it.'" We all quickly said amen, and then Mom grabbed a

Bible. The phrase was from Psalm 81:10, although none of us had known it at the time. Mom said that she felt at peace about the situation, a peace that she had not experienced for a long time.

Of course, it remained to be seen how God would make good on His word.

We had some dried oatmeal (that, even when cooked, is nasty stuff without at least some milk), a little bit of bread, and a can of canned fruit. It was our practice to buy powdered milk in the box and then mix it with water for our oatmeal. So Mom checked the box and discovered just a little powder left in the bottom. It was not enough to mix up a batch of milk for the morning, but because she never threw anything away, there it sat. Obviously breakfast the next day would be gummy oatmeal and canned fruit. Yummy! At least we would have something to eat.

The next morning Mom stood stirring oatmeal in a simmering pot when she got a strange, quizzical expression on her face. "I just had the oddest thought," she announced. "I feel as if I've just been told to go thump on the side of the milk box and then mix up milk. But I know there isn't enough for a batch of milk. Well, it's strange, but I'll do it." Opening the pantry, she took out the milk box, whacked on the side of it with the flat of her hand, and then proceeded to measure out a couple cups of powered milk into the measuring cup. All of our eyes grew wide as we watched the powder flowing and flowing from the spout. When she had enough for the milk, she set the box onto the counter and mixed up a nice, frothy pitcher of milk for our glasses and our oatmeal. We added canned fruit, and the meal was delicious. Checking the milk box revealed that the level of powder was the same as before: just a thin layer in the bottom, not enough to make any quantity of milk. Mom, again never one to throw anything away, shoved the box back into the pantry.

As lunchtime approached, we wondered what we would eat. A knock on the door answered that question.

A woman stood in the doorway with a curious expression on her face. "I know this will sound very strange," she said, "because I live quite a ways down the road, and I don't know you folks. But this morning I had the strongest impression that I must go out to my garden and fill up some boxes with vegetables. Then I was impressed to drive up the road, going where I did not know, and when I got in front of your house, I realized that this was the place. I'm sorry if this sounds completely crazy, but do you have any need of some vegetables? I also have some cans of fruit in the trunk."

Mom almost slumped to the floor in shock. Inviting the woman in, she then explained our situation. After some weeping and prayers of thanksgiving, we went out to the woman's car. In her trunk she had packed boxes and boxes of vegetables. But from my point of view, the best was yet to come. She invited us to have lunch at her house.

To this day I remember that she had made a lentil stew, with crushed tomatoes and delicious seasonings. She also had homemade bread. We ate and ate, and Mom cried as she kept thinking of the passage "Open your mouth wide, and I will fill it." As the woman dropped us off at our house again, she handed us the ingredients for bread along with some dried beans and lentils. In the kitchen Mom set to work making bread.

The next morning breakfast would again be oatmeal and fruit. Once more Mom thumped on the side of the milk box, and again she poured out enough powder for another pitcherful. When we checked the level inside the box when we were finished, once more we saw just a thin layer in the bottom.

For weeks this went on. The woman's gift of food, carefully prepared, kept us in good stead, and every morning we managed to get just enough powdered milk from the box for one more batch.

Eventually the crisis passed, more money came in, and we actually went to the store to purchase groceries. We even bought another box of powdered milk. It was the right thing to do.

The next morning Mom poured the last of the powder from the first box into the measuring cup, and for the first time in weeks, the box was empty. Indeed, it hadn't even contained a half cup of powder. With some ceremony we threw the now-empty box away. The box was not magical, but it did seem to symbolize God's care for us.

During the entire crisis we didn't miss a single meal.

And to this day, savory lentil stew is one of my favorite dishes.

Persevering Prayer: Why?

Perseverance is one of the most central principles in our petitions to God. As Mom grew more and more concerned, her prayers took on more and more intensity, until the day she in effect threw God's promises back into His face.

Why did He not respond sooner? Or why in the case of Elijah on Mount Carmel (1 Kings 18:42-46) did God require seven prayers before answering? And why did Jacob have to wrestle with the Lord all night long before finally insisting, "I will not let you go unless you bless me" and only *then* receive a blessing and a new name (Gen. 32:26, NASB)? The Bible has so many stories of delay that we have to ask ourselves, Why does the Lord not respond as soon as we pray in our great need?

We find the answer in the implications drawn from a single, simple fact: we live in a world torn by war. Sure, the warfare is spiritual, so we are often unaware or insensitive to it. Furthermore, we intentionally and carefully erect walls of comfort and security around ourselves as best we can, the better to pretend that we don't live in a war zone. As we settle into a comfortable chair alongside good friends for a pleasant evening, it is more than just difficult to remember that our enemy, "the devil, prowls about like a roaring lion, seeking someone to devour" (1 Peter 5:8, NASB).

The conflict often seems so distant from us, so much an abstraction, that its reality registers only in a crisis, and usually by that time our comfortable lifestyle has virtually disabled our ability to wrestle with God, to prevail with Him. As a result, we find ourselves weak in faith and amazed when the enemy penetrates our barriers and actually strikes us low. The crisis often finds us not "prayer warriors," but instead "babes weak in the faith," unable to persevere, and demanding a quick and easy solution to our problems.

One major implication from the spiritual war is that we often have to wait on the Lord while a spiritual conflict wages behind the scenes, unknown to us, as we pray for the Lord to accomplish what we ask.

Consider the unseen battle surrounding the prophet Daniel. In Daniel 10:12, 13, we find that he has been praying for three weeks to gain an understanding of a vision. He has not received an answer . . . after three weeks of fervent prayer! Finally, an angel comes to explain: "Then he said to me, 'Do not be afraid, Daniel, for from the first day that you set your heart on understanding this and on humbling yourself before your God, your words were heard, and I have come in response to your words. But the prince of the kingdom of Persia was withstanding me for twenty-one days; then behold, Michael, one of the chief princes, came to help me, for I had been left there with the kings of Persia. Now I have come to give you an understanding of what will happen to your people in the latter days, for the vision pertains to the days yet future' " (verses 13, 14, NASB).

The prophet prays to understand the vision, but does not get an immediate response. Why? Because something was resisting the heavenly agencies. Who is this "prince of the kingdom of Persia"? The marginal reference to Daniel 10:13 suggests that the "prince of the kingdom of Persia" should most probably be understood as a powerful satanic angel. God sent His angel to provide Daniel with his requested answer immediately as the prophet started his supplications, but Satan, realizing what was at stake, sent his own mighty angel to keep God's angel from reaching Daniel. It was only when the Lord sent another angel—an archangel, Michael—that God's angel was able to provide Daniel with the answer to his prayer. And, after giving the prophet his answer, God's angel would return to continue the struggle against Satan's agent. Real warfare is going on, and it affects how our prayers get answered.

But how can anyone, even someone as mighty as Satan, possibly resist God? Why didn't God just employ 50 or more powerful angels to overcome Satan's angel in this case? Well, presumably, however many angels God sent, Satan would dispatch enough to resist them. The supply of angels on both sides is limited (shocking thought, isn't it?), and angels are engaged in many activities around the world and in heaven. The turning point in the struggle came only when God sent the archangel, Michael. So why didn't He just delegate the task to Michael in the first place? Or why did God bother with using angels at all? Why not just employ His omnipotence directly? After all, the number of His angels is limited, but His personal power is not. The answers to those questions are a bit more complex.

To address them, let us now consider the case of Job, which reveals more of the subtlety of the spiritual conflict that engages us.

Job and the Nature of Spiritual Conflict

The story of Job has triggered much commentary over the centuries, so I do not presume to contribute anything new here. The point I find significant for our purposes, however, is that God displays His people in pride and shows them off. In the cosmic struggle God has His champions on earth, and He displays their faith before the enemy, before His own gathered hosts, and before others on our planet. He proudly demonstrates the perseverance of their faith in Him.

Think about the delays you have experienced and the prices you have paid in terms of the cosmic conflict. To illustrate, if the United States Army decides that a particular hill needs to be swept clean of the enemy, it can send in the infantry, or it can nuke the hill. Both will effectively rid it of the enemy. However, nuking it is a devastating, brute-force approach, carrying with it many implications for how the rest of the world will view the U.S.

In the cosmic conflict between good and evil, it matters much to God how the universe perceives Him. I will say more about this

39

later, but an important principle of the conflict is that God values free will above all things—it is the most precious thing in the universe. Think about the fact that Satan succeeded in deceiving one third of the heavenly angels (Isa. 14:12-20; Rev. 12:4). How can heaven or earth regard God as anything but the arbitrary despot Satan claims if every time Satan begins to win a little, God just sweeps in and nukes the situation? God cares to be recognized as the fair and reasonable being that He is, so that His creatures do not serve Him out of blind fear. By giving His creation freedom, He risks misunderstanding, and so the way God deals with them provides the evidence they need to serve Him out of love and respect rather than blind fear.

And in His choice to employ His servants to do His work, instead of just "nuking the hill," God reveals (among other things) that He values the most careful, subtle approach to situations rather than a heavy-handed, brute-force method just to make things His way.

The cosmic conflict has always been about evidence. And God has always designed that His creation will detect and believe the truth about Him because of the weight of evidence. Even in the face of Satan's lies, God continues to employ evidence as His sole weapon, as He urges the conscience and woos the reasoning mind. Although God is all-powerful and able to make things just the way He would like them to be, He restrains Himself to make room for free will in the universe. When He could employ nukes, instead He dispatches His infantry. He builds His case in each life, He establishes the evidence to overthrow Satan's lies, and He allows Satan's perspectives and tactics to develop and reveal their actual results. God waits for us to decide based upon our own evaluation of the evidence.

Job is God's foot soldier in the conflict, and the patriarch waits with perseverance as the Lord writes a story with his life.

God exalts that in the life of Job He can display that out of the pit of hell He has rescued some so completely that they have entirely overcome Satan's grand lie: God is not telling you the whole truth and is withholding some great good from you. Job is a profound example of a person who has overcome Satan's lie so thoroughly that he can say with assurance: "Though he slay me, yet will I trust in him" (Job 13:15). The patriarch has come to trust the Lord so completely that he has utter confidence in God's good will toward him, and he does not doubt that fact regardless of circumstances, appearances, or feelings.

So Job had the power to persevere as a good soldier, as did Jacob, Moses, and Jesus. What is the nature of this power, and, more important, how do we obtain it for ourselves so that we can triumph in the cosmic conflict as they did?

Wrestling With God

Consider the audacity of Jacob, who struggled all night against God. His hip out of joint, he is exhausted and in severe pain and realizes that the Lord can strike him down in an instant. Yet it is not fear of more pain or of death that Jacob feels. Rather, he clings to God in desperation born out of the fear that he will lose this amazing opportunity to get something special from the Lord. What transpires during that nightlong encounter? As only wrestlers know, during a match you come to understand the other person. You begin to sense how they are going to respond, how they think ahead to their next move, and how they prioritize their tactics. Evenly matched wrestlers often talk, chiding each other, yet a growing respect and knowledge will develop. More than one friendship has emerged on the wrestling mat. Jacob wrestles with the Lord, and through the long night comes to know Him. He sees His justice and mercy, recognizing that the being he struggles against can annihilate him in an instant, yet He does not. And through the long night Jacob learns much about himself. Struggling with the Lord, he comes to see himself as he truly is: manipulative and deceitful. Instead of trusting God, he has spent his life arranging circumstances as best he can to benefit himself, even at the cost of others. So far

41

from being a man of faith, on the night of the struggle Jacob seeks God in justified fear of the righteous wrath of his cheated brother.

Yet, in order for God to enable him to take his place in the lineage of faith, a true son of Abraham, the Lord must create a profound change in Jacob. He must transform him from "one who supplants" into *Israel,* or "he who strives with God." After the striving, after showing Jacob himself and saving him from, and lifting him above, himself, the Lord gives Israel his new heart and his new name. God grants him favor with Esau, and Israel emerges from the crisis forgiven both by God and by his brother. Along with this forgiveness—and always a part of it—Jacob emerges a reformed man. His heart has been changed.

God loves it when His people have the audacity to cling to Him until they gain victory and blessing. He loves it when they know His heart well enough that they can offer His own promises back to Him as *the* reason He should answer their prayers, because they believe in the Word of God to accomplish just what it says, which is the essence of true faith.

The principle of perseverance is this: If you will count yourself a soldier in the army of God, then remember that *victory never happens without a struggle.* What comes easily to us cannot be counted a victory. If there is no resistance, nothing to overcome, then there is no triumph. The comfortable, everyday, easy living we experience most of the time does not challenge us, and it certainly does not threaten us to our core. Yet it is a core change that we need. This is why the Bible says that God cursed the ground (Gen. 3:17). Only struggle, pain, and striving could bring us to confront the vast pit of darkness that had opened in our natures. And only through struggle could we ultimately obtain pure faith and thereby victory over our lower natures. Although we often forget this fundamental reality, we deserve death just as much as Jacob did. Each transgression we commit makes us yet again worthy of death, and it is a struggle to wipe that stain from our lives—one that cost the very life of God! Yet we take sin lightly and go beboppin' into His presence to display to Him our "good" lives and use that tainted currency to buy from our bubble-gum machine "god" what we desire. Instead we must learn to struggle, and we must learn the price of dependency and submission to a sovereign God.

That is why God dislocated Jacob's hip and left him lame for the rest of his life. With each painful step Israel remembered with deep gratitude that he had wrestled with God and emerged with the blessing and a new name. Each agonizing step reminded him of his utter dependency upon God, and he felt close to Him because of the ongoing reminder that His touch could have been one of death, yet wasn't.

Why did God not touch Jacob in some way that would bring him ongoing pleasure instead of incessant pain? We might as well ask what happened to the initial budding of "faith" demonstrated by some of my family after the healing of my sister Cathy's tongue. Somehow, in our perversity, we think in our world of sin that health and prosperity are just the way things should be. Tongues should be whole and undamaged, so when one gets restored to that state we somehow quickly forget how that took place—the happy, healthy status quo is what matters to us. Quickly we lose our sense of dependency on God, and thus we lose His blessing.

But note this point carefully: God blesses Israel by giving him a lifelong mark of his dependency, a reminder of the closeness of the struggle, a symbol of the death that should have been but wasn't. Israel stands in awe that he wrestled with Him and lived. Instead of feeling that the Lord should have treated him better, he lives in daily amazement that God touched him and deigned to bless him at all, that the Creator lowered Himself to the level of wrestling with him and letting Himself be known. As a result Israel relishes the pain that constantly reminds him of God's ownership of him and of the desperate struggle that redefines him.

If we too would be part of the lineage of faith—that of spiritual Israel—we must learn to "strive with God." We must wrestle with

Him and prevail, and thereby come to know both Him and ourselves. Only those who have done so can adopt the surname of Israel.

The Price of Gethsemane

Jesus Himself endured struggles and strived with God throughout His time on earth. Witness His final struggles in Gethsemane. The cup trembles in His hand as He considers the awful price to be paid for humanity. Throughout Jesus' time on earth Satan has tempted Him again and again with alternative, easy ways to "win" back the human race. From His trial in the wilderness and through the many attempts on the part of the crowds and even His own disciples to direct His path away from the cross, Satan has tried to convince Jesus that the "victory" can be won without a struggle. How many times has Christ rebuked Satan, telling him to "get behind" Him, because Jesus knows the price He must pay? And there in Gethsemane, sweating blood in His soul anguish, the cup trembles as Jesus recoils from that price.

Jesus is mighty in prayer, and He prays with all the strength of His persistence that God will grant Him some way out, that the Father will make a way of escape for Him as well as for humanity. And what is this price He must pay otherwise? Does Jesus shrink from the pain, from the humiliation? No, Jesus recoils from eternal separation from God.

In John 3:14, 15 Jesus declares of Himself: "As Moses lifted up the serpent in the wilderness, even so must the Son of Man be lifted up; that whoever believes will in Him have eternal life" (NASB). Here He alludes to the incident in Numbers 21:8, 9, in which the snakebitten people had only to turn and gaze upon a bronze serpent erected on a pole to receive healing.

The serpent is a symbol of Satan and of sin. Bitten by serpents, the people were dying from sin and in their sins, yet Moses does not erect a lamb for them to see. Instead he puts up a serpent—a symbol of sin for them to gaze upon and live. We ask ourselves, *Why a serpent?*

We find the clues in several places. Romans 8:3 tells us: "For what the Law could not do, weak as it was through the flesh, God did: sending His own Son in the likeness of sinful flesh and as an offering for sin, He condemned sin in the flesh" (NASB). And in 2 Corinthians 5:21 we read: "He made Him who knew no sin to be sin on our behalf, that we might become the righteousness of God in Him" (NASB).

See Jesus clinging to the ground in Gethsemane. Having lived a perfect, sinless life, He must offer it in exchange for the sinful lives of all humanity. He must die, for the wages of sin is death. But this death cannot be the "sleep" that Jesus labels the first death. Everyone dies that kind of death. It has the hope of resurrection and ultimate salvation. Jesus would have nothing to fear from such sleep. No, what He shrinks from is something else.

Revelation 20 speaks of the resurrection and judgment of the dead, and verses 13 through 15 declare: "And the sea gave up the dead which were in it, and death and Hades gave up the dead which were in them; and they were judged, every one of them according to their deeds. Then death and Hades were thrown into the lake of fire. This is the second death, the lake of fire. And if anyone's name was not found written in the book of life, he was thrown into the lake of fire" (NASB). All the dead must be resurrected for the execution of final judgment. Some rise to eternal life, but most are brought back to life so that they can experience the "second death," the annihilation that has no hope of resurrection. In the second death, as Hebrews 10: 27 tells us, there is only the certainty of "the fury of a fire which will consume the adversaries" (NASB).

The second death is final, eternal, hopeless separation from God, and the Bible promises it to all who have "trampled under foot the Son of God, and [have] regarded as unclean the blood of the covenant by which he was sanctified, and [have] insulted the Spirit of grace" (verse 29, NASB).

Think about the force of the serpent symbol again. On the cross

Jesus consented to have all the sins of the world heaped upon Him, all the sins that ever had been committed, and all the sins that ever could and would be committed. Jesus *became* SIN. His perfect sinless life was exchanged for sin itself, which is how all-encompassing the sacrifice had to be. So Jesus consented to become sin itself.

Then, in those dark hours on the cross, shrouded from view, the entire wrath of God poured out upon sin in the form of Jesus. God "condemned sin in [Jesus'] flesh" (Rom. 8:3, NASB), and in the process Jesus experienced the hopeless, utter separation from God that is the second death. Hear Him cry out in an anguish He paid the price to spare us from: "My God, my God, why hast thou forsaken me?" (Matt. 27:46). After a life of submission to and utter faith in His Father, Jesus finally reaches the climax of the lifelong struggle: Will He endure the crushing sense of God's utter condemnation of sin—of *Himself* (for He has *become* sin)? In Gethsemane Jesus senses that the burden of sin He bears will separate Him forever from His Father, and that there can be no promised resurrection for Him.

Having realized in Gethsemane the price to be paid, He experiences it on the cross. And having chosen in Gethsemane to drink the cup, on the cross He drains its last drops, thus experiencing every horror of the wrath of God in condemnation of sin. He knows firsthand utter, hopeless separation from God. Jesus did not die to save us from the first death—from His time until now all have died. No, He died to save us from the second death, because He bore it in His flesh.

Yet the pure faith of Jesus pushes back the darkness as it utterly transcends circumstance, appearance, and feeling. He has no earthly reason to believe in His resurrection, and Satan torments His soul with the thought that God's hatred of sin is so great that He cannot be saved from this final death. All the evidence opposes His resurrection—that is, all the evidence except what the Word of God says. And Jesus believes *solely* in the Word of God. Despite the sense of utter separation, He commits His soul to His Father, trusting in the promised resurrection even though He dies feeling the utter hopelessness of the second death. On the cross we see the vast divide between feeling and faith. Feelings come and go, but faith transcends all and clings to the one unassailable evidence: the Word of God.

Even as He experienced the horrors of the second death so that none of us need to, Jesus gained the victory of faith, because He believed that the Word of God could do what it said, and that therefore He would be resurrected and reunited with His Father. I say again and again, genuine faith is acting on the belief that the Word of God is true. The faith of Jesus penetrated the deepest darkness ever known to cling solely to the Word of God, and this enabled Him to cry out in victory, "It is finished!" (John 19:30), and then commend His spirit to God. Thus Jesus gained the final victory.

There is no victory without a struggle. But God has designed our struggles to lead us to victories of faith. So God makes us wrestle with Him, as did Jacob, until He can produce in us faith and thereby the power to gain victory.

Spiritual warfare rages in the universe, and we are caught up in the middle of it. Indeed, sometimes it feels as if it is about us. The Lord allows His efforts on our behalf to be withstood by the enemy for a time—but only as long as He deems it necessary to build our perseverance and thus our faith in Him. Meanwhile He employs us as His infantry to sweep the hills of the world clean of His enemies, all the while carefully ensuring that He does not violate the principle of free will. He uses our lives to provide evidence that can contribute to reaching others. And in our struggles He works with us toward the day that, like Jesus, we will have completely overcome Satan's first lie. He strives to build in us a faith that penetrates and transcends circumstances, appearances, and feelings until it lays hold only on the Word of God to do just what it says.

Chapter 4

DON'T JUMP

At summer camp I learned to rock-climb, a pursuit that became a discipline for me both physically and spiritually. From that summer on, climbing became the means of God's salvation of me. I believe that He used it to save me from a life wasted on drinking and drugs, and from becoming like everybody I knew. In fact, for several years I didn't have a single association that wasn't involved in the hard drug scene. Climbing gave me different perspectives and priorities, and God employed its many metaphors to enrich and guide my life out of that spiritual pit.

Eventually I became a skilled enough climber that I aspired to include tackling El Capitan, in Yosemite Valley, California. I had found a wonderful climbing partner, named Mark Smith, and we were training and gearing up for a major ascent that later became fairly famous (or infamous, depending upon which side of the controversy you find most compelling).[1]

Our preparation for this climb included such things as jumping off bridges (roped, of course). Mark and I knew that we would be taking many long falls during our climb, and we wanted to train the fear of falling out of ourselves as much as possible. So we would go out to various bridges, rig up ropes, tie into our harness systems, and hurtle off into space. I can tell you that there is something very counterintuitive about leaping off of a stationary object such as a bridge. And the "elevator going down" sensation just never got totally familiar.

One day we found ourselves staring over the guardrail of the Big

Tujunga Canyon Bridge in southern California. I don't remember the bridge's exact height, but it seems that it was about 200 feet above the creekbed. It was certainly high enough that we could finally go for a really long jump. The construction of the bridge was seemingly ideal. A huge concrete arch spanned the canyon, with the base of each side embedded in the canyon walls, and the roadway traversed horizontally over the apex of the arch. So by anchoring our ropes at the apex of the arch, we would have a wide-open space into which we could fall between the legs of the arch.

Now, it was not our practice to jump straight down our ropes. Instead, we would move off to the side of our anchors and then leap. The swinging fall was much easier on our bodies, as the impact forces were much smaller. Besides, we had come to really like the feeling of swinging after the initial dropping sensation.

The Big Tujunga Canyon Bridge was seemingly perfect for our purposes, but, not being totally stupid, we realized that the possibility existed that a long swing could actually propel us into one of the legs of the main arch. Though the possibility seemed pretty remote, we decided to perform an initial test before actually jumping.

We anchored our ropes at the best spot at the top of the arch and then added enough rocks to one of our large canvas bags to make the bag weigh about 60 pounds (we didn't want to haul much more weight back up after the experiment). Then we walked back about 40 feet from our anchor (we didn't want to have to haul it farther than that), tied the canvas bag into the rope end, lifted the bag over the guardrail, and dropped it free. The bag dropped, caught, and then swung sideways just as predicted. In fact, the trajectory was even better than we thought it might be, because the bag didn't swing in under the bridge toward the main support arch.

Satisfied, we hauled the bag up and got ourselves ready for our own jumps. A coin flip nominated me to go first, so I walked back up the bridge about 80 feet (about as far as we felt we could safely swing, given the narrow canyon walls) and tied into the rope. My heart racing, I stepped over the guardrail and began calming my pre-flight jitters. With each bridge jump I always had to go through a bit of "psyching up" to be able just to step off into space.

Something strange always takes place in me when I'm about to jump, and this time was no exception. I have to go through a process of thinking like someone who jumps off of bridges rather than as someone who walks along the sidewalks of bridges. As I stood at the edge, staring into the abyss, I could already sense what that long drop would feel like, a mixture of discomfort, exhilaration, and almost panic all at the same time. I was forcing myself to do something that is totally outside of everyday events and experiences, and my gut has been programmed to rebel against doing what I was planning to do. But I was ready. Just as I reached the point of stepping off as I had done dozens of times before from other bridges, suddenly an utterly riveting "voice" spoke in my head, shouting, DON'T JUMP!

Recoiling, I almost fell off anyway. Still standing there at the edge, I felt myself suddenly shaking and filled with adrenaline. What in the world had just happened?

As I attempted to think it through, I tried to convince myself that it was just fear talking. But I knew that I had never heard a "voice" that compelling before, and it didn't seem part of me at all. What to do? By now it had become a matter of principle that I must go ahead and jump. I could not back down just because I was scared. After again going through each point of the setup in my mind and reviewing our earlier dropped-bag test, I was ready once more.

But as I got set to step off, all the usual feelings swirling up inside me, once more that mental voice boomed, DON'T JUMP! Grabbing the guardrail, I knew that I could no longer pretend that it was just my nerves. There was simply no mistaking that it was not something that I was manufacturing inside of myself. I could not jump. Feeling defeated and frustrated, I climbed back over the guardrail to the safety of the sidewalk.

Mark approached me with a look of amazement on his face.

"What's up, Rich? I've never seen you back down from anything before. Is this one that scary?"

Although I tried to explain, it sounded lame and manufactured even to me. I could not convey the intensity of the voice. Having given up, I would let Mark take his turn.

But, seeing something in my face, he sensed that something unusual was going on. He set up for his jump by tying into the rope only about 50 feet from our anchors rather than the 80 feet I had planned. Standing by the anchors, I leaned over the guardrail to watch his jump.

Once over the guardrail, he paused just a second, then stepped off. He dropped until the rope caught and jerked him into a sideways trajectory. In horror I realized that he was swinging in under the bridge, toward the arch, and that he was going really fast. In fact, he was hurtling faster than the bag had. His arc took him to the arch, where he bent his knees to absorb the impact, then bounced off. After that first contact, Mark's swings diminished rapidly and soon he hung straight under the anchors. A quick ascent up the ropes brought him back to the sidewalk, but the wide-eyed look of shock never left him.

Standing on the bridge together, we struggled to comprehend what had just happened. Because of the bag drop, we had been confident that we would end our first swing nowhere near that arch.

At this point Mark had some data points to work with, and, being an engineering student, he had the mathematical background to perform the necessary calculations. Given the trajectories we had observed, and considering the much longer swing I would have taken than he had, with its attendant increase in velocity, Mark was able to calculate that if my trajectory had taken me under the bridge as his had, I would have hit the arch at about 50 miles per hour. It would have reduced me to just a skin-sack of crushed bones after that first swing.

"Don't jump." Two simple words: obey them and live; disobey

them and die. How often does our future hang in such a balance?

Having thought about those two words countless times in the decades since that event, I will always be convinced that God intervened to save me. I guess that critics might say that I might well have not swung under the bridge as Mark had. They might argue that his calculations could have been entirely mistaken—that, like the bag, I would not have ended up anywhere near the arch. Or, taking a different tack, they might claim that my intuitions were finely enough honed that I *sensed* something terribly amiss and warned myself in a way that I could not ignore. It seems to me that all such explanations are straining to account for something not explainable in such terms at all.

I believe that the odds of Mark's calculations being in error were slim to none. Swinging under the bridge was exactly where I would have gone, because I don't think it was possible to step off of the bridge in the same perfectly perpendicular way that we had dropped the bag (and I'm actually shocked that we hadn't noticed that aspect of our test before). In fact, our bag drop test was something of a formality. I believe that the bag and I would have taken very different trajectories for a number of different reasons that we should have thought through, and would have done so if we had not become so used to jumping off of bridges. And that becoming accustomed is itself a strong argument against my intuitions being what saved me. In fact, all my intuitions about jumping had been trained to conclude something like this: "It's going to look weird, it's going to feel weird, and it's going to be weird; but it's going to turn out just fine." There is no way, given all of the data I had available to me, that I could have had any intuitive sense that this time something was terribly amiss. Intuition does not strike me as a reasonable explanation.

Furthermore, since that day I have heard that same compelling voice at other times and in other contexts. As a result I have learned to always heed it. I have discovered that it is not a function of my own mind, because it tells me things I *must* know at that time that I could not otherwise have known.

The voice of the Lord is usually a "still small voice," as the Lord is quite the gentleman in His dealings with us. He rarely speaks with His might and power to disrupt our chosen path, because He respects our free will so much. But at times He does intervene, and I have heard both sides of God's voice. He has saved me more than once through both approaches.

The Nature of Evidence

With so much at stake in the cosmic conflict as well as in each of our individual lives, why does God not just stop us more often? Why does He not value our salvation a bit more and our free will a bit less, so that He can find the right balance to save everybody? And why is it that most people will be lost, even though it is God's highest priority to save them?

The question comes down to a matter of evidence and its evaluation. Contrary to what many mistakenly or disparagingly call "faith," true faith is founded on evidence. As I said earlier, I cannot actually muster up any faith that I have a million dollars in my pocket right now, because I have no evidence to suggest that such a thing is true. Believing such a thing at this moment would be delusional, not a matter of faith. True faith is not just a blind "leaping off of the diving board," so to speak. Blind leaps are presumptuous, because we have no reason to suppose that the pool has any water in it.

On the other hand, it takes no faith for me to believe in the Pythagorean theorem or that one plus one always equals two. About such propositions I have genuine knowledge.[2] The truth of any proposition reflects a continuum of evidence. At one end of the continuum I find no evidence in support of something. Believing in this case is either delusional or presumptuous. At the other end of the continuum I have ample support for a proposition. In this case "believing" would be just another word for "knowing" or "being certain," and *not* believing such a proposition would be delusional. What we call "faith," then, is believing in the truth of a proposition when the evidence is somewhere between the two ends of the continuum.

In the context of a discussion about evidence, let us consider carefully my current miracle story.

Although I prepared to jump with a large body of evidence about what the outcome would be, I did not realize that all that evidence was in error and that it was all leading me to my death. ("There is a way that seems right . . . ") But here is the really interesting point about God's "stopping me" with His voice: He did nothing more than add another bit of evidence to the mix. God did not forcibly keep me from jumping. Instead, He just delayed my decision long enough so that I could consider one more thing.

Now I ask you, how many people would have rationalized that voice away and leaped anyway? I shudder as I think of how close I was to doing that very thing, and I thank God for the second warning. But part of the evidence He gave me was *in* the second warning. By the very fact of the second warning, I knew deep inside that this voice must trump the entire body of previous evidence. Yet how many people would have jumped even after the second warning?

In our "scientifically enlightened" age we think that what counts as "evidence" should be quite "objective."[3] I certainly had not assembled an exhaustive body of scientific evidence indicating the safety of jumping, but what data I had gathered seemed reasonably reliable. The scientific method certainly does not preclude mistakes. So I had reasonably good evidence to suggest that jumping off of that bridge would be safe. Yet, in finally deciding not to jump, I chose to overlook all the objective evidence I had assembled and allow what I took to be the voice of God to overrule all of it. I can hear the Christians reading this paragraph saying something like "Yes, and the voice of God should always trump all other 'evidence.'"

When "Objective" Evidence Doesn't Work

We must be very careful now. People have committed all sorts of atrocities and acts of apparent stupidity in the name of God and sup-posedly according to His direction. The bastions of "objectivity" often tout this fact as the strongest reason to conclude that "the voice of God" as people perceive it is completely subjective and therefore unreliable. "Objectively" speaking, they would say that I "lucked out" when, whatever originated my "impression," that "voice" turned out to be correct. They would say that from a really "objective" point of view, just a more careful analysis of the actual data available to me would have had the same effect as the "voice" did. In this case, it seems that the "voice" harmonized with the "objective" facts of the matter. But it is often the case that a "voice" or other "evidence" seems to lead us in opposition to what others would call the "objec-tive" facts of the matter. When our impressions or our interpretations of the Bible differ from the "objective evidence," that is when the problem of what counts as evidence becomes acute.

For example, the (highly disconcerting to most scientists) fact of the matter is that the vast majority of people in the United States sim-ply do not believe that evolutionary theory fully accounts for human origins. Science tries to convince us that evolution is an "objective fact" that we should, as reasonable people, accept. Yet our country is filled with otherwise reasonable people who just don't buy it.

Scientists think that if people were properly educated about evo-lutionary theory, they would just naturally believe it. And some evi-dence supports the idea. For example, the *Minnesota Daily* reported on April 21, 2005: "A recent poll by the *Minnesota Daily* concluded that university students are much more likely to believe in evolution than the rest of the U.S. public." The numbers are revealing: "83 percent of university students believe in the theory that humans evolve over time. The remaining 17 percent of respondents believe that God cre-ated man 10,000 years ago and that humans have not evolved."

However, while the poll seems to signify that the more educated a person is, the more likely it is that the individual will believe that evolution alone accounts for human origins, that is not actually the case. This *Minnesota Daily* poll actually conflated two questions that many other polls keep separate: whether evolution alone accounts for human origins, and whether God works *through* evolution to produce human beings. The *Minnesota Daily* poll phrases the alternatives this way: "Man has evolved, either with or without God's guidance," and "God created man in his present form, and man has not evolved."

Thus the *Minnesota Daily* numbers actually correlate closely with more general polls of Americans, ones that keep the contrast between pure evolution and God's involvement quite separate. On October 23, 2005, a CBS poll reported that "most Americans do not accept the theory of evolution. Instead, 51 percent of Americans say God created humans in their present form, and another three in 10 say that while humans evolved, God guided the process. Just 15 percent say that humans evolved, and that God was not involved." So it appears that only the minorities (15 and 17 percent) at the extremes have an unequivocal position. Most Americans, whether university students or not, still believe that God must have played *some* role in the creation/development of human beings.

At this point it appears that the scientists have only themselves (or the content of the theory itself) to blame, because for decades they have largely had their way with public education. Yet while generations of children have been taught according to the evolutionary theory textbooks (produced by the scientists), the vast majority still grow up *not* to believe that evolutionary theory is a completely sufficient account. Furthermore, we are constantly inundated with evolutionary theory in all forms of public media. Even the word "evolution" itself has come to denote virtually any sort of change (usually improvement) over time. Despite an amazingly sweeping and pervasive educational campaign in favor of evolutionary theory, though, something else seems to be getting into people's minds to keep them from believing in it. What is this something? And what can science do to combat it?

Well, scientists might take some comfort in the March 8, 2006, report of a Gallup poll. Frank Newport, from the Gallup Web site, writes: "Surveys repeatedly show that a substantial portion of Americans do not believe that the theory of evolution best explains where life came from . . . Those with lower levels of education, those who attend church regularly, those who are 65 and older, and those who identify with the Republican Party are more likely to believe that God created humans 'as is,' than are those who do not share these characteristics."

So it appears that scientists do have a number of avenues available to convert the people of the United States to their version of a "rational" viewpoint. For example, they can keep on "educating," although even the *Minnesota Daily* report, properly understood, seems to indicate that such an approach is not having the desired effect. Perhaps they can try to convince people to quit going to church, although that would seem to presuppose the very effect they would be trying to create with this approach. Scientists can put their hopes in the budding "rationality" of the young, although somehow by the time they get a college education the significant majority still disbelieve in evolutionary theory's complete explanatory power. Or they can try to convert people away from the Republican Party. This last method seems to be the most hopeful, since it is seemingly the one thing that scientists can do that either doesn't beg the question (as affecting church attendance does) or hasn't already been shown ineffective. Now, of course, we must wonder if this means that scientists would have to conclude that Democrats are more "rational" than Republicans.

I am, of course, speaking largely tongue-in-cheek in the last paragraph. However, scientists do face a significant problem insofar as their educational program doesn't seem to be having the desired results. (Perhaps this will take a bit of the urgency out of the current push for so-called intelligent design being taught in public schools.)

Is more or stricter education about evolutionary theory what is needed to convince people of its "objective fact"? I don't believe so. I think that the issue of *evidence,* the issue of that *something* that is keeping people from completely buying evolutionary theory, is manifestly more complex than scientists are prepared to acknowledge.

One significant problem is that science wields such terms as "objective fact" like a club, hoping to wow "rational" people into believing. Yet rational people recognize that the space shuttle *doesn't* blow up only *most* of the time.[4] People intuitively sense that whatever it is that science is doing, it is not telling us the ultimate truths of the universe. And no amount of education is going to convince most people that science is accomplishing something that it most certainly is not, namely, getting humans in touch with those ultimate and objective truths.[5]

This is the basis of a profound tension that many feel toward science. People recognize that science "works" in that it produces "advances" in technology. In that sense, science seems to be "on to something," and thus "true" as far as it goes. But there's the rub: *as far as it goes.* The purely naturalistic paradigm that is the foundation of science strikes most people as incomplete, even if they can not articulate the problem in those terms. Intuitively human beings sense that there is more to the world than meets the eye (or the microscope, or experiment, etc.). They recognize at least at an intuitive level that when all the available scientific evidence is assembled and evaluated, as in the case of my miracle story in this chapter, even "all" the evidence still leaves something out, and the evaluation of that evidence cannot ever be properly "objective."

As a result, despite all its many and legitimate triumphs science continues to suffer a credibility gap, and that gap is exactly the width of the gulf most people perceive between the naturalistic paradigm and all there actually is to know about the universe. For them, all the "truths" of science still leave open a lot of space for the "voice of God" or "revelation" or other supernaturalistic forces to count as evidence.[6] And, even more disconcerting to scientists, it is a fact that for most people the perceived "voice of God" still trumps all the other evidence. For them, internal "impressions" count as strong "evidence," even when those impressions exist wildly apart from the "objective facts" of science. Indeed, what they call "faith" just is believing in their internal impressions, and "being strong in the faith" just is clinging to the "truth" of those impressions boldly, even defiantly, in the face of evidence to the contrary.

But is this faith?

Intellectual Honesty

Now we find ourselves on very dangerous ground indeed! A misstep to either side can result in intellectual or spiritual disaster. On the one hand, we can become so gullible that our "faith" is an ignorant travesty just waiting to be exploded or manipulated. But on the other hand, we can become so "educated" and skeptical that we lack the capacity to discern or act upon God's interventions when He does intervene in our lives. Either side is destructive to genuine faith and thus imperils our souls.

In the face of this dilemma, some will advocate "finding a balance," which means something like "having a tendency to see God's interventions, but not being too credulous." After all, as in cases of Pascal's Wager sort of thinking, it's less dangerous to assume that an event is a function of God's providence than to conclude that it's not. Thus if there is danger of error on the matter, it is more cautious to lean toward the side of "faith" than toward thinking too critically or "objectively," lest we get sucked into a skeptical vortex.

But let us consider the implications of such a default position. I want to explore how unsafe this position really is, and to do so I will briefly engage us in one side of one of the classic philosophy of religion debates of all time. In so doing, we will come to see that true faith must be more intellectually involved and much less gullible than is the counterfeit accepted by most Christians today.

Yet we will also see that this fact does not suggest that true faith must be more "scientifically minded" in order to be more "objective." The dichotomy between science and faith is a false one. Science and faith are not, as Stephen J. Gould argues in *Rocks of Ages,* "nonoverlapping magisteria." The magisteria of science constantly makes claims attempting to constrain the "proper" exercise of faith, in effect telling faith what it is "justified" to accept as true. And religious faith properly impinges upon and even trumps the claims of science regarding matters wherever science itself rests upon a type of faith. Moreover, the magisteria of science is not the one of "objective truth," contrary to Gould's assertions. For many reasons I cannot go into in this present book, I simply deny both the objectivity and the truth of many of science's more strident claims, while faith (revelation) does provide genuinely objective (God's eye) truths. Finally, we have at our disposal a spectrum of truth-gathering devices apart from either science or faith. But again a detailed discussion of that subject is for another book. What is important for us now is to get clear upon the proper relationship between evidence of all sorts and what we choose to believe. Let us keep in mind as we proceed, however, that the empirical[7] claims of science are just one sort of evidence in the spectrum of data points relevant to a given question, and that sort of evidence really enjoys no special merit just in virtue of its being scientific. For a more developed discussion of evidence and modes of knowledge, please turn to the very back of the book and the appendix: "Lockean Model of Knowledge."

For now, let's talk about the principles of intellectual honesty. William Kingdon Clifford was a famous British mathematician and philosopher. Although he lived only 34 years, in even that brief time he displayed a wealth of genius. He invented "geometric algebra," which underlies our current discipline of mathematical physics. Decades before Einstein developed his geometric theory of gravity, Clifford had already suggested that gravitation was a function of geometry. Even in William James' attempted refutation of a famous article by Clifford, James referred to him as the *enfant terrible* (the "terrible in-

fant," or, in other words, the "child prodigy"), acknowledging the respect accorded Clifford in his own lifetime. In 1877 Clifford wrote
"The Ethics of Belief," the article that will concern us here.[8]

He opens the article with a story, and he is such a delightful
writer that it is worth telling in his own words:

"A shipowner was about to send to sea an emigrant ship. He
knew that she was old, and not overwell built at the first; that she had
seen many seas and climes, and often had needed repairs. Doubts had
been suggested to him that possibly she was not seaworthy. These
doubts preyed upon his mind, and made him unhappy; he thought
that perhaps he ought to have her thoroughly overhauled and refit-
ted, even though this should put him to great expense. Before the
ship sailed, however, he succeeded in overcoming these melancholy
reflections. He said to himself that she had gone safely through so
many voyages and weathered so many storms that it was idle to suppose she would not come safely home from this trip also. He would
put his trust in Providence, which could hardly fail to protect all these
unhappy families that were leaving their fatherland to seek for better
times elsewhere. He would dismiss from his mind all ungenerous sus-
picions about the honesty of builders and contractors. In such ways
he acquired a sincere and comfortable conviction that his vessel was
thoroughly safe and seaworthy; he watched her departure with a light
heart, and benevolent wishes for the success of the exiles in their
strange new home that was to be; and he got his insurance money
when she went down in midocean and told no tales."

Clifford expresses legitimate horror at the shipowner's convenient belief and resulting action, and we are certainly inclined to agree
with him that "surely . . . he was verily guilty of the death of those
men." We agree that the "impressions" that the shipowner used to
trump the other evidence were not legitimate. But what makes
Clifford's essay fascinating and profound is that he explores the nature of the guilt that we should ascribe to the shipowner. Initially we
think that *because the ship went down* (because the "impression" came

apart from the facts), the shipowner is guilty. Clifford does not let him off the hook so easily, however:

"Let us alter the case a little, and suppose that the ship was not unsound after all; that she made her voyage safely, and many others after it. Will that diminish the guilt of her owner? Not one jot. When an action is once done, it is right or wrong forever; no accidental failure of its good or evil fruits can possibly alter that. The man would not have been innocent; he would only have been not found out."

The idea that consequences are not the foundation of morality is certainly in harmony with Christian principles, but Clifford is after much bigger game than even this conclusion. You see, most people have no problem thinking that our external actions are what must be ethically evaluated. Clifford argues instead that the very act of believing, of choosing what one will believe, is itself the "action" that determines the rightness or wrongness of all the external behavior that follows on its heels:

"The question of right or wrong has to do with the origin of his belief, not the matter of it; not what it was, but how he got it; not whether it turned out to be true or false, but whether he had a right to believe on such evidence as was before him."

The idea that morality inheres in our believing itself, that our actions are just an outworking of our believing, is initially a bit shocking. But Clifford's most astounding point is that "right" and "true" as well as "wrong" and "false" can be separate things. We tend to think that "right" beliefs are the "true" ones, and "wrong" beliefs are the "false" ones. Clifford concludes, however, that it is the method of obtaining a belief that makes it right or wrong, regardless of whether the belief happens to be true. The rightness or wrongness of the shipowner's belief, and the rightness or the wrongness of the resulting actions, were fixed at the point of decision. Yet the truth or falsity of the shipowner's belief was purely a matter of later circumstance.

Thomas Nagel argues in "Moral Luck" that circumstances (luck) should not play a role in moral evaluations, but that we are intuitively drawn to let luck have such a part. Accounting for the tension between our intuitions is the problem of moral luck.[9] Consider the case of a drunk driver. He staggers out of a bar in the wee hours, barely manages to open his car door, collapses into the seat, eventually fits the key into the ignition, and starts on his way home. In the first scenario the drunk driver hits and kills a woman crossing the street. Had he been sober he would have never failed to notice and would have easily avoided the woman. But in the second scenario the drunk driver happens to whiz through the intersection just one second before the woman steps off the curb, so he avoids the accident entirely and makes it home with no mishap.

Usually we tend to ascribe more "blame" to the man in the first scenario. But we also recognize that there is no difference in any aspect of what the man had control over. In both scenarios he chose and acted exactly the same. What can be evaluated about the man is fixed before he ever encounters the intersection. His choices and actions appear to have their moral weight already determined entirely apart from whether or not he (and the woman) were merely lucky.

Clifford urges us to recognize that "getting lucky" has nothing to do with morality. Our actions are a necessary product of our beliefs, so if our actions have moral weight prior to their outcomes, then our beliefs have moral weight prior to their expressions in actions. Thus, ultimately, moral evaluation must occur at a much deeper level than that of visible deeds or behavior, and certainly long before those actions produce the fruit of consequences. Christ Himself suggested the same thing in His sermon on the mount, but it seems that even we Christians fail to see the implications of it.

If you consider every terrible thing done to Christ Himself, you will see the same pattern emerge again and again leading up to each abuse: ample evidence is provided to convince a reasonable person that Jesus is the Son of God and the Christ. The perpetrators of evil ignore this evidence and fixate upon other evidence (for example, passages in the Old Testament that point to Christ's kingly role). Christ heaps miracles upon miracles, and His very use of Scripture is convincing to some but not to the majority. Because the leaders and the people greatly want the Messiah be a king, they cannot accept the lowly Christ who avoids coronation. Slowly but surely their minds turn more toward their disbelief. They reject more and more evidence that thwarts their chosen conclusion. Finally, the cherished belief turns into action and results in the murder of the Son of God. But, note this carefully, the murder was not the wrong thing. Rather, the choice of beliefs that led to the murder was the wrong thing! As Christ Himself taught, whether or not the believing led to the outward act of murder, murder had still occurred in the heart of the believer (this was Christ's point in the Sermon on the Mount). The shipowner committed himself to the deaths of the passengers, regardless of whether or not they happened to die, by believing a position opposed to the best and total weight of evidence that he had before him.

What is the nature of this "commitment" that goes hand in hand with all of our beliefs? As Clifford puts it:

"Nor is it truly a belief at all which has not some influence upon the actions of him who holds it. He who truly believes that which prompts him to an action has looked upon the action to lust after it, he has committed it already in his heart. If a belief is not realized immediately in open deeds, it is stored up for the guidance of the future. It goes to make a part of that aggregate of beliefs which is the link between sensation and action at every moment of all our lives, and which is so organized and compacted together that no part of it can be isolated from the rest, but every new addition modifies the structure of the whole. No real belief, however trifling and fragmentary it may seem, is ever truly insignificant; it prepares us to receive more of its like, confirms those which resembled it before, and weakens others; and so gradually it lays a stealthy train in our inmost thoughts, which may someday explode into overt action, and leave its stamp upon our character forever."

Please pause and take the time to read that passage again. I am serious. Carefully consider it.[10] Clifford clearly develops Christ's own intent in linking the "thoughts of the heart" with morality. It is the *believing* that matters. The resulting actions (if they occur at all) merely reveal the innermost beliefs. Furthermore, unless you assume that morality should properly be founded upon luck, then you will agree with Clifford (and Christ) that the truth or falsity of a belief is not where the moral weight of a belief resides. The fact that the drunkard believes (on the basis of no good evidence) that he will get home without mishap in no way lessens his guilt, regardless of whether or not that belief happens to turn out to be true. His getting home without mishap cannot make his belief right, and it is not the unlucky mishap that makes his belief wrong.

Where are we so far? We have realized that moral weight inheres in beliefs, that actions and outcomes are actually only indirect indicators of what the beliefs might have been, and that whether or not beliefs happen to be true or false is not the proper basis of their moral significance. If the truth or falsity of a belief is not what determines its rightness or wrongness, then what is?

Clifford's answer (again, I think, a reflection of what Christ taught) is that the *method* of obtaining a belief is what makes a belief right or wrong. Let's think of it this way. It is often the case that I am forced to make some active decision between two alternatives. Usually I can do no better than simply weigh out the evidence supporting each side. In doing so, I must be as careful as possible not to let bias and simple desires skew the weight of evidence. In other words, I must not "lust after" one side or the other. As questions and doubts present themselves, I must honestly assess them—not avoid them or pretend that they don't exist. I must be flexible in my thinking, rather than dogmatic, giving the evidence an honest hearing and allowing my mind to be open to other possibilities that I might have never seen otherwise. By employing this method, I am intellectually honest.

MFAUP-3

Now, I can already hear some gasping, "Well! I don't intend that my mind should become so open that all my brains fall out!" But I am not advocating being gullible. In fact, if you will remember, I began this discussion to demonstrate that much of what passes for "faith" today is nothing more than being gullible. As with the shipowner's "sincere belief," much of what is "sincerely believed" today is the result of intentional (often even dogmatic) gullibility. Opening your mind to alternative possibilities to what you sincerely believe, however, is the antidote to gullibility rather than the root of it. However, the danger to right believing comes at us from both sides, as I noted earlier in this chapter. On the one side, we simply accept beliefs that agree with our previous ones. We tend to be un-thinkingly gullible regarding like beliefs. On the other side, we can become so skeptical that no weight of evidence is ever sufficient to convince us to hold (and act upon) a belief.[11] So let us be just as afraid of *both* skepticism and gullibility.

Consider that dichotomy in terms of miracle stories. Suppose I tell the incident of my sister's tongue being healed to an audience that includes both Christians and agnostics. Let us examine the typical responses of both groups.

At the end of the narrative the Christians uncritically exclaim, "Praise Jesus," and they turn to the agnostics in triumph to ask, "In the face of such a miracle, how could you fail to believe?"

As for the agnostics, they carefully and in couched terms reply, "Very interesting story. H'mmm . . . I wonder how accurate Jensen's recollection is of the events after so many years. I wonder if the story is even fundamentally true in its important details."

The Christian responds, "Can't you see how good God is? Think of it—his sister's tongue was almost cut in half, and it was healed instantly!"

The agnostic replies, "Maybe, but let's grant for a moment that everything happened just as Jensen says. Even so, it's not necessarily or even likely the case that the Judeo-Christian 'God' you are referring to was responsible for it. There are many other alternatives."

Aghast, the Christian stammers, "His mom prayed to *God*. Hello! And *God* answered."

Stoically the agnostic deflects the horror. "Whether or not she prayed to what she thought was the Judeo-Christian God, that fact says nothing about what was actually responsible for the healing. After all, even quantum theory tells us that there is a tiny chance of such an event occurring just randomly. It's just really, really hard to know what to make of such an event. To be honest, I see no reason to think that the Judeo-Christian God had anything to do with it."

And you can see the point by now. The typical Christian tends to accept miracle stories uncritically, and the agnostic often approaches them hypercritically. But flip the coin over, start talking about evolutionary theory, and watch how the roles and responses exactly reverse, with the "agnostic" now dogmatically asserting that evolutionary theory is a fact, and the Christian attempting to poke holes in the theory. In both contexts, both sides ignore and uncritically accept evidence, being gullible and credulous in their own specific ways while applying their biases to the weight of evidence at hand.

As Clifford well emphasized: "No real belief, however trifling and fragmentary it may seem, is ever truly insignificant; it prepares us to receive more of its like, confirms those which resembled it before, and weakens others." Thus it behooves us as thinkers, not as "Christian thinkers" or as "agnostic thinkers," or as any other particular type of thinkers, but as thinkers simpliciter, that we carefully consider the whole weight of evidence affecting our beliefs about a question.

The matter is even weightier than I have suggested so far. Clifford continues:

"And no one man's belief is in any case a private matter which concerns himself alone. Our lives are guided by that general conception of the course of things which has been created by society for social purposes. Our words, our phrases, our forms and processes and modes of thought, are common property, fashioned and perfected from age to age; an heirloom which every succeeding generation inherits as a precious deposit and a sacred trust to be handed on to the next one, not unchanged but enlarged and purified, with some clear marks of its proper handiwork. Into this, for good or ill, is woven every belief of every man who has speech of his fellows. An awful privilege, and an awful responsibility, that we should help to create the world in which posterity will live."

It is in light of this solemn responsibility that Clifford can press it home to each of us:

"It is not only the leader of men, statesman, philosopher, or poet, that owes this bounden duty to mankind. Every rustic who delivers in the village alehouse his slow, infrequent sentences may help to kill or keep alive the fatal superstitions which clog his race. Every hard-worked wife of an artisan may transmit to her children beliefs which shall knit society together, or rend it in pieces. No simplicity of mind, no obscurity of station, can escape the universal duty of questioning all that we believe."

But now Clifford seems to have gone too far. "Questioning all that we believe"? Not only do we wonder if this is even possible, we question whether it could possibly be required that we do so! Is Clifford just being hyperbolic here and really doesn't mean to sound as vociferous as he does? No, he presses the point home more and more intentionally and vigorously:

"If I let myself believe anything on insufficient evidence, there may be no great harm done by the mere belief; it may be true after all, or I may never have occasion to exhibit it in outward acts. But I cannot help doing this great wrong toward Man, that I make myself credulous. The danger to society is not merely that it should believe wrong things, though that is great enough; but that it should become credulous, and lose the habit of testing things and inquiring into them; for then it must sink back into savagery."

And, in a passage that should be particularly poignant to Christians, Clifford details the fundamental nature of the great evil of credulity:

"Men speak the truth to one another when each reveres the truth in his own mind and in the other's mind; but how shall my friend revere the truth in my mind when I myself am careless about it, when I believe things because I want to believe them, and because they are comforting and pleasant? Will he not learn to cry, 'Peace,' to me, when there is no peace? By such a course I shall surround myself with a thick atmosphere of falsehood and fraud, and in that I must live. It may matter little to me, in my cloud-castle of sweet illusions and darling lies; but it matters much to Man that I have made my neighbours ready to deceive. The credulous man is father to the liar and the cheat; he lives in the bosom of this his family, and it is no marvel if he should become even as they are. So closely are our duties knit together, that whoso shall keep the whole law, and yet offend in one point, he is guilty of all."

When considered from that perspective, our interrelations are so intimate, and the tide of society so affected by the beliefs (and resulting speech and actions) of us all, that it now seems difficult for Clifford to *over*state his case:

"If a man, holding a belief which he was taught in childhood or persuaded of afterwards, keeps down and pushes away any doubts which arise about it in his mind, purposely avoids the reading of books and the company of men that call in question or discuss it, and regards as impious those questions which cannot easily be asked without disturbing it—the life of that man is one long sin against mankind.

"If this judgment seems harsh when applied to those simple souls who have never known better, who have been brought up from the cradle with a horror of doubt, and taught that their eternal welfare depends on what they believe, then it leads to the very serious question, *Who hath made Israel to sin?*"

Clifford condemns credulity in both Christians and agnostics alike. Looking around society today, both in and out of the scholarly community and both in and out of the church, I have seen plenty of guilt to go around. Agnostics embrace what they call "doubt," even as they are utterly unwilling to acknowledge the profound weight of evidence on the side of the Christian. Christians, by contrast, can quickly adopt the comfortable sentiments espoused from the pulpit and from most Christian literature, sentiments that assure them of eternal life and a bubble-gum machine god who expects nothing more of him than "only believe," as though that "belief" is a mere assent to the "truth." Such "Christians" view questions with deep distrust and regard doubts as arising from the devil, allowing them to ignore questions or anything that disturbs them. Yet even if all doubt is of the devil, the way to overcome it is not to pretend that it does not exist.

Consider how God would have preferred the confrontation in the Garden of Eden to go.

Satan: You shall not surely die. God knows that when you eat of this fruit, you will become as He is (and as I have become), knowing everything, even those things He doesn't want you to know.

Eve: Maybe you are right, but at the moment I have no actual reason to think so. Instead, everything in me resonates with what God has called "good." What He terms right and true and good seem to me to be right and true and good.

Satan: Ah, gullible one! Of course it seems that way to you, because you don't know the very things that God wants to keep from you. If you could see things as I do, you would find your true freedom.

Eve: Perhaps, but I don't detect any constraints on my freedom now. Sure, God said to not eat of this one tree, but that's hardly a constraint on my freedom! God created everything, including me, so of course it's His right to withhold this one tree from me if He wants to. In fact, considering it that way makes me realize that it is solely His right to define all the boundaries. Nevertheless, I experience profound freedom.

Satan: Now you're being obtuse. Just because you feel free doesn't mean that you are. Knowledge is power, and if you don't have the knowledge, you can't be really free because you are really powerless. There are so many things you could choose if only you would decide to eat this fruit.

Eve: So you are suggesting that my choices would expand if I would only decide to disobey God? Then it seems to me that what you are saying is that everything comes down to this one choice: eat the fruit or don't eat the fruit. Then you have thwarted yourself, serpent, because you were just telling me that I'm not really free. But in order for me to be absolutely free, as you suggest, you must already admit my absolute freedom! Having more choices to make doesn't change the fact that each choice is just like this choice. In each choice I am totally free to decide. And in each choice the matter comes down to whether or not to obey God. So it becomes clear that this debate was never about freedom or power at all. It is only about whether or not to disobey God right here and right now, and you have not yet given me any reason to suggest that it would be better for me to do so. Again, all the weight of evidence I have suggests that it would be a profound mistake to do so. I grow tired of this debate. Maybe I will see you around some other time, but for now, goodbye.

Now, I'm not saying that we should debate endlessly with Satan, or that any of us need to be particularly intellectually sophisticated in our dealings with him, as my example might seem to suggest. What I am arguing is that when empowered with the Word of God (properly understood and employed), we need not fear to meet the temptations or assaults of Satan upon our faith. The temptation of Christ in the wilderness reveals an important point about doubts and temptations, one that will quiet some of the fear about what Clifford is suggesting. Doubts and temptations both come to us in species. That is, we don't have to answer each and every particular example or form of a doubt in order to have addressed a species of doubt.

For example, I have come to reject all forms of consequentialism[12] in ethics. Thus I don't need to evaluate carefully every new variety of utilitarianism[13] that emerges. Once I identify an ethical theory as being

71

consequentialistic, I can reject that theory because I have sweeping and devastating reasons to reject all forms of consequentialism.

In the same way, Eve would not have needed to stand arguing with the serpent about every imaginable point of contention. Having caught the creature in one significant deception about the basic nature of his temptation, she would have been justified simply to return to God, ask Him about other points of concern, and reject the serpent's message. Just as soon as Christ recognized that each of Satan's temptations in the wilderness involved just another variation of the same fundamental species, He rejected Satan's efforts and drove the devil away.

People are rightly skeptical about the more strident and sweeping claims of science. We have ample reason to think (although it is beyond the scope of this book to discuss) that the claims of science are not about "ultimate" or "objective" reality at all. Most people rightly believe that there is "something more" to the universe than science's purely naturalistic paradigm can admit. Does that open the door to phrenology, astrology, the paranormal (in its most tawdry forms), and so on? Conversely, we may ask what entitles us to believe that the Bible is the "Word of God," as opposed to the many other supposedly sacred scriptures from other religions. As you see clearly now, no matter what you believe on any given subject, some will regard you as gullible and others will consider you as skeptical.

Another issue in the science versus Christianity debate currently raging in North America is that Christians who pride themselves on rejecting the evidences of science are the same people who will dogmatically trot out miracle stories as the basis for their "faith." But consider this fact: "signs and wonders" are just more sensory experiences—more evidences of the senses. The interpretation of those experiences is what makes for the supposed faith. Nothing in principle makes miracle stories different from scientific ones. *Both* rely upon empirical evidence (the senses) to draw conclusions. And *both* deal with evidence that is unreliable in principle. Consequently, there is something deeply disingenuous about either scientists or Christians bashing on each other with the same club. Christians have much better "weapons" at their disposal than miracle stories, and I will have much more to say about that point as we proceed.

Where should we draw the intellectual line? When do we know that we have honestly considered questions and doubts that threaten our beliefs? And when do we have assurance that we are neither gullible nor skeptical, but that we are instead intellectually honest? There is no pat answer, and I would be lying if I tried to claim there was or to formulate one. Perhaps this is one reason Scripture tells us to work out our own salvation "with fear and trembling" (Phil. 2:12).

However, before this sounds as if, in the face of profound questions, I have nothing whatsoever of value to offer, let me mitigate what I have just said with some actual practical advice.

Our goal is to form coherent worldviews. We want our various beliefs to "hang together" into a harmonious whole, in which the entire fabric is woven into a design that most correctly reflects the way things really are. However, we find ourselves looking for the "first threads" of that tapestry. We want our tapestry to be one in which merely plucking at our "first threads" does not cause the whole thing to unravel. And that is possible to accomplish. There are not an unlimited number of alternatives extant as potential "first threads." As a result, we can evaluate the foundations of various belief systems (always maintaining a willingness to revisit the issues in the face of additional evidence), and determine the relative plausibility of each. Each has its own accounts of everything from metaphysics[14] to ethics, and each has to integrate with the actual physical evidence that we do have (which is, by the way, a subset of what science claims to have). While a responsible investigation does take time, and it will often require more study than we had initially expected, that investigation is possible for each of us. And each of us is merely gullible if we unthinkingly accept either the Bible or science as among our "first threads" prior to engaging in some serious study.

I believe that I can speak from experience on this. Having received my entire philosophical education in secular universities, I honestly gave atheism and agnosticism a fair shot. More than once I had a professor comment, "You have the promise to be a really good philosopher—if only we could get you past this superstitious theism."[15] I took that admonition seriously, and I honestly considered purely secular accounts of ethics, physics, language, and so on. Also I talked with many former believers and considered why they had rejected theism. Meanwhile, I read the many theistic responses to the secular perspectives, written by such excellent and famous philosophers as Alvin Plantinga, Saul Kripke, and Philip Quinn (among many others).[16] In addition, I have considered non-Christian religions as well as many varieties of Christian denominations.

As a result I have come to believe (with an emphasis on the process) that Quinn is more generally correct than he intended when he states that theists "have had the better of the argument." Christians need not run scared from doubts or questions. My study has convinced me that we need not fear science when it questions the literal Genesis account of Creation. I know that Christianity and a literal interpretation of Genesis are intellectually defensible and respectable. But I say all this by way of encouragement for you to engage in that process for yourself. My study cannot substitute for your own. Be intellectually honest, and in so being you will elevate the process of thinking of those around you. The only alternative is for you to settle in more dogmatic fashion into your own comfortable beliefs (whatever they may be), and then there is no difference in principle between you and the religious leaders who orchestrated the murder of the Son of God. If you believe *anything* dogmatically, without willingness even to consider at any time that you might be in error, then you have literally closed off the primary avenue by which the Holy Spirit can reach your reasoning mind with new revelations of truth. None of us are in such an epistemically privileged position[17] that we can consider ourselves immune from error, and so for each of us, knowledge of God arises from careful, thoughtful consideration of all the evidence. When you stop examining the evidence we find in the world around us, you halt the process of understanding God and seeing His perspectives. Therefore, you must be intellectually honest, or your life is indeed "one long sin against mankind" and against the God who gave you the marvelous ability to really know Him.

---

[1] See *Wings of Steel* (Hagerstown, Md.: Review and Herald Pub. Assn., 1994).

[2] I will not be dragged into an epistemological morass here. I am well aware of skeptical arguments against even this simple claim, and this book is not the place to debate them. For the purposes of this book, our everyday usage of words such as "knowledge" will serve just fine.

[3] It is worth noting at this point that what most people mean by "objective" is really intersubjective. If "all" or some version of "most" people agree about something, then that is commonly taken as an "objective" fact. But a huge difference exists between genuine objectivity and intersubjectivity. It is beyond the scope of this book to delve into such details, but one of the fundamental problems with how people perceive the nature of science is that they conflate intersubjectivity and objectivity, and then they use that latter term in error. However, I will boldly assert for the purposes of this book that the Bible tells us about the most important, genuinely objective facts of the universe.

[4] I am well aware that scientists will blame engineers for things not working as they are supposed to. Engineers will in turn blame manufacturers, and manufacturers their materials suppliers, who will in turn claim that the engineers and installers did not use the materials as specified. But when all the finger-pointing loops are finished, and everybody has ensured that they are pointing at somebody else, the fact remains that science is about how and why things seem to work as they do. And things do not always behave as they seem usually to do. Every scientific theory is laden with "anomalies," and the import of such anomalies is, conveniently, taken to be exactly what the relevant scientists say their import is.

[5] Of course, Nobel-winning physicists, such as Stephen Weinberg, would beg to differ. However, unfortunately, as *Dreams of a Final Theory* demonstrates, being a top physicist does not make you a good philosopher, and the book is absolutely riddled with question-begging assumptions and other basic philosophical errors.

[6] There is so much to say about what it is that science actually does, and the relation of science to Christian faith, that I must postpone such discussion for a future volume. However, the interested reader can begin to explore the philosophy of science, particularly regarding naturalism and evolutionary theory, both from a non-Christian and Christian point of view, by reading anything from Stephen Jay Gould, Richard Dawkins, Daniel C. Dennett, Phillip E. Johnson, Michael Behe, Roger Penrose, and the works listed in the bibliographies supplied by these authors. I would also point you to the specific volumes: Thomas S. Kuhn, *The Structure of Scientific Revolutions* (Chicago: University of Chicago Press, 1996); Robert Klee, ed., *Scientific Inquiry: Readings in the Philosophy of Science* (New York: Oxford University Press, 1999); Robert T. Pennock, ed., *Intelligent Design*

Creationism and Its Critics (London: The MIT Press, 2001); and Michael Denton, *Evolution: a Theory in Crisis* (Bethesda, Md.: Adler & Adler, 1986). These should get you started, although they are just a start.

[7] The term *empirical* just means knowledge obtained "from experience," and can also be called *a posteriori*. It contrasts with *a priori*, which means knowledge obtained "prior to experience." In the case of science, the "experience" is that of the senses, although many philosophical theories include some form of "inner experience," which signifies awareness of our own inner states.

[8] For our purposes we will not discuss James' response to Clifford's article "The Ethics of Belief." In studying and teaching the debate for years, I have come to conclude that James is actually arguing past Clifford in all significant respects, so that James does not succeed in really addressing Clifford's main points. Thus I will not take the space here for a fully developed debate. The interested reader can easily pursue it.

[9] A large amount of literature exists on this subject, and I am not even skimming the surface of it. See Thomas Nagel, Bernard Williams, and Susan Wolf (and their associated bibliographies) for an introduction to this literature.

[10] I find it ironic that the foregoing passage so harmonizes with Christ's own teachings on this subject, yet James took Clifford to be threatening the very core of religious believing.

[11] I think that this is the danger that James perceived in Clifford's article—that using Clifford's approach to believing would thrust us into a deep skepticism from which no amount of evidence could ever be "sufficient." Clifford, however, never suggests any such thing, and he even thwarts this danger by explicitly stating that one is entitled to hold any belief as long as he or she is willing at any time to consider evidence contrary to that belief. Thus he advocates a nondogmatic stance rather than skepticism.

[12] Ethical consequentialism is a branch of ethical theorizing that prioritizes the good over the right. This is to say, that right and wrong are defined in terms of good and bad, in which the right thing to do is to produce a good outcome. There are many theories about the good, and there are many theories about how to produce good consequences. The various flavors of utilitarianism are the most well-known versions of consequentialistic ethical theories. If, as I do, one rejects all forms of good-prior-to-right ethical theorizing, then one may immediately ignore all forms of consequentialism.

[13] Among consequentialistic ethical theories, utilitarianism is the most well known and popular. The basic way that utilitarianism produces good consequences is to "maximize utility," in which what counts as "utility" can be any of the various "goods," depending upon the flavor of utilitarianism. For example, hedonistic utilitarianism asserts that the right thing to do is whatever maximizes pleasure. (It should be noted that the "maximizing" in utilitarianism seeks to encompass the entire set of moral entities, and some philosophers include animals in the set of moral entities.) We can categorize the various versions of utilitarianism according to what each asserts is the primary good and the theorized mechanism by which that good is to be maximized.

[14] Metaphysics is the study of reality, of existence. A metaphysical study concerns itself with the actual facts of what exists, not just how things appear to us.

[15] Fortunately, if my letters of recommendation from my professors are any indication, they decided that I was a good philosopher despite the fact that I ultimately came down on the side of theism.

[16] It appears that one *can* be a "really good" philosopher even with a commitment to theism.

[17] Epistemology is the study of knowledge and truth. An epistemological study concerns itself with what we can know (and why) and how we come to know anything at all. So an epistemically privileged position is a "God's-eye" sort of view that enables genuine, indubitable knowledge

Chapter 5

DON'T FALL

By the time I had reached my mid-20s climbing occupied most of my attention. It is really beyond the scope of this book to describe the value I saw (and still do see) in the skill, but it drove me to find my limits and to know myself.

One day I decided to make good on an idea that I had harbored for some time. I wanted to "free-solo" a 1,200-foot-high cliff in Yosemite. Free-soloing meant that I would be climbing the cliff with no rope—a fall would almost undoubtedly be fatal.

Before you conclude that I'm totally insane, I should say that my proposed route was well within my abilities. I had climbed other routes of that grade of difficulty for years without falling, and I had already taken this particular route several times without incident. Because I knew the route well, the only challenge I foresaw was that of "keeping my head together" when climbing without a rope.

Climbing is actually as much a mental as it is a physical game. So I was enthusiastic to experience the route free-solo.

For the first 700 feet of climbing I was basically romping up the wall. The level of difficulty was what I had expected and remembered, well within my comfort limits. The joy of moving quickly, with no pauses to set protection placements, anchors, belays, or for bringing a partner up, was exhilarating. But about 700 feet up the wall I had an important decision to make.

The last time I had climbed the route it had a famous section called the "rotten log pitch." The climb reaches a small, dirt-covered ledge. On that ledge a pine tree had once grown about 40 feet tall and then died. When the tree had finally fallen over off of the ledge, amazingly it had dropped *across* the wall in such a trajectory that it had caught on the edge of a higher ledge. The base had remained on the original ledge, and the tree trunk had wedged firmly on the edge of the higher ledge, producing a suspended "bridge" of sorts angling up and across the blank wall about 30 feet, connecting the two ledges. From the upper ledge the climbing became much easier, so the fallen log acted as a bridge between the harder lower sections of the route and the easier upper ones.

The problem with the rotten log was that through the decades it had indeed become more and more rotten. Since the log was suspended about 10 feet away from the main wall, traversing its length up to the higher ledge became a more and more horrific prospect as the years went by. I had personally observed several very good climbers catch their first sight of the rotten log, visualize themselves astride its creaking, groaning, bouncing length, look down the more than 300 feet of steep, blank rock to the next ledge system below, and just decide not to do it! Through the years many climbers had retreated from that spot rather than shinny their way up the rotten log pitch. It was a standing joke in the Yosemite Valley climbing scene that some poor sap was going to ride that log down when it finally crumbled loose from its perch on the higher ledge, and that would be one wild ride until the rope caught and plucked the climber free from the hurtling mass of death.

The rotten log became so bad that climbers determined to find another way to reach the higher ledge systems, and ultimately they worked out an alternative route from the lower ledge using some smaller and much harder crack systems. Experts rated the alternative path two grades harder than any other section of the route, and many climbers who could cope with the route's lower rating could not manage the difficulty of the alternative section. So for them the rotten log pitch was the only way up the route.

One day the rotten log was no more. I never heard of anybody riding it down, and I'm sure that story would have been widely circulated had it actually happened. I presume that winter snows simply accomplished the inevitable, and word quickly spread that the only way up the route now was via the alternative crack system.

As I started up the route I well knew that I would need to employ the alternative crack system from the lower ledge. It was for me the only unknown section of the route, but even its difficulty grade was well within my abilities, so I had decided in advance that I would simply take that section particularly carefully, and then the upper section of the route would be just more of a romp.

Eventually I found myself on the lower ledge, staring at the upper ledge where the rotten log had once rested. Looking down at the sweeping exposure, I realized that I probably would not have had the guts to shinny up the rotten log free-solo anyway, so it did not matter that it was gone.

Turning to the small crack leading up from the ledge, I centered myself. This was much more serious climbing, and I entered a new frame of mind.

As I worked my way up, one crack would lead to another, then another. It was important to me that I be able to reverse my progress all the way back to the starting ledge, and then, of course, to the ground if I should encounter a section that I was unwilling to attempt. I often climbed up several feet, then reversed my moves, connecting them in my mind with those that had come before, thus assuring myself that I could work my way back down to the ledge if necessary.

Eventually I had climbed more than 100 feet up from the ledge, and I really did not relish the prospect of retracing it back down. So I felt more and more committed the higher above the ledge I got.

Finally I was within about five feet of a higher ledge that connected to the easier climbing on the upper section of the route. My ascent of the alternative crack system was almost complete. One obstacle lay between me and the easy romp to the summit.

At the top of the crack system a small "ceiling" jutted horizontally out from the wall. To reach the ledge above, I would have to climb out almost horizontally, following the cracks and small holds, until the wall rounded back over to vertical again. From that point I would be able to reach over and grab the edge of that higher ledge, pull myself up onto it, and the difficulties would be behind me.

As I glanced down the hundreds of feet to the lower ledge system that would be my first bounce if I fell from that overhanging section, I could feel the seriousness of the situation, but I knew the grade of difficulty, and I was confident in my ability to overcome this last obstacle. Nevertheless, as I started working out the final moves to surmount the overhanging section, I was careful to ensure that I could reverse them if necessary.

Up and down, up and down. I pushed one move higher each time, until I knew I could regain the relative security of the crack system underneath the overhang. But there would be a spot beyond which I knew I could not reverse the sequence. At some point I would have to swing my feet loose and commit to pulling up onto the ledge, and from there it would be next to impossible for me to regain my footing and reverse the moves.

So I stayed in the lower crack for a moment, contemplating. The choice was clear: commit to the final move over the overhang or reverse my way 800 feet back to the ground.

It wasn't much of a choice. I believed that final move to be well within my abilities, and there was arguably more danger in down-climbing hundreds of feet back to the ground. I started up.

Quickly I repeated the overhanging moves to the point of commitment, let my feet loose, pulled up with both hands, then reached up and over with my right hand for the edge of the ledge, expecting to find a surface edge to grab on to, and discovered . . . sloping, rounded, mossy, wet, sandy . . . Holding myself in a one-arm pull-up with my left arm, I frantically felt everywhere I could up there, but there simply was no decent handhold. Everything I could feel was worthless.

As I lowered myself down to allow myself to grip with my right hand again, the first cold wave of fear washed over me. Hanging there from both hands, feet dangling over the abyss, I quickly thought through my options. The clock was now ticking. I knew I did not have stamina to remain there for long. I could only attempt that pull-up and one-arm hang maybe two or three more times. While I could try to reverse the moves out of there, I realized that I could expend a lot of energy doing it, and if it wasn't successful I wouldn't have anything left even to attempt getting onto the ledge again. The clock was still ticking.

Finally committing everything I had to making it up onto the ledge, I decided this time *carefully* to explore my handhold options above, reserving enough strength to lower down, hang for a few moments, and then *make* the move on my last attempt.

I pulled up, locked off with my left arm, and reached up again with my right hand. Then I worked carefully across the rounded edge of the ledge as far as I could reach in both directions. Nothing. A few spots would probably have been good handholds if they had been dry and clean. But, wet and mossy and gravel-covered as they were then, they were useless.

When I lowered back to regrip with my right hand again, an icy chill swept over my entire being. I knew that I was going to die. Somehow I had gotten myself into a situation without any escape. I certainly did not have the energy to try to reverse my way out of the overhang now, and the residual energy I had for my one last attempt over the last move was waning fast. Worse, even that last vestige of fading energy was worthless, because I had no way to use it. I was out of options.

In all my years of climbing difficult routes I have never prayed for God to make protection placements stay in the wall, or help an anchor to hold, or to intervene in supernatural ways. I have prayed for good judgment. I have prayed for protection from elements entirely beyond my control. But I have never prayed before or since as I did that moment.

Every shred of my existence suddenly focused upon God, and I clung to Him as my *only* hope of salvation. My prayer was necessarily quick, but what it lacked in eloquence it more than made up for in fervency: "My Lord, You see how I got here. I wasn't being stupid, but even so, I'm not justifying my need of Your help now. I ask for Your help because I *need* it, and for no other reason. If You don't help me now, I'm dead, so it's entirely up to You. I'm going to try once more—for what, I don't know, because there is nothing up there for me. Lord, make something happen for me, please!"

My arms and fingers felt wooden, and a great, heavy ball of icy lead weighed in my center. But I pulled up with everything I had . . . to try . . . I knew not what . . . and . . .

Everything went black.

When I awoke, I was lying on my back on the upper ledge.

Pushing myself up, I looked around, baffled. For several minutes I sat there in dazed awe. Then, from my new vantage point on the ledge, I began to survey what my possible handhold options had been. My awe deepened as I saw the water trickling down from the wall above, pooling up on the ledge, and then trickling in small rivulets over and into all the pockets that might have otherwise been handholds. Moss and gravel had collected in each one. Perhaps in dry conditions I might have concentrated my efforts on cleaning out the best pocket enough to hang on to it and pull up with it, but in the current conditions that would have been a waste of energy.

How had I made it onto the ledge? What had happened to me while I was unconscious, and how could I have possibly climbed anything while in that condition?

I made my way to the top, hiked the trail back down to the valley floor, and then found my climbing partner, Mark, to tell him the whole story. To this day we remain without a naturalistic theory of how I could have survived.

The plot thickened several months after my free-solo ascent. In dry conditions, another climber (I don't remember who it was at this point) and I climbed the route together, primarily to check out that particular section. We ascended with typical roped belays and anchors, the leader using protection placements to catch him in the event of a fall. When we reached that fateful section, the other climber led the way. He reached the overhanging spot and placed protection, clipped the rope into the protection, and was thus safe from a long fall. He then began to work out the moves onto the upper ledge. The holds were still gravelly, but they were dry. He fell twice before working the sequence of moves out. Once on the ledge, he anchored himself and began to belay me up.

As I climbed this time I had none of the stress from the previous ascent. I was calm and relaxed. I had a top-rope, a rope from above to keep me from falling should I slip. You can have no better protection when climbing. So when I reached the overhang, I had none of the trauma from before. I was able to take my time and use the holds that the other climber had cleared out from his efforts. Even so, I fell once, and was caught by the rope, before working the sequence out.

To this very moment, as I write, I have no idea how I lived through my free-solo ascent and how God saved me. But I have no doubt that He did!

Miracle Stories and Faith

I have found that God intervenes most dramatically when I am used up. I don't mean when I *feel* used up, but when I *am* used up. It is when I have put forth my best efforts (and those efforts are honestly the best I have) that God intervenes and saves me.

Now, I'm not making such a point as "When I fall short of victory, then God's forgiveness makes it as though I have overcome." No, quite the contrary. I'm saying instead that when I am committed to victory (over sin or over circumstances), and I have honestly employed everything I have in the struggle, then I am assured of actual victory because God is determined that I shall not fall!

But imagine what would have happened in my story if I would have just hung there praying without commitment, unwilling to put forth every last vestige of energy within me to survive. My prayer would have been quite different: "God, there's no point in me trying because I can't make this. It's too hard for me, and I'm going to fall anyway, so I'm just going to let go now. Only You can catch me as I fall, because I give up now." Would God have honored such a prayer? I believe that such an approach to Him would be as if Jesus had succumbed to Satan's temptation to throw Himself off of the top of the Temple: presumptuous!

Or I could have just hung there in quiet desperation, waiting for the inevitable, my numbing limbs finally becoming so saturated with lactic acid that the nerves could no longer get their signals through and, like the rotten log, I turned into a hurtling mass of death.

The Bible indicates that God does not miraculously intervene on behalf of those who have given up the struggle. Instead, Scripture repeatedly urges us to invest every last fiber of our beings in the struggle to overcome self and sin and the world *and* to depend upon God to make our efforts victorious: "You have not yet resisted to the point of shedding blood, in your striving against sin" (Heb. 12:4, NASB).

Most of the time the Lord's help gives our efforts victory much less dramatically. Consequently, it is easy for us to slip into *feeling* as if we are gaining victories on our own. Then in a crisis we conclude that a temptation or circumstance is too much for us and that we are too weak to gain a victory. Rather than clinging to the Lord in final desperation, determined that we shall have His salvation, we gamely "struggle on," until our strength gives out and we fail. So far from our cry mirroring Jacob's "I will not let thee go, except thou bless me" (Gen. 32:26), our pitiful wail is "You have let me go and left me to face this on my own, and I cannot, so see, I fail."

Of course, there is no greater evidence of the Lord's presence than when He performs a miracle for us. Right? So we pray for miracles.

A fairly famous climber (I will call him JB to protect the guilty) once published an article in one of the climbing magazines pro- claiming his atheism. JB recounted how he had been climbing El Capitan in Yosemite. At one point he was using Jumars to ascend a rope that was attached above him. Jumars are camming devices that slide up a rope easily, but clamp onto the rope when a person pulls down on them. So the ingenious device allows a person literally to "walk" up an attached, dangling rope.

As JB was Jumarring his way up the rope, he looked up about 50 feet above him to see that the rope was rubbing back and forth over the edge of a piton (a metal spike driven into a crack in the rock). With each motion, JB would bounce up and down on the rope, and the up-and-down stretching of the rope scraped it against the piton, slowly sawing it in two.

JB recounts his prayer: "God, if You help me to live through this, I will believe in You." After his prayer JB began moving slowly and carefully up the rope, attempting to keep his bouncing to a bare minimum. He reached the point that it was almost sawn through and passed it. "It was then that I knew there is no God," he says.

Convinced that there had been no supernatural intervention, JB felt confident to conclude that God does not exist.

How many of us have fallen for the same faulty logic? Oh, per- haps we don't make the mistake as flagrantly as JB did. Perhaps we don't conclude that God doesn't exist. Instead, our mistake is more subtle. In the absence of the desired miracle, we perceive that we are alone and unhelped. We pitch our "faith" on the occurrence of mir- acles, and when they are not as dramatic or immediate as we desire, we feel abandoned, and our "faith" takes a beating.

On the other hand, we simply love to hear miracles like the one I just told in this chapter, because it reminds us that God still does intervene . . . at least for some people at some times. And there the downhill slide begins. While such stories remind us that God exists, they only make His seeming disregard for us all the more unnerving and even outrageous. To the extent we are honest with God, each of us has at times raged at Him, "You *could* do something about this situation, if You only *would!* What's Your problem? Can't You see that I need a miracle *now?*" And if the situation then seems to quietly resolve itself, our "faith" suffers, and we feel a bit more alone and a bit less likely to believe that God hears us and has our best interest at heart.

JB lived through his crisis, yet in the absence of a dramatic miracle he perceived that there was no God. On the other extreme, to salvage their "faith," many Christians search out "miracles" in everyday, naturalistic, causal events to convince themselves that there is a God (in their lives).

The likes of JB and his existentialist ilk embrace the void, revel in the meaninglessness of their lives, and denigrate the "weak-minded" who "use God as a crutch." Sadly, JB is right about many Christians who are attempting to use Him as a support. But He is no bubble-gum machine! He cannot be manipulated into producing events for us in exchange for believing in Him, living a "good life," performing some noble deed, or standing up for Him against the enemy.

And the harsh reality that many of us have not learned to accept is that at present we *do* live in a sinful world, and most of the time God allows causality to take its course. God hates it when a precious pet gets run over by a car. He hates seeing people dying in agony from cancer and other afflictions. The litany of all the tragedies in the world that God hates is endless. But in most situations He allows causality to take its course. And, more important, He permits us to exercise our freedom to introduce new causal chains into the world, which so often produce their fruit of more evils and tragedies.

So let's consider the causal chains that our freedom creates in the world. We would consider JB to be arrogant and presumptuous if he had prayed for God to save him and then kept ascending his rope by jumping and bouncing as much as he could. Yet so often we do the same thing by setting into effect causal chains that we then discover produce undesired effects, whereupon we pray for God in effect to cancel out causality and make our decisions (which really do affect the world) as though they had never been. We pray for God to perform miracles to save us, and then our "faith" takes a beating when He does not do so. And our causal chains touch not only ourselves—they reach out to bind others and affect the rest of the world. Should God intervene every time someone else's causal chain affects me in some way I don't like?

Am I suggesting that we should not pray for miracles, that we should not pray for God to rescue us from situations of our own making? No! As my own story in this chapter should make strikingly clear, I believe that we should "pray without ceasing," always calling upon the Lord to rescue us. However, what I am saying now is that our faith should not be bound up with the results of our praying!

This is a strange thought, isn't it? After all, in the church today isn't "answered prayer" the single most commonly cited basis for "building our faith"? If "answered prayer" isn't going to be the basis of our faith, then what could be? Isn't my suggestion here just a recipe for making a shipwreck of faith?

On the contrary, severing the connection between the apparent answers to our prayers and the strength of our faith is the only hope we have of securing a genuine faith-based relationship with God that will withstand any trial or temptation. I will say much more about this basic point as we continue. However, it is critical that we stop linking the strength of our faith with our perception of consequences.

Hanging there on the very threshold of death, I prayed with complete attention upon God. My prayer was no frivolous asking for Him to reveal Himself, to prove Himself to me. My prayer was no attempt to put enough quarters in the machine, so to speak, recounting all the reasons He owed me salvation. My prayer had no veiled threat to God that if He didn't save me I wouldn't like Him anymore. And even as I write this I say that I did not offer that prayer itself as a "prayer well-prayed" enough to demand the desired answer from God. Hanging there, I could offer only the utter desperation of my need, and I had no capacity to demand anything from Him. I realized that He was well within His rights and His typical mode of action to let causality take its course. Yet, in my desperation, I believed in Him. I clung to Him knowing that He could save me. And, ultimately, I pulled up that last time, exerting everything left in me, but *resigned to whatever fate God should choose for me.*

That is the essence of acting in true faith. True faith clings to God and depends upon Him for the most positive outcome (whatever that is from God's perspective). But it also resigns itself to whatever God decides. True faith exerts *every* effort to make the perceived good come about, even when it knows that the effort will not be sufficient. Then, having fought the best possible fight, it accepts God's decision. The outcome, the result of our praying and our clinging, is not the issue. True faith is believing in and clinging to God regardless of circumstance or consequence. Such faith cannot be effectively assailed, much less broken.

Then what is the value of miracle stories? After all, I have no reason to expect, to demand, of God that any such thing will happen in response to *my* prayers.

First, let us relinquish the idea that miracles prove anything about God. If this were that sort of book, I would demonstrate to you with profound and compelling rigor that even if my miracle stories could get you justification for belief in the supernatural realm, they could not provide support for believing in a particularly Judeo-Christian God. There are countless supernatural alternatives to the Judeo-Christian God as the acting source of supernaturally produced events. We quote only part of the verse as we tell our "miracle" stories: "Faith cometh by hearing" (Rom. 10:17), as though the "hearing" of the verse means hearing miracle stories. But the passage continues, "and hearing by the word of God." The Word of God is the sole and sufficient basis for true faith. Miracle stories cannot play that role.

So, then, what is the value of miracle stories? They are faith-building only insofar as they are the Word of God. Indeed, the Bible is chock-full of miracle stories, but mark this point carefully: the miracle stories in the Bible themselves need justification. By this I mean that we must ask ourselves what entitles us to believe that those stories are true. It will not do simply to reply, "Well, they are in the Bible, and the Bible is true, so those stories must be true."

Before you go running scared from yet another philosopher obviously trying to destroy your faith, hear me out a bit longer. This book is about building your faith, and I'm *not* suggesting that the Bible and its stories aren't true.

What I'm noting is the fact that before we can believe the miracle stories in the Bible as being the Word of God, we first have to ascertain that the Bible is itself true. It will not do to say that the Bible is true because the miracle stories in it prove that a good and powerful God was behind its writing. Such a response is deeply circular and demonstrates nothing. For example, I have actually heard this line of "logic" floated from the pulpit: "We know that God exists because the Bible says it is so. When we are asked how we are so confident that the Bible is correct about this, we may calmly reply that it must be so because the Bible is the Word of God." I'm not making it up—I have heard many variations of this and similar themes.

Fortunately we can do much better than this to defend the truth of the Bible against its critics, but what we *cannot* do is trot out the miracle stories in the Bible as the evidence to believe that Scripture is true!

This book is not about defending the truth of the Bible, but the point here is that we only have reason to believe in the truth of the miracle stories once we already believe in the credibility of the Bible as a whole. Its miracle stories don't build genuine faith until *after* we already have faith in the Word of God. Thus faith as a function of the Word of God comes first, and the value we gain from the miracle stories occurs after that. We must first believe that the Word of God is true.

Here is the problem with most of the miracle stories I hear from other people. Those telling them lack credibility. I am not convinced that the stories happened substantially as the people claim, and, even if I can get that far, I find that the events are often not about what I would call genuine miracles. As a result, such stories cannot be genuinely faith-building, because they lack the trustworthiness to count as the Word of God to me.

I hear someone saying, "OK, Jensen, you're more of a skeptic than most, but a lot of people do find their faith being strengthened by such stories. You might be better off if you believed in such stories more."

Perhaps, but remember our previous chapter about intellectual honesty. People believe all sorts of things that they don't have any right to accept. They believe because for whatever reason it suits them to do so, but the weight of evidence they have at their disposal does not justify their belief.

The problem with the mass of miracle stories told in churches today is that they lead people to believe all sorts of false things about God, while at the same time they encourage the "believers" to become, as Clifford puts it, "credulous," more inclined to accept other things that they have no right to believe. And believing *wrongly* is not genuine faith. Genuine faith is not a matter of defiantly clinging to your particular belief in spite of the mass of evidence against it.

False things about God I have heard stated directly through "lost keys" sorts of "miracle" stories (for example, during children's stories in church) include: "So just pray, because if you really and honestly pray, God will give you what you ask for." Really? How is this not a bubble-gum-machine view of God? How, then, are children to hang on to faith when they pray for God to find and save their lost kitty, and the kitty turns up flat as a pancake thanks to a losing encounter with Mister Mack Truck? Oh, then the parents rush to generate all sorts of ad hoc explanations for the event: "Well, honey, maybe Fluffy was really dying from a terrible disease that we didn't know about, and so God let Fluffy die a quick and painless death instead of a long, slow, horrible death that would cost us hundreds of dollars before it was all over." Whaaat? *Any* explanation at that point simply punts on the child's burning question: "So is it really true that

God will give me *anything* I really and honestly pray for?" And it doesn't take very many incidents of a child being told that something is *certainly* true, and they find out later that it *cannot* be, before the "teller of the true" is unmasked as the panderer of the false. Coming to realize this, our young people then face a desperate struggle with a false dichotomy: on the one hand they must decide to be uncritically gullible in order to stay "in the faith," while on the other hand they must choose to reject Christianity totally because it seems founded upon a mass of fables and outright lies. I have heard so many students grappling with this false dichotomy that I am genuinely sickened to think of the sweeping effect our miracle stories, and the theology we derive from them, have had on our youth.

In my years of teaching at a Christian university I became convinced (largely from the mouths of the students themselves) that the reason our young people are leaving the churches in droves has nothing to do with a clunky, outdated worship style or the music we have or allow in our services. The primary and fundamental reason that we are losing so many of our young people is that they have encountered no substantial reason to believe that can withstand scrutiny. All the miracle stories they have heard growing up have not only not convinced them. Such accounts (and, worse, the theological theorizing that emerges from them) have provided evidence to substantiate their deepest fears about our religiosity: either God does not exist; or He is distant, unconcerned, arbitrary, unreliable, and therefore generally not relevant to living life.

If we want to save a generation of college-age people now (and the younger ones that will become them later), what they do *not* need is yet another helping of miracle stories. Rather, they must have philosophically rigorous evidence* (which *is* available) that the Bible provides the most sensible and plausible picture of the way the universe works and the values by which it is governed. That evidence is not and cannot be provided by miracle stories. Miracle stories are to be themselves believed only *after* the source of the stories is deemed credible. Not until we have a foundation of other reliable evidence can we consider miracle stories in their proper context. And, to put it bluntly (and accurately), most miracles stories told today are *in*-credible, and the picture of God they paint is a travesty.

The Bible portrays principles of how God deals with His universe. It does not depict a distant, uncaring, arbitrary, and unreliable God. Instead, there are "rules to the game," so to speak, and we can know and understand those that apply to us. Jesus promised that we would know the truth and that it would set us free. Then we can enjoy freedom and power that is amazing and relevant to our lives right now, but they are only available when we understand the principles revealed in the Word of God and live our lives in harmony with them. Every "miracle" story must prove to be in harmony with those principles, or we must discard it as false or as not a genuine miracle at all. *Questionable* miracle stories cannot fill the role of being the "Word of God" to us, so they cannot in principle be faith-building. And, as I will develop in upcoming chapters, genuine, mature faith does not depend on miracle stories at all.

---

* This is distinguished from wishful thinking, undue emphasis resulting from bias, or a host of other ways to distort interpretations in order to meet one's own goals. A philosopher emphasizes rationality, which in this case means an emphasis upon coherency. "Rigorous" in this setting means that the inferences one performs are rational and not fallacious. So before I can believe in the Bible as the "Word of God" with philosophical rigor, I must first evaluate a sizable mass of evidence, explore alternatives, and conclude by the weight of evidence and the inferences drawn from it that the biblical picture of reality is the most coherent account. "Coherentism" does have its problems, but so do all epistemological theories when thought of as complete accounts. Certainly for a worldview to be putatively correct, it must be at least coherent. Amazingly, many popular worldviews don't get over even this low bar.

Chapter 6

LULLABY AND GOOD NIGHT

I have argued so far that genuine faith is not a function of consequences and does not arise from miracle stories (and I will yet say more about this point). Also I have emphasized that genuine faith is not a matter of getting things from God (and again I will have more to say about this point, too). Furthermore, I have also stressed that genuine faith involves decisions to believe in (and act in harmony with) the truth of various propositions according to the weight of evidence. So I am driving at the idea that genuine faith is a matter of having a particular perspective, a collection of right and true beliefs (in Clifford's sense) that we hold and act upon. Thus I am developing the idea that genuine faith is, simply, a matter of coming to see and respond to things in harmony with God's perspective—that is, we have intellectually honestly come to see and react to things as He does.

While I will expand and support these ideas as we proceed and explore their implications, I want it to be clear at this point where we are heading. So it is time to consider seriously the notion of a perspective, that collection of beliefs that make up what we commonly call a "worldview."

The Search for Security

Three primary perspectives clamor for primacy in our lives. Initially you might find what I say about them simplistic. However, as you read on, I expect you will discover more depth and import in my observations about these competing perspectives.

The (at least Western contemporary) world tells us that life consists of surrounding ourselves with as much comfort and security as possible. The purpose of life involves such things as to reproduce, provide for ourselves and our families, help our kids start at least one rung higher on the ladder than we did, and have a good life.

The "good life" includes such things as a nice house and car, perhaps a boat, a gas barbecue on the back deck, maybe an RV or two, comfortable furniture, a flat-panel TV, some tasteful wines, a nice soaking tub in the master bath, and the list goes on and on. Acquiring the amenities of the good life is called "consuming," and consuming is one of the primary responsibilities of a good citizen, because it is what keeps our economy strong. Of course, the purpose of the good life is that we share its amenities and comforts with friends and family during "good times" that we enjoy some evenings and on the weekends.

Meanwhile, we should spend most of our time during the week "producing." Such producing is vital, because it is the foundation of our nation's gross domestic product (our national wealth) and is the basis of our capacity to individually live the good life. On the one hand we "produce," and on the other hand we "consume." It all works so nicely and neatly. So ideally we strive to get a good education at a good school, land a good job, start making shrewd investments, build that nest egg, acquire excellent health and life insurance, see to it that our significant purchases are insured, exercise at the gym or spa, eat right, get enough sleep, and so on. Our goal is to produce wealth and do everything in our power to protect it, thereby surrounding ourselves, our loved ones, and (in our small way) our nation with "security" to enjoy the good times, which is what life is about.

Here we have the purely materialistic version of the good life, although other varieties do exist. For example, we might call the "good life" building respect and reputation in our chosen profession, or producing things (such as books) that will outlive us. Our kids might seem paramount in our lives, and we certainly hope they will survive us. Yet no matter what the prime motivator seems to be, the "good life" never actually strays very far from materialistic concerns, because those concerns are fundamental to our success at whatever we define as the good life. Any way the "Worldly" perspective is cashed out, material security lies at the core of it.

Security in all its forms is most coveted, and the need for security has become more consciously apparent to the average person in these post-September 11 times. Such "security" ensures that nothing unfairly or prematurely (whatever that means) wrests the good life away from us. After all, we've worked to produce, and now the good life should be ours to enjoy. Our Worldly perspective tells us that our reward for producing is the good life, and the role of a good government is to keep us secure so that we can expect to enjoy the "good times," however we define them.

The Worldly approach asserts that we should *expect* security. Working hard and playing by the rules guarantees that we will accumulate wealth and enjoy good times in our "good life." Our efforts and that of our governments are devoted to ensuring this result.

Perhaps something goes wrong, and the good times come to a screeching halt. Cancer or a heart attack strikes, a downsizing or layoff occurs, an accident takes place, or any one of an amazing number of other devastating possibilities raises its ugly head in the midst of our lives. Shock and horror flood us, and when the fairness of the universe gets called into question, we turn to something bigger than ourselves for answers. Thus the Worldly perspective urges us to turn to our doctors, our lawyers, our unions, our insurance companies, and/or to the government for the solutions to get back our sense of security.

But we find that while government cares much about production in general, it has little concern for individual producers. Insurance companies value us only so far as we are profitable for them, and many a person has found what they thought to be excellent insurance to have exceptions, limitations, and loopholes that protect the company rather than the person. We find that physicians are hamstrung by the lawyers and by the insurance companies, so we don't even get the treatments the doctors would deem best. In short, everywhere we turn, we discover that the system that supposedly secures us has profound faults and limitations that we were not even fully aware of prior to our own particular crisis.

Of course, if security can be restored within the system and it brings back our good times, then it bolsters our Worldly perspective, and we resume life with a deeper sense of security than ever before. But if things don't work out that way, or if we are perceptive enough, we realize in a flash that there was no way in principle for us to foresee the potential for crisis well enough to actually ensure security against it.

The Worldly perspective is not utterly naive. It recognizes that we cannot cure every illness (but the system is working on it), that we cannot avert every catastrophe (again, the system is working on it), and that we cannot avoid every interruption in the good times (and the system is working on that, too). From the Worldly perspective, though, we just come to believe that the odds are low that we will be the ones to suffer devastating illness, catastrophe, layoff, etc. And we enjoy a basic confidence bordering on faith that the system is robust enough to solve virtually any problem. In fact, when one is confronted by incurable illness, the first and most pressing question out of that person's mouth is something like "But Doc, you have some new procedure. Right? I mean, I've been hearing about so many advances. There's something . . . Right?" And questions like this reveal the deep and abiding faith we have that the system really won't utterly fail us in the crunch.

However, if the system totally breaks down in our case and our past sense of security cannot be restored, then we feel betrayed. A crisis of faith occurs as the realization presses upon us that our faith in the system was misplaced. Despair and confusion sets in. We still look for answers in something bigger than ourselves, but when the only "bigger" system we know has failed, what answers can we hope to find?

While by necessity I have somewhat oversimplified the Worldly perspective, I have presented the caricature in order to paint the actual reality in stark tones. The Worldly perspective *is* about producing, consuming, and seeking security so as to enjoy good times. When the good times end, this perspective has no answers. The existentialists rub their hands smugly and say, "See? We've told you all along that life is bleak, empty, and without answers or meaning. Now you've gotta just buck up and 'embrace the void.' You shoulda done it sooner, and then this wouldn't be such a shock."* But we sense that it is an odd answer when "embracing the void" bears no resemblance to any motivation for seeking security, or in fact for seeking anything at all. Someone who truly "embraces the void" isn't motivated to seek good times. This sort of person instead commits suicide, and suicide is the great problem that existentialism has yet to solve. In a world viewed as devoid of objective values, a perceptive person can "embrace the void" only with despair (no matter how successfully one keeps a stiff upper lip), and the good life really acts only as a series of Band-Aids frantically applied over the growing and seeping holes and wounds in our psyches.

No, in the crunch the Worldly perspective has no real solutions. It can offer only "death with dignity," whatever that means, and the hope that we might find some meaning in the whole mess by investing our lives in something that is meaningful to us beyond our own brief existence. Our kids, a cause, or some great accomplishment can make the Worldly perspective seem like more than it is, since such "investing in the future" helps us to evade the meaninglessness of our present.

But if the Worldly perspective is correct, then the whole universe is uncaringly hurtling toward maximum entropy, and sometime long before that occurs, nothing that has ever mattered to us will still exist. Where is the meaning or value in our investment in our kids, the cause, or the great accomplishment then? One cannot borrow meaning and value from the future and use that to invest the present moment with it, not when each moment in the future has the same zero meaning and value that the things of the present mo-

MFAUP-4

ment have. Long before that maximum entropy the Worldly perspective will have demonstrated its utter moral bankruptcy, and we can know even right now that the whole pyramid of borrowed future value must collapse into nothingness.

So all that the Worldly perspective has to offer is that we seek to secure the good life and the good times that life brings now, and revel in whatever wholly subjective "value" we can conjure up for ourselves, because there is nothing else. And when that desperate sense of security gets stripped away, the result is a loss of faith of epic proportions.

By contrast, the "Worldly Theistic" perspective seems much more sophisticated and robust. It enjoys all the good times advantages of the Worldly perspective . . . but it adds theistic "answers" to the security problem. And it solves the fundamental dilemma of the Worldly perspective by adding a confidence in objective, lasting values and meaning to life.

The Worldly Theistic perspective assures us (by any number of theological devices, including miracle stories, in any of a vast number of religions) that God wants us to be comfortable, happy, and prosperous. As a result the Worldly Theist also goes to a good school, lands a good job, starts making shrewd investments, builds that nest egg, acquires excellent health and life insurance, sees to it that significant purchases are insured, exercises at the gym or spa, eats right, gets enough sleep, and so on. The Worldly Theist also believes in striving to attain "security" but has an ace in the hole: a relationship with God is the ultimate security for the good life.

Our relationship with God guarantees that the universe is ultimately fair and working in our best interest. Christians quote those passages from the Bible that promise us health and prosperity if we will stay close to God. Muslims cite passages from the Koran that offer them heavenly bliss if they will perform the works of God (including, in some extreme readings, that a suicide bomber will have a fabulously erotic eternity). So the Worldly Theist adds to the secular security measures additional ones: going to the right church or religious institution, maintaining godly relationships, helping in the community, living a moral life, abiding by the golden rule, praying and reading scriptures regularly, witnessing or proselytizing, and so on.

The Worldly Theistic perspective assures us that not only do we have government, insurance companies, and so on looking out for us, but we have God Himself as well.

The problem with the Worldly Theistic perspective is that when this system fails, the crisis of faith is far more devastating. A person struggling with the Worldly perspective can always turn to God for the first time. But those let down by the Worldly Theistic perspective have found that even God has been a failure! If He hasn't held up His end —if even He has abandoned you—where else do you have to turn?

Somehow Worldly Theists have come to believe that God is like a bubble-gum machine. They attempt to put in enough piety, prayers, good works, and the right attitude to motivate Him to give them the affirmative answers to prayer and the good times that they seek. And the anger and distrust against Him when such things are not forthcoming is impressive indeed. Yet we must have great sympathy and compassion with Worldly Theists, because God does. Almost all true Christians have had the Worldly Theistic perspective during at least some part of their lives.

What, then, is the solution to the crisis of faith? What perspective can provide us with the security we seek and the assurance that God's part of the system never breaks down?

The Christian perspective has many similarities to the first two worldviews. To some there may appear little outward difference. The Christian might well go to a good school, land a good job, start making shrewd investments, build that nest egg, acquire excellent health and life insurance, see to it that significant purchases get insured, exercise at the gym or spa, eat right, obtain enough sleep, and so on. The difference in the Christian's perspective is that the Christian has both a different definition and assessment of *security*.

Security in Christianity

While the Worldly Theist clings to that subset of his or her Scriptures that promises health and prosperity to those that serve God (and is shocked when things don't work out that way), the true Christian recognizes in the Bible God's perspective of our lives here on earth: simply, that we live in a battlefield. Scripture constantly reminds God's people that they will endure trouble, persecution, trial, temptation, and attacks from Satan on every front. True Christians recognize that they have signed up for military duty, and the risks of wounds and death are high indeed.

What soldier storming the beaches of Normandy *expected* to come away unscathed? The most impressive character to me in the movie *Braveheart*—apart from William Wallace, of course—is the father of William's best friend. Early in the movie he is shot in the chest with an arrow. Although it staggers him, he fights on. Later, in another encounter, we see the entire front half of his left hand axed off. Though it elicits a yell, he fiercely fights on. Even the wounds that ultimately kill him in a final skirmish do not keep him from finishing that battle. Here is a man who recognizes that he can *expect* to get wounded in battle, that it is just the minimal price a warrior pays. He is a man who is committed to the fight regardless of what it will cost him. Yet somehow we "Onward Christian Soldiers" find ourselves slipping into the false perspective that because Christ "overcame the world," that fact means that we can expect a cushy and protected time of it.

So let's get clear exactly what Christ meant when He said that He had overcome the world. Clarity on this point will ground our proper expectations for genuine security. Such understanding will therefore make us immune to any crisis of faith.

Overcoming the World

Do you think that I am painting too grim a picture and that my focus upon war is overly morbid and tending to steal away the joy that Christians are supposed to feel? Perhaps you ascribe to the notion that "Christ won at the cross, and so the war is over"? If so, then I pray your faith survives when the first devastating blow intrudes into your life—because it is coming!

Unless, of course, Satan has instead determined that the most effective way to keep you out of the battle is to make you oblivious to it. With some he destroys their faith by frontal attacks that cause them to question God's goodness and the truth of His Word. Much more commonly and subtly, though, he deals with the faith of others by never letting it grow, by keeping them lulled with the false sense of security that arises from an amazing lack of difficulties. Such people never grasp who God is or see for themselves the truth of His Word.

David and Solomon both noticed how the wicked seem to prosper, but not only the blatantly wicked do so. The nominal also go blissfully through life. Satan is well aware that if he arranges circumstances such that the "believer" never has to wrestle with God, then he or she remains weak and actually *faith*less. So if your life seems pretty nice, and your prayer life lacks any sense of wrestling, be afraid—be very afraid! Satan is attempting to lure you into a fatal sleep, the result of which will be those fateful last words from the Lord: "I never knew you" (Matt. 7:23). Jacob got his new name by wrestling with God, and it is only by wrestling with Him that He will know you and give you your new and glorious name.

The Bible says that all who will live godly in Christ Jesus will suffer persecution. Thus if your life has no battle in it at all, it can mean only that Satan sees you as no threat to his cause. His best tactic in that event is to let you think of yourself as a "good" person, even a "good Christian," as he lulls you further asleep, leaving you feeling more and more secure. Remember how Satan dealt with Eve? "Noooo . . . just don't worry. There's no threat . . . you will not surely die, as God claims. I have something better for you. I have an increase of knowledge, freedom, and power (and, thus, security) for you. You don't have to remain in your lowly, under-God's-thumb state. You too can be like God."

The parallels today are many and varied, but the same smooth, soft tone accompanies every line: "Look at how successful you are. You've got money, great kids, and the time and security to enjoy it all. See how much God loves you to give you all these things. He wants you to enjoy them. Remember the Garden of Eden? He created you to enjoy wonderful things. That's what you are for! So enjoy, just enjoy." And the lie is so hard to detect, because God *does* love for His people to be happy and healthy and to have their needs met. But there is a lie there, and it's lulling all the same. Since the fall, humanity has been engaged in a desperate struggle against a terrible foe. What was principally true before the Fall is primarily untrue since the Fall. Satan led us into the Fall, and then he has spent millennia denying the implications of it.

Since the Fall God has cursed the ground. The world is filled with pain and death and decay. Each of us now bears only faintly the image of God, and Satan seeks to completely efface even that in each of us. As a result, it takes heroic effort on God's part to reach each of us, and it requires heroic effort from each of us to so much as lift our hands heavenward. True faith has become weak, almost nonexistent, and difficult to develop. Utterly self-absorbed and comfort-seeking, we are inclined to do nothing to cooperate with God in developing the sort of character that would fit us to dwell with perfectly holy beings. Having come to view sin lightly, we have lost sight of the absolute abhorrence that God has for it and have forgotten what a tiny, simple act of disobedience started the whole mess. We rest secure in our sense that God can wink at our grievous, willful, intentional sins, because of the sacrifice of Christ. Furthermore, we no longer grasp the magnitude of the price that God had to pay to erase even that one, tiny, seemingly insignificant act of transgression, and so we crucify Christ afresh with our ongoing willful sins. And in the face of all this, Satan attempts to convince us through a comfortable life that the war is over.

But it has not ended for any of us. Each of us has a battle to fight for our own souls and for those around us. While Christ has won in a general sense, each one of us still has to apply that victory to our own lives and to those in our sphere of influence. If you believe that the war is over, then Satan has already won in your life. The only way to gain victory now is to wake up and take up the fight.

Rise up to meet Satan in your own life and in the lives of those you come into contact with daily, and see how instantly he becomes a roaring lion instead of purring false security in your ear. Observe how quickly he withdraws his comforting hand from your life and your possessions, only to make it into an iron-hard fist to smash back at you. *All* who will live godly in Christ Jesus *will* suffer persecution.

Why does God allow Satan such liberty? And why does it seem that He does nothing to protect us from such blows? One might as well ask, Why did He dislocate Jacob's hip socket before He blessed him? That is the more pressing question, after all.

The reason is simple, and I have touched on it already. Our only, and I repeat, *only* safety in the war comes when we cling desperately to Him. It's humbling to really grasp this truth, but the basis of our redemption is humiliation. Sin began in the universe as a function of pride, and humiliation and dependency is the foundation of our redemption. Jesus Himself endured humiliation beyond measure and absolute dependency upon God. To go from being one with God in all ways to being a mere human being, submitting to the most despicable abuses . . . Are we better than our Master? Pride and independence led to the first human sin, and only the path of humiliation and utter dependence can effect our salvation now. Picture Jesus clinging desperately to His Father in Gethsemane, and then again on the cross, and ask yourself, Are we better than our Master?

The Lord in His wisdom knows just what each of us needs to endure to bring us forth as "gold tried in the fire." Satan lies and urges us to seek security of place, power, position, wealth, family, and of every other worldly good. But the Bible tells us that we will have no security *for* or *in* such things, that we are in a cosmic war,

103

and that we should expect to lose any of these things at any given moment. In the same way that an experienced sergeant will strip from his recruits what they think are the necessities so that he can harden them for battle, the Lord wisely removes from us (allowing Satan to beat on us) whatever He knows will make us soft and unable to be a warrior for Him. But the story of Job demonstrates the careful oversight that God employs as He allows Satan to tempt, batter, try, and persecute us. Yet even then God deals tenderly with us, knowing just exactly how to get the gold and remove the dross from our lives.

While Satan delights in causing suffering, God mourns with us, cries with us, and sympathizes with our pains; and He limits Satan in all of his attempts to utterly destroy us. In the same way that God suffered with Jesus on the cross and saved Him, He agonizes with us in our trials and will save us. Just as the suffering of the cross was necessary to the grand plan of salvation, our suffering is necessary to our particular plan of salvation—not for merit, but for dependency. Christ's suffering earned us the opportunity to be saved, while our suffering draws us to cling to God so that we can be saved. We must come to the point at which we fully grasp our fallen state and cling to God with the fervency that Jesus had, yet we are so amazingly inclined to be confident and independent in our false sense of security.

How has it been for you so far? Are you aware from painful experience that you are in a battle for your life? Or are you being lulled to sleep?

What is the nature of genuine, mature faith? It is *not* about security in anything even remotely resembling what the world calls security. To share the perspective of God, to enjoy genuine faith, we must be prepared to be humbled, to be dependent, and to be a true warrior in the battles of the Lord. Warriors don't expect or seek after security, and they are not surprised or disconcerted when their Commander leads them into fierce battles in which they get wounded or even killed. The perspective of genuine faith is that God is always good and that His

Word is always true, regardless of circumstances and situations. Thus, like a good warrior, the one with genuine faith is prepared to pay any price in the grand cause of his Commander.

Perhaps some are thinking now that all this focus upon battle and being a warrior doesn't touch the hearts and lives of the women in the service of God. Some might say that the warrior model just doesn't fit their role in God's church. Any perspective that doesn't address the role of the majority of God's church must be in error. Right?

On the contrary, the perspective I have been developing thus far is perfectly appropriate for women in the church, although I will admit that we do not usually address them in this way. Women, however, can be and are warriors in every sense of that term.

If you, a woman, are reading to this point, and you don't see yourself as a warrior, let me turn your mind toward a side of you that you may have missed. Imagine a woman's reaction if one of her kids is in danger. What woman will *not* become a lioness in defense of her cubs? Will she not be prepared to fight all the forces of humankind or hell itself to rescue or defend her child? You can have that same warrior perspective about the cause of God!

Consider the woman warriors down through history, and for a modern-day example, just look to those in the nation of Israel. Whatever you think of Israel today, the fact remains that women serve ably alongside their male counterparts in military service, and they are fearsome warriors in their own right.

While many societies intentionally "protect" women and de-emphasize their warrior natures, the fact remains that all women have a warrior inside, and all can (and must) gird up their own armor and join the battles of the Lord.

One final point bears mention about the warrior perspective. We must all be very careful that any conflicts we find ourselves fighting are indeed "battles of the Lord" rather than just our own personal hobby-horses. Seek the Lord, and be sure that any fights you take up are really based upon divine principles. Remember when James and John asked Jesus to rain fire from heaven down on a village that had rejected them, and Jesus rebuked them (Luke 9:54, 55)? Consider all the "holy" wars that have been fought (and are still being waged) that are based upon the fundamental principle of coercion. Will you, by your efforts, attempt to force people to believe and behave like you? If your version of fighting the battles of the Lord has you enslaving the consciences of others, then you are unwittingly battling on Satan's side. God values free will and the right to choose intelligently above all things in the universe. So be careful to keep your role in the struggle against evil one of mentoring, educating, advising, and urging others to abandon their sins, rather than an attempt to compel people to think and behave as you believe they should. Be certain that the "persecution" that springs up against you is not just a legitimate reaction on the part of people who rightly discern that you are attempting to mold their consciences to conform to your ideals.

In the battles of the Lord the Holy Spirit is the force, and we are to be merely channels for Him to let it flow through. Unfortunately, too many "warriors" go out to battle the world lacking the Holy Spirit, and, failing to abide by godly principles, they attempt to be the force for change. But the government of God is not founded or maintained by coercion. The "force" of the Holy Spirit is, as we discussed earlier, His power to touch hearts and minds with additional data points for consideration. But He always leaves people free to choose.

That said, the cause of God is in need of warriors, and all those who take the name of Christ should see themselves and act as warriors who are ready to be used and used up in the battles of the Lord. Christ has overcome the world, and the world is now in desperate need of men and women who will take up the challenge of securing and occupying the territory that He has won (both in the world and in their own hearts and lives). The world needs men *and* women who will stand boldly for the truth and by their examples and educational efforts seek to draw others from the side of Satan to the service of the Great Commander.

---

* I am well aware that not every response to the implications of a lack of objective values can be forced exactly into an "existentialistic" box. However, being an ethicist, I have done a more-thorough-than-average (even for a philosopher) survey of the literature of values, and I have seen the same basic themes threading through all attempts to construct a philosophy of purely subjective values. I don't think it is unfair or a gross oversimplification to cast all such philosophies as "existentialistic," even though this or that subjective value theory might depart from this or that existentialist theory in one way or another. The hard core of existentialism threads its way through all other subjective value theories, and I don't apologize for my conflation in this context.

Chapter 7

GENUINE FAITH

We are now in a position to get to the bedrock of genuine faith. The loss of faith that humanity experienced at the Fall in the Garden of Eden is to be replaced by the emergence of pure, victorious faith that completely overcomes the first satanic lie. Pure mature faith will express that God does have our good uppermost in mind, and that His Word is always, without exception, true. So let us see exactly where our steps in this book have been leading so far.

The great contrast between the fallen, or lower, nature and the divine nature is that between manipulation and faith. Fallen nature is fundamentally manipulative in seeking its desires (including its craving for security, as we see in the Worldly Theistic perspective) by whatever means, while the divine nature is fundamentally forthright and submissive in expressing its desires. Manipulation is as opposed to faith as rebellion is to submission. The problem is that both manipulation and rebellion can be subtle indeed.

Manipulation Versus Faith

Satan's first lie centered on an insidious introduction of the manipulative perspective: "You can do an end run around God by having a relationship with Him as equal to equal. Then He will be forced to deal with you differently—there will be no more of this 'obedience' business, because you will be as He is and know what He knows." The whole idea here was (and is) that you can extract from God what He is not willingly giving you. (Of course, the manipulative perspective also seeks to get things from other people by any means necessary.)

To get at the heart of this contrast between manipulation and faith, let me tell you about my infant nephew and niece (call them Dick and Jane).

Dick and Jane are both old enough to sit up in their high chairs, but they don't talk at all yet. The other day at breakfast both decided to go on a hunger strike. Any good food their mom set before them went straight to the floor. After a while of this, their mom decided it was naptime. Into their cribs they went. An impressive screaming fit, in stereo, ensued. Being strong, their mom just left them to throw their respective tantrums. Just about the point that naptime was over, the screaming stopped. Their mom got them both up and into their playpen. Within minutes they had rejected all of their toys and ejected them over the playpen wall. More screaming erupted. Resisting their psychological pressure, their mom just left the toys outside the playpen. Still more screaming. At lunch all the good food was dashed to the floor again, as the hunger strike continued. Back they went into the playpen, with the toys back inside. Nope, all the toys came flying out again, spurned with great prejudice. More screaming (amazingly, none of it from their mom yet). Eventually suppertime arrived. By this time Dick and Jane finally folded. They ate what their mother offered them, had a pleasant evening, and went to bed with no further incident.

How many parents have exhausted themselves trying to figure out what their kids wanted, so that the hunger strikes and/or screaming would stop? And how many have had a deep suspicion that they were being manipulated, but have had no idea what to do to regain control? (And, make no mistake, parents intuitively know that they should be in control.) Is it even possible that a tiny infant can be manipulative? Doesn't manipulation require some fairly higher-order mental processes, abilities that we think infants lack?

Having watched the behavior of our own cat, Yojo, not to mention countless infants and children, I have become convinced that manipulation is one of the most fundamental skills imparted by the lower nature. Far from involving "higher-order" processes, manipulation is profoundly intuitive and basic—even an animal can do it unconsciously.

Manipulation, however, does require some prerequisite experiences that can act as the basis for understanding what will be effective (whether consciously understood or not). Such experiences ground all attempts at manipulation: (1) the manipulator believes that the manipulatee has the power to grant the manipulator's desires; (2) the manipulator believes that the manipulatee has some sort of desire to grant the manipulator's desires; (3) the manipulator believes that he or she knows what is best for himself or herself, and so the manipulatee must be induced to provide that as opposed to whatever the manipulatee might otherwise offer; (4) finally, the manipulator believes that manipulation is the best method to get what is desired from the manipulatee.

All of these elements are present in an attempt to manipulate. If you are uncomfortable with the word "believes" when applied to animals, then just replace it with "perceives," or whatever similar term suits your fancy. The end result is the same. Yojo will engage in some fairly impressive hunger strikes, crying, and other histrionics in order to convince Dana or me that canned cat food is in order instead of yet another batch of dry. But we are strong, and the hunger strikes always fail in the end. It's as though Yojo is trying to say, "I want canned food, and I'm not eating this dry junk anymore. I know you care about me, so you will be horrified to see that I refuse to eat. Worried that I'm sick, you will wring your hands and attempt to figure out what is wrong. By then you will fall all over yourselves trying to find something that I will eat. Eventually you will capitulate and give me the canned food, and then, finally, I will relieve your trauma by deigning to eat it." Now, I'm fairly sure that Yojo doesn't think all this through consciously, but the behavior indicates that something like this mental program is being run at some deep level.

Dick and Jane are in effect saying the same sort of thing by sending all their food to the floor. And they are demanding a certain sort of attention (perhaps to be held or read to) when they hurl all their toys from the playpen. But notice that there is no point to such histrionics at all (and they are never employed by genuinely in-need animals or children) unless the manipulator is convinced that the best hope of getting the desired thing is by employing such tactics. The manipulator rejects what he or she already has (thus risking losing it) in order to impress the manipulatee enough to elicit what is desired.

Thus the operative element of the manipulator's perspective is the fourth point: the manipulator believes that the manipulation is the best (read: most likely to succeed) method to extract from the manipulatee what is desired. The other elements actually underlie this point. They give the manipulator the sense that the manipulatee might be susceptible to the attempted manipulation. The manipulator must believe (at some level) that the manipulatee has the power and desire to provide, and the manipulator must believe that the desired thing must be extracted from the manipulatee instead of whatever other thing the manipulatee might think is best to provide. This third element is what motivates the fourth, making the manipulator believe that the manipulation is necessary to getting the desired thing. The manipulator assumes that, even though the manipulatee does have the manipulator's best interest at heart and will provide something accordingly, the manipulatee will tend to get it all wrong and so must be induced by some mechanism to override default behaviors in order to come into line with the manipulator's wishes. The manipulator must consider the manipulatee as both caring and inept. If the manipulatee were not caring, there would be no reason to suppose that he or she would respond to any appeal, and if the manipulatee were not perceived to be inept, there would be no need for the manipulator to employ any mechanism for behavior modification.

Thus we see that at the core the manipulation is a psychological tactic to influence the behavior of a perceived interested (probably even caring) yet inept provider. The manipulator attempts to sway the manipulatee by employing some psychological tactic in order to extract what the manipulator wants. But it all presupposes a core confidence—the manipulator believes that he or she understands the manipulatee and so can devise the most appropriate tactic. Little children quickly realize that their parents are there for the purpose of meeting their needs and that their parents are deeply emotionally invested in this function. It's a short step indeed for a kid to begin experimenting with tactics to probe the recesses of this emotional investment to see what it might produce.

When a kid yells at a parent for the first time, "I hate you," it is usually a lower nature and cruel attempt to bring the parent to his or her knees, groveling for acceptance and prepared to capitulate, so deeply does the kid believe in the emotional investment of the parent. While at the moment it might feel true to the kid as well, and so could be viewed as nothing more than a truthful utterance, the fact of the matter is that the kid knowingly risks much by yelling such a hurtful thing. The kid deeply understands that such a statement is "wheeling out the big gun" and that it will likely have some sort of profound effect. He or she puts in jeopardy what he or she already has in the hope of gaining something "better." But the child does so in the belief that the caring part of the parent will rise to the bait and that instant death or dismemberment will likely not result.

Now, it bears emphasizing that we must distinguish manipulation from simply asking for the desired thing. And it is not simply accepting what one already has, in the confidence that the provider will offer what is best. Yojo, Dick, and Jane cannot ask in the traditional sense of that term. But unlike a genuinely needy animal or child, all three of them certainly can, and do, reject (with extreme prejudice) what they already have in an effort to get something else. The antithesis of manipulating is asking and accepting. Manipulation employs some tactic for rejection and extraction.

We live in a child-parent sort of relationship with God. Like classic manipulators, we approach Him believing that He can provide things for us, that He desires to present us with good things, and (at least implicitly) we need to get Him to grant us what we want instead of what He otherwise might give. Thus, like classic manipulators, we often pray with a sense that we must employ some sort of manipulation to extract from God what we believe is best for us. We see examples in prayers: "Do this, and I'll believe in You" or "Do this, and I'll do x, y, and/or z for You." Sometimes we yell at God, "I hate You," and at the time we might genuinely believe it of ourselves, although we hope that He will do something to make us not hate Him. Perhaps we might enter periods in which we don't talk to Him in the hope that He will do something impressive to break down the wall between Him and us. Other times we flee and flee and flee in an attempt to see just how far God will chase us. Perhaps we even say such things as "If You can't or won't do this for me, then I want nothing to do with You," in which, again, we might believe that about ourselves but hope that God will be brought to capitulate. In every case, we are motivated by a fundamental sense that we know what is best for us, that God somehow isn't getting it right and that we can employ some tactic to obtain what we want.

Furthermore, we seem to see in the Bible that God has even appreciated and rewarded such tactics. We cite stories of Abraham, Moses, and even Sampson as illustrations of people who appear to have manipulated Him successfully. And we use such examples as evidence that He is susceptible to manipulation, and thus that it is at least one effective tactic by which to manage our relationship with Him. And there it is: we want to control our relationship with Him, and we will employ whatever tactics we think will help us to do it.

But does genuine, mature faith include manipulation in dealing with God? Do the biblical examples demonstrate the sort of relationship God aspires to have with each of us? What are we to make of the apparent manipulation of God that we see in the Bible?

Rather than to argue directly about whether or not various biblical stories illustrate successful manipulative tactics, I want to focus upon the sort of perspective that grounds a mature, genuine faith. It sharply contrasts with manipulation in all its forms, and the point will become clear that manipulation is the polar opposite of faith.

Consider Jesus asking God for the resurrection of Lazarus, or Him wrestling with the Father in Gethsemane. Read the prayer of Jesus in John 17. These are among the most poignant examples of the perspective Jesus reveals in His own relationship with God.

Jesus had unwavering confidence in God's power to do anything and everything necessary to ensure the best results. He was convinced that His Father was aware of and committed to obtaining the best outcome (regardless of how consequences might seem or feel at any given time). Furthermore, Jesus was absolutely committed to submitting to the divine will in every circumstance. When He prayed, it was not to extract anything from God, but to request from Him in accordance with the Father's will. Thus Jesus prayed to align Himself with God's will instead of to align the divine will with His own.

This last point is so significant that it bears deeper inspection. The amazing thing about the prayer of Jesus in Gethsemane is that He pleaded for another alternative, requesting God to change the plan, so to speak. Yet He immediately followed that request with an expression of submission. Considering the stakes, we marvel at the simplicity and forthrightness of Christ's Gethsemane prayer. We observe no manipulation of any sort. Instead, Jesus forthrightly puts His personal desires on the table, asks God if they can be accommodated, and then instantly submits to the Father's will, subordinating His own desires to the divine will. The Gethsemane prayer is the highest example we have of genuine, mature faith. It was the necessary prerequisite for the victory on the cross.

In Christ's life in general, and in this prayer in particular, we find no evidence of manipulation. Rather we discover in it the fundamental principles of mature, genuine faith: forthrightness, honesty, and submission to God. Christ was willing to pay any price in the great battle. We see in His life, as it can be our privilege to enjoy in our own lives, that He utterly rejected both parts of the first grand lie. He was so convinced of God's goodness and power that He was prepared to sacrifice His own eternal existence in order to submit to the divine will. Such utter confidence in and submission to God is obviously the opposite of efforts to manipulatively extract something from Him.

Why, then, does God tolerate, even seemingly reward, our prayers when we are at our most feeble and manipulative? The answer will be obvious to any good parent: you simply can't expect mature responses from an infant. An infant is the embodiment of the lower nature. Utterly selfish and determined to extract what they want from their parents, infants grow up into children that are master psychologists determined to find any cracks in their parents' armor. If you think this paints too bleak a picture of the early parent-child relationship, then I assert that some form of ignorance, naïveté, or capitulation has affected your perspective. Parents genuinely engaged in subduing their children's lower (fallen) nature are well aware that it is a battle, and it is a conflict that the parent (representing self-control and the higher nature) must win. Without breaking their children, the parents must subdue (and teach their children how to subdue for themselves) that ever-present lower nature.

In our present age of permissiveness and an ever-threatening specter of being reported to Child Protective Services, parents often feel helpless in the face of increasing rebelliousness and manipulative behaviors from their children. But they must decisively meet the issue head-on when the child is an infant, and the ongoing skirmishes must be fought with principled firmness.

Parents can wean children from manipulative approaches by early demonstrations of how a forthright, submissive approach is more healthy and productive. But what is paramount is that parents never actually let themselves be manipulated. They must always maintain their sovereignty, so that it is clear that a child's attempts to manipulate were not successful as manipulations. That is, parents can feel free to make any bargain or engage in any argument that seems appropriate, as long as the child knows that the adults are consciously deciding what to do rather than having something extracted from them.

The flip side of this coin is that parents must train genuine intellectual honesty in the budding minds of their children. When adults manipulate or cow children into believing that what a parent says is true, the ultimate backlash is guaranteed. The children's minds will not always be under parental thumbs. It is our privilege to provide evidence to our young people, and we must encourage them to evaluate that evidence. Rewards and punishments for having or rejecting certain beliefs are forms of manipulation and actually encourage blind, dogmatic believing rather than intellectual honesty. So while it is correct to expect a certain appropriateness of behavior from our children, we must also be very careful that we handle their developing perspectives with grace and intellectual honesty.

We should bring this nonmanipulative sort of perspective to our biblical examples. We see God listening to His (at times) childish people, occasionally making bargains with them, but never allowing Himself actually to be manipulated. God remains clearly sovereign, and when He decides, it is clear that He does so out of His own perspectives. "God is not mocked" (Gal. 6:7), and He is not extracted from!

Meanwhile, God appeals to the minds of His people. Gently and patiently He helps us to understand Him and grasp His viewpoint. He deals with us as children when we are children, but He expects us to grow and mature also. What might seem cute in a toddler can be irritating in a teenager. Just so, what God winks at in our spiritual childhood He finds inappropriate and unacceptable when we should have matured. But His goal is ever to lead us away from manipulation (and its attendant rebellion) and toward mature, genuine faith (and its accompanying submission). Let us recognize the spiritual weakness of God's people and focus on the true standard of faith: the life of Christ.

As we grow in faith and knowledge of God, we will cease to ask for signs and wonders as the basis of our religious experience. We will treat miracle stories appropriately, praising God when they are credible and being unaffected when they are not. Our faith will neither rise nor fall with the apparent "answers" to our prayers, and we will rest in the unshakable confidence that God's Word is true and that He has our best interest ever uppermost in His mind.

Such a faith is not only profoundly liberating; it is infinitely empowering as well. It derives from a deep understanding of who God is and what His will is. With such faith we can pray from His perspectives, which will enable us to know when we should ask Him to "move mountains" and when we should instead ask Him to "move us." We can pray for miracles when that is appropriate, knowing that He has the power to grant our requests. But such prayers are not tests, and they involve no faith building, because such prayers already presume the faith to pray them forthrightly and submissively. Mature faith frees God to do things for us that He would otherwise not do, because He knows that we will not misunderstand Him or think that we have extracted something from Him. God is free, then, to exercise amazing power in our lives because we are in harmony with Him and are not attempting to rise above Him. Then we can "ask what we will," knowing that He will grant our requests—because then they will be free from all taint of selfishness and manipulation.

Consequentialism Versus Faith

Sadly, we tend to have matters exactly backwards. We ask God to display amazing power in our lives, assuming that then we will have faith. We think we will come to know God by His doing for us what we ask/extract from Him. Instead, the Bible says that we build faith by knowing God, that we come to know His through His Word, and that we submit to Him as we come to know Him. The answers to our prayers, then, are the result of faith rather than the foundation of it.

I can think of no better example of this principle than the biblical story found in Judges 19 and 20. Because of its length, I will not quote it here, but I encourage you to read it for yourself. I will briefly paraphrase the account.

The Bible says that "in those days, when there was no king in Israel" (Judges 19:1) a Levite from the hill country in Ephraim got married.* His wife, however, left him, "played the harlot" (verse 2, NASB), and ultimately returned to the home of her parents in Bethlehem in Judah.

After four months the Levite went to "the girl's" parents, talked gently with his wife, and eventually convinced her to return to Ephraim with him. After enjoying several days of hospitality in the home of her parents, the couple (with the Levite's servant) finally departed in the afternoon. After traveling until near darkness, they approached Jebus (Jerusalem), a Jebusite city. The servant urged the Levite to spend the night there, but the Levite refused. Instead, they pressed on until they arrived at Gibeah, a Benjamite settlement. Entering Gibeah after sundown, they sat in the open square, hoping that someone would offer them lodging for the night (the expected practice in the ancient Near East).

As darkness settled, strangely nobody offered to take them in. But finally an old man returned from his fields and offered the group his hospitality.

As they were all eating and drinking that night, some evil and unruly men from the city began banging on the old man's door, insisting that he send the Levite out to them so that they could have homosexual relations with him. Apparently in fear for his whole household, the old man begged them to not do such an evil thing, and when they seemed determined, he offered his own daughter to them, rather than to send the Levite out (the ancient code of hospitality required a host to protect his guest at all costs).

When the Levite heard this, he was horrified that his host would make such an offer, and instead he "seized his concubine and brought her out to them" (verse 25, NASB). (We could certainly have much to say about the horror of this act, but, as you will see, this is not the focus of the story.) Then, while the Levite and his host spent the night inside, the evil men raped the poor girl until dawn broke. When they finally released her, she staggered to the threshold of the old man's house and (apparently) died.

At "full daylight" (verse 26, NASB) the Levite arose and went out to find the girl dead. He took her body home to Ephraim and there cut her up into 12 pieces. Then he sent the pieces throughout the land of Israel as a cry for justice.

Now, here is where the story gets very interesting indeed. It has been horrible so far, but the sons of Israel rise up in righteous indignation and gather in their desire to hold the evil men of Gibeah accountable for their crime. The account of their efforts to "punish them for all the disgraceful acts that they have committed in Israel" (Judges 20:10, NASB) reveals the fundamental principle of faith.

The Israelites gathered soldiers from all the tribes except Benjamin. After they cast lots to form a fighting force numbering one tenth of their total numbers, that group went to Gibeah "united as one man" (verse 11, NASB) in the cause of justice.

You would think that the people of Gibeah would immediately hand over the "worthless fellows" (verse 13, NASB) responsible for the crime, but instead they decided to resist. Men from the tribe of Benjamin assembled from all the surrounding cities and prepared to fight the other tribes. A civil war loomed.

Confronted by the prospect of actual war against their own kin, the Israelites were deeply concerned about whether or not they were pursuing the right course. They withdrew from the field of battle to Bethel (where the ark of the covenant was located) to ask God what to do. Now, mark this point carefully: "Then the Lord said, 'Judah shall go up first'" (verse 18, NASB). God Himself told the Israelites to pursue their present course, to fight the Benjamites, and that the delegation from Judah should attack first.

Encouraged, the Israelites returned to Gibeah and prepared to enjoy victory in their quest for justice. And in the ensuing battle, not only did the Benjamites prevail but they did so after slaughtering 22,000 men of Israel (verse 21, NASB).

And "the sons of Israel went up and wept before the Lord until evening, and inquired of the Lord, saying, 'Shall we again draw near for battle against the sons of my brother Benjamin?' And the Lord said, 'Go up against him'" (verse 23, NASB).

Surely victory was at last assured. Right? Nope. In the next encounter the tribe of Benjamin killed 18,000 Israelites.

Again the Israelites assembled in Bethel, and again they wept before the Lord. This time they add fasting and sacrifices. And again they asked if the Lord was with them in their quest. "Shall I yet again go out to battle against the sons of my brother Benjamin, or shall I cease?" Phinehas, one of their leaders, asked (verse 28, NASB). Once more the Lord instructed them to attack, but now He added that in this battle they would be victorious.

The next day, after laying a clever trap for the Benjamites, Israel did triumph. The slaughter left only 600 Benjamites still alive, and the Israelites set Gibeah and "all the cities which they found" on fire (verse 48, NASB). Thus Israel ultimately cleansed this great evil from the land.

So let's summarize. Its righteous indignation aroused, the rest of the tribes of Israel determine to exercise justice. In counsel with God, the Lord tells them to proceed. But the Benjamites cut them down in their effort. Israel again asks God what it should do, and once more the Lord commands them to proceed. They go down to defeat yet again. When they pray to God a third time, He again commands them to attack. This time, after having lost 40,000 men so far, they finally prevail. What are we to conclude from such a story?

The incident strikes me as the most baffling in the entire Bible. My wife and I have prayed long over this narrative, trying to understand how God could knowingly send 40,000 brave soldiers to their deaths in pursuit of legitimate justice. It is clear that He was behind the Israelites in their quest—His messages to them are unwavering: "Go forth." At no point do we find the slightest hint that

God is punishing Israel for their violent quest, nor do we find their methods called into question. There appears to be no difference between God's relationship to Israel at the first and final inquiry at Bethel. Reading the story as a function of God "backhanding Israel even as He smites Benjamin," or something like that, simply won't do as an explanation.

No, the obvious interpretation is that Israel righteously sought to hold the evildoers accountable to justice. Benjamin had precipitously escalated the conflict by supporting the evildoers. Although Israel was not immediately prepared for civil war, God encouraged the rest of the tribes to meet Benjamin's response. But Israel went down to defeat twice before finally executing justice upon Benjamin. What could God possibly be telling us with this story? Why would He send 40,000 men to their deaths when so many other times He had enabled quick, easy victories for Israel?

Finally my wife and I have come to see this incident as one of the prime exemplars in the Bible of the contrast between the principles of manipulation and faith.

You see, the vast majority of so-called Christians have "faith" in God just so long as things are going as they think things should. I have so often heard "miracle stories" that go like this: "So we knew that we would have to step out in faith. We signed the papers and purchased the television station, knowing that we had no way to come up with the $1.2 million that we were now in debt for. Then, just the day before the payment was due, a check arrived to cover the amount. God is good, and He rewards those who step out in faith."

Faith, as I have been casting it, is acting on the belief that the Word of God is true. But when Israel did so, they went down to defeat. And not once, but *twice!* They believed God, and they were slaughtered for it. And notice how honest Scripture is. The Bible actually tells us the story of this civil war, yet how many times do we hear "miracle stories" of those who have stepped out in faith only to lose the television station, suffer death and defeat, come down with cancer or some other devastating disease, be ejected from the country, and so on and so on? We hear the miracle stories that have "happy endings" because we assume that they are the only ones that "build our faith." But the Bible is brutally honest as it tells this baffling story, and we had better in all honesty deal with the questions it raises.

Is the Lord really with us, we wonder, when we are seemingly defeated in our godly quests? When all seems dark and Satan seems to be pulling his own victories out of a hat? Does the Lord *really* love us when disaster strikes, when we lose our job, when we are struck down with disease, when a heart attack ends the life of a great saint, or when our beloved spouse gets killed in an auto accident? Where is there any evidence of that love and care when evil is arrayed against us and seems to prevail? For example, where was God's love for Jeremiah when his enemies cast him into the pit? Or where was God's love for John the Baptist during his beheading? And most of all, where was God's love for Jesus when all of God's wrath against sin poured out on Him on the cross?

We are simply caught up in consequentialistic thinking! When things are going well, we believe in God's love and care, and when things turn bad, we conclude that the Lord has deserted us, and we experience a crisis of faith. We tie our "faith" to consequences and perceived outcomes, and thus we cling to miracle stories to bolster our faith, when they actually have the opposite effect. Because we hang our "faith" on consequences, "believing" when circumstances turn out the way they should, we find that we actually have no sustaining faith when things fall apart.

Imagine the reaction if Israel had abandoned their quest for justice after the second encounter. They would have lost 40,000 men, and then would have slunk home defeated and questioning: "What gives? The Lord *said* we should go up and fight, and then He just lets us get smashed!" What if they would have quit at that point? What would the Word of the Lord have meant to them then and forevermore? Or what if they would have gone up the third time to battle, but the Lord had deigned to give them the victory only at the fourth encounter, a fourth encounter that they never attempted? Suppose they went up four times when yet the Lord intended them to have the victory on the fifth engagement. When *should* they have quit? At what point should they have evaluated the consequences and thereby decided that God actually was not with them, despite what the "Word of the Lord" seemed to indicate?

"Never!" you say? As long as the clear Word of the Lord told them to proceed, they should proceed, you reply? Simple to say, but much harder to live. Do you live like that? Or do you begin to doubt the "clear Word of the Lord" when consequences seem arrayed against you?

It is true that we often have reason to question whether we are stepping out in faith or in presumption. But there is a way to tell the difference: obedience. When we are obeying God, abiding by clear principles or even His direct word, our "stepping out" is never presumptuous. What makes this civil war story so devastating is that the Israelites were obeying—both the clear dictates of justice and the clear Word of the Lord specific to their situation. And even so, they got slaughtered. They questioned, received assurance, and went forward in their quest. And still they went down to humiliating defeat.

God asks you through this story, What price are you prepared to pay to serve Me—to do what I say, what you know is right? Are you a fair-weather "Christian," or are you a true soldier of Christ who will strive for justice, righteousness, and victory no matter what your fate? Are you someone who is only after the glory of victorious campaigns, or are you willing to take arrows to the chest, have half your hand cleaved off, and then ultimately succumb to your deadly wounds so that you die just as the campaign seems to be lost?

Maybe the price *you* will have to pay is that you will maintain your genuine, mature faith before the watching universe now, as Satan has free reign to hack you down. Perhaps you will be one of the 40,000 cut down in the quest for justice. Imagine what it would

have been like to be in the second battle. Having already experienced defeat in the first encounter, now you find yourself dying of
horrible wounds and seeing your brothers fleeing yet again. All is
lost! Do you die thinking that both the quest and your death were
for nothing? What can possibly ground your faith then?

Then your faith can rest on nothing except the fact that you
fought under the banner of the Lord. You threw yourself into His
battles because He told you to. Then your faith can cling to nothing
but the bare Word of the Lord, and *this is always and ever will be the
only foundation for genuine and mature faith*. Regardless of appearances
or circumstances, faith is always a matter of acting on the belief that
the Lord is good and that His Word is always true.

It is a marvelously incomprehensible thing to stand before the
King of the universe and have Him honor you by placing a crown
on your head to declare before the assembled throng, "Well done,
thou good and faithful servant!" What price are you willing to pay
to obtain *that* honor?

Do you question why some people seem to enjoy miracles and
wonders in their lives, yet the Lord seems to grant you only pain,
hardship, and disappointment? Do others seem to be "blessed of
God," and you wonder where His blessings are in your life? Are you
going through a crisis now? Do you have a devastating disease, or has
a loved one just been diagnosed with one? Has a horrible crime or
accident left you or someone you love scared or disfigured? Have
you just lost your job or even your career, and financial disaster
looms? Satan has his way in the world in many terrible forms, and
we cannot avoid the pressing questions: Why has no miracle appeared in my case? Why does the Lord not seem to hear my cry
now? Has my life been a waste? What does the "grand cause" matter if *this* terrible thing is to be the outcome in my life? Think about
what it must have felt like to the men of Israel dying horribly on the
second battlefield. Every doubt and question you could ever have
must have been pressing upon them as their breath slipped away.

And consider the fear of those still alive as they asked the Lord yet again at Bethel, "Should we continue, or should we cease?" In effect, their prayer contained the question: "Will You allow us *all* to be slaughtered, or is there some final victory to be had here?"

Each time the men of Israel believed in God's Word, and each time they ignored consequences and events. They went forth believing that they were soldiers of the Lord, individually prepared to pay whatever price He demanded of them in order to fight this battle for justice. Determined to submit themselves to Him, they were willing to pay any price.

Perhaps it doesn't feel so lofty in your case. Feeling little and insignificant, you can see no way in which you are "fighting the battle of the Lord." So your private suffering seems to have no grand purpose that you can cling to. Job must have felt the same way, and only much later were God's people in a position to realize what a profound role he played in the grand cosmic conflict. Whatever you are going through now, however much heaven seems as brass over your head, you can rest assured that the Lord loves you and will strengthen you to be faithful in your trial. Regardless of circumstances or apparent outcomes, you can know that you are blessed of the Lord and that heaven will honor your faith and faithfulness for all eternity. Genuine, mature faith grasps hold of the unseen realities and clings solely to the Word of God. Will a miracle or other divine intervention sweep in to solve your personal crisis? I cannot know. But I do know this: whether or not God intervenes, that fact has nothing whatsoever to do with your relation to Him or to the foundation of your faith.

So what role do miracles play in the development of mature, genuine faith? They are not the *foundation* of faith—they are a *result* of it. I am positive that when Peter healed the crippled man, the disciple didn't gape in awe and think, *Wow! God is with me. He* does *love me. And He is powerful and willing to exercise His power through me.* No! The opposite was the case: Peter was already confident and assured of the facts about God and His relationship to him, and therefore the apostle could be confident that miracles would be the result. And in the life of post-Pentecost Peter we see that neither circumstances nor adversity threatened his faith. Instead, we can summarize the story of adversity in his life as one "rejoicing that [he] had been considered worthy to suffer shame for His name" (Acts 5:41, NASB).

The story of the war between Israel and the Benjamites begs you to consider the foundation of your own faith. Daily you confront the fact that you live in a world at war, and if you will be a good soldier of Christ, you may be called upon to be cut down in any one of a vast number of horrible ways. Would you wrestle with God to obtain the desired blessing if you knew that one result would be that He would dislocate your hip in order to give you a constant dependency upon Him? If your faith would withstand adversity, trial, and temptation; if you would be victorious; if you would be crowned in the end by your King as a good and faithful servant, then you must put away every trace of the perspective that God exists to serve you and give you a good life. Instead, you must gain the perspective that faith is entirely a function of knowing and acting upon the Word of God regardless of consequences. As Matthew 12:39 warns us: "An evil and adulterous generation craves for a sign" (NASB). The tribal war story in Judges forces us to question the extent to which we put our confidence in "signs" or in apparent consequences.

Mature, genuine faith is one that can endure the test of both Eden and Gethsemane. Thus we do not believe miracle stories in order to understand and believe in God better. Rather, we understand and believe in God through His Word, and thus we can properly interpret and understand miracle stories.

While most people continue to ask for signs and wonders, attempting to manipulate God in various and subtle ways, it is our privilege to enjoy a real, forthright, honest, and submissive relationship with Him. Such a relationship, if we are prepared to pay the price for it, is the source of all power. It enables God to employ His infinite power in and around us. Are you prepared to relate to God as Jesus did in Gethsemane? Are you prepared to serve Him as a warrior, enduring whatever wounds come your way? And are you prepared to rest your faith *solely* upon His Word, regardless of consequences, and submit to His will for your life? If so, then you are ready to experience the richness of God's power in your life!

---

* The actual word is "concubine," indicating a wife of lesser legal status.

Chapter 8

ALL POWER

B y now it might seem that I have been portraying the true Christian life as devoid of joyful experiences and of evidences from the Lord's wondrous working in our lives. I can understand how one might misunderstand me in this way, but nothing could be further from the truth. Instead, I seek to depict the true Christian life as one in which the Lord is actually enabled to employ His wondrous power in more and more marvelous ways. Only those endowed with genuine faith can actually experience the true richness, joy, and power of Christianity.

I have reserved the best for last. In the Bible we see that faith is an active principle: "by faith Abraham did" this, and "by faith Moses did" that. And we read that "faith cometh by hearing, and hearing by the Word of God" (Rom. 10:17). I have repeatedly emphasized the Word of God, and it is time to grasp its practical realities. It is clear that understanding the nature of the Word of God is the basis of all the power that faith harnesses in order that the faithful might do and be what the Lord wills for them. Therefore, recognizing the nature of the Word of God is the centerpiece of making sense of the active principle of mature, genuine faith. When we understand, believe, and act as though we believe the Word of God, then we have mature, genuine faith that can employ all the power that God has made available to us.

While most Christians seek ongoing evidences that the Lord loves them and has their best interest at heart, they fail to take hold of the true source of power for their lives. But what exactly is that power?

What Is the Word?

When you hold the Bible in your hand, what do you think of it? We call it the "Word of God," but what does that mean? Is it a collection of stories designed to give us some moral principles and general guidance for life? Or is it a compilation of allegories, not to be taken too literally, and always to be measured against the "reliable" claims of science? What really is the Bible? Let us examine some of the claims that Scripture makes for itself, and then we will clearly see what Christians are entitled to hope for from it. In the process we will discover the practical reality of genuine, mature faith.

Let us begin at the very beginning, looking at the Creation account in Genesis 1. I want to focus on one particular aspect of that account: how did everything come into being? What was the active power of God that brought things into existence?

Again and again we encounter the same formula: "Then God said . . . " And then the thing declared comes into being, just as He commanded. So what is the creative power of God? His word.

The exception to this in Genesis is the creation of humanity. Everything surrounding the human race—all the accoutrements of their existence—God made by His word alone. But notice the intimacy with which He created the first man and woman (Gen. 2). The only other creative act we have recorded in the Bible in which God touched something into existence was His writing out His law with His finger. Otherwise, God speaks, and thus things come to be.

Many passages of Scripture support the idea that the word of God has creative power in itself to go out and accomplish the thing spoken of. We will survey some of them, because such a notion is initially very counterintuitive to us. When we speak, our words have no power in themselves. If I announce, "My pen will now move from the left to the right side of my desk," I can wait for that to happen as long as I like, but my saying it won't make it happen. That pen isn't going to move according to my will unless I physically reach out and shift it. My words might reflect my will, but they are not the power of my will. In God's case, by contrast, His word is the power of His will. His words have power in themselves to make His will reality. I know that this sounds strange, but let's look at more biblical evidence.

God precedes Isaiah 55:11 by expressing how His ways and thinking are so much different than ours (verses 8, 9). And the primary difference—the thing that is to give Israel hope during its captivity in Babylon—is that God's word has the power in itself to make the prophesied redemption and restoration of Israel real in due time: "So shall My word be which goes forth from My mouth; it shall not return to Me empty, without accomplishing what I desire, and without succeeding in the matter for which I sent it" (NASB). Notice that God is assuring His people that when He speaks, His word itself will accomplish what it says. Just as He can create with His word, He can make future events reality by His word. His word fulfills itself by the power invested in it.

How can this be? Hebrews 4:12 gives some insight: "For the word of God is living and active and sharper than any two-edged sword" (NASB). The Lord declares that His word is different from our word because it is living and active. It has in itself all His divine power to accomplish the very thing that the word says.

Matthew 8:1-3 depicts a leper cleansed by the word: "'I am willing; be cleansed.' And immediately his leprosy was cleansed" (verse 3, NASB). How much time elapsed from the word of God and the fulfillment of that word? "Immediately"! When God wills it, His word instantly acts to perform what it declares, and when He states what the future will be, His word acts at the appointed time to perform what it announces.

In Matthew 9:1-8 we see Jesus forgive, and then as proof of the power of His word to make forgiveness reality, He heals the paralytic by His word. The word of Jesus alone is sufficient to calm the storm in Matthew 8:23-27. And His disciples marveled because even the wind and the waves obeyed His word.

Hebrews 1:1-4 explains the foundations of reality to us, as God tells us how He created our reality and even now sustains it. Speaking of Jesus, the writer says: "His Son, whom He appointed heir of all things, through whom also He made the world. And He is the radiance of His glory and the exact representation of His nature, and upholds all things by the word of His power." As John 1 explains to us, Jesus is the part of the Godhead that made all things by His word. Scripture calls Him "the Word" because it is by His word that things are as they are. And this passage in Hebrews clarifies that the word of God sustains all ongoing reality.

What does Hebrews say is the power of God? "The word of his power" (Heb. 1:3). God's word is the way in which His will becomes reality, a principle further amplified in Colossians 1:3-6. Speaking of the word of God, Paul refers to the "word of truth" as accomplishing this in believers: ". . . constantly bearing fruit and increasing, even as it has been doing in you also since the day you heard of it and understood the grace of God in truth" (verse 6, NASB).

Notice that the word of God is what makes the change inside the believer. Just as God's word has in itself creative power, it also has in itself re-creative power. The word of God forgives, uplifts, and sanctifies the believer: "For the word of the cross is foolishness to those who are perishing, but to us who are being saved it is the power of God" (1 Cor. 1:18, NASB). The word of God is the power of God. As James 1:18 says: "In the exercise of His will He brought us forth by the word of truth, so that we would be, as it were, the first fruits among His creatures" (NASB). How does God bring us forth as new creations? Again, "by the word of truth." The word "by" signifies that the will of God is made real using His word. His word is the motive force that makes real what the word declares.

Given what God says about His own word, what then is genuine faith? Many Bible stories clearly reveal the answer, but none more powerfully and obviously than the incident of the Roman centurion in Matthew 8:5-13.

In this story a Roman soldier approaches Jesus to ask for the healing of his sick servant. Jesus offers to come personally to heal the servant. But amazingly, the officer refuses. Instead, the centurion tells Jesus that he understands the nature of authority and, most important, the power of the word of authority. He acknowledges that he fully recognizes that Jesus' word is sufficient to accomplish the thing the word says, and that He doesn't need to do *anything* more than speak the word in order to make the spoken thing real. Amazed by the centurion's depth of comprehension, Jesus states flatly that He has not found such faith in all of Israel. The pagan (and hated Roman) grasps the nature of genuine faith better than all of the "chosen" of Israel when he recognizes that the word of God has in itself the power to do what it announces.

What Jesus calls faith in this story is simple: acting on the belief that the word of God has power in itself to do what it says.

This principle has amazing implications for every aspect of our lives. First, it is clear that the word of God is the mechanism by which we are being saved. As 1 Peter 1:23-25 declares: "For you have been born again not of seed which is perishable but imperishable, that is, through the living and enduring word of God" (verse 23, NASB). We have already seen that the word of God is itself living and powerful, and here we see explicitly that it is because of (through, or by) the "living and enduring" word that believers are born again. The disciple continues to press the point home: "'But the word of the Lord endures forever.' And this is the word which was preached to you" (verse 25, NASB).

Remember the verse I have been emphasizing throughout this book: "So faith comes from hearing, and hearing by the word of Christ" (Rom. 10:17, NASB). The point is now plain. Hearing and grasping the word of God, and acting on the belief that it is true, is genuine faith. Genuine faith recognizes, and lets its perspectives be shaped by, the reality that the word of God has power in itself to do what it says.

I ask again: When you hold the Bible, what is it to you? Do you recognize the amazing power there in your hands?

I certainly do not minimize the need of prayer, as I have made clear throughout this book. But it is also the case that many Christians do not experience the power of God in their lives as they might because they spend time praying and asking for God to do in and for them what He has already given them His Word to do for them. They simply don't recognize the power of the Bible in their lives. Second Timothy 3:5 describes the evil people of the last days as "holding to a form of godliness, although they have denied its power" (NASB).

Some of the implications of this "radical" reliance on the bare Word of God can be shocking.

Evolutionary Theism

For example, it has become fashionable and "intellectually sophisticated" to be a theistic evolutionist in the face of the claims of evolutionary theory.* I mentioned this in chapter 4, but I want to zero in on this point more carefully now, because I believe that theistic evolution is just a form of "denying the power" of the word of God to do what it says; and that denial is the basis of an utter lack of faith, regardless of how much praying goes on. That sort of lack of faith infects every aspect of a theistic evolutionist's life and theology.

A young man told me recently, "I wouldn't care if it turned out that God spat upon the ground, and from that point evolution took over. That wouldn't change my perspective of God in the slightest." And, like him, many people sincerely believe that they can have it both ways: they can have (some version of) God as well as evolutionary theory. What such people don't understand is that such an amalgamation is *not* intellectually sophisticated—instead, it is a confused abomination of both evolutionary theory and the claims and power of Scripture.

Evolutionists reject such a combination of a "divine starting point" with evolutionary theory because they are committed to a purely naturalistic paradigm that leaves no place for (and has no need of) God in their explanations. Hard-core evolutionists treat such a view with derision as a useless distortion of evolutionary theory.

Theists should reject such a view because of how it guts the point and power of Scripture. Theistic evolutionists assume that they are quite intelligent to suggest that the seven days of Creation actually signify seven indeterminate time periods during which the process of evolution took place. Countless practical problems challenge such a view (including that the very order of the "days" would also have to be manipulated), but, as I will demonstrate, the theological implications are staggering and utterly unacceptable to any genuine Christian.

How much time passed from Jesus saying "Be cleansed" to the leper being cleansed? The transformation was immediate. Or consider how much time lapsed from Christ speaking the word of healing to the centurion to his servant being healed. The Bible declares, "That very hour," which is just another way of saying "right then." When the word of God says for something to be done, it is done. The Lord has no need of indefinite periods of time or naturalistic processes to add to the power of His word. In the same way that evolutionists reject God from their naturalistic accounts, theists should reject naturalistic additions to the Bible's supernatural accounts. The amalgamation of naturalism and supernaturalism in "theistic evolution" is a bastardization of *both* perspectives.

Victory Over Sin

As I said, the theological implications of minimizing or denying the power of the Word of God are devastating. Yet every day Christians are swayed every which way by misinterpretations of the Bible and by the claims of science, so that they do not know where their anchor is anymore. Our anchor is the Word of God, but it must be properly understand and integrated into the life.

Consider your own victory over temptation. The Bible makes some astounding claims, yet we are not willing to take them seriously, because we are afraid. The Bible urges us: "He who has suffered in the flesh has ceased from sin, so as to live the rest of the time in the flesh no longer for the lusts of men, but for the will of God" (1 Peter 4:1, 2, NASB). Scripture emphasizes the power of the Word of God in our sanctification by declaring, "For by these He has granted to us His precious and magnificent promises, so that by them you may become partakers of the divine nature, having escaped the corruption that is in the world by lust" (2 Peter 1:4, NASB). "Let this mind be in you which was also in Christ Jesus" (Phil. 2:5, NKJV), and then the passage goes on to talk of the humility and obedience of Christ. Galatians 5:16 states flatly: "But I say, walk by the Spirit, and you will not carry out the desire of the flesh" (NASB). After telling the people about the internal, spiritual implications of the law of God, Jesus announces, "Therefore you are to be perfect, as your heavenly Father is perfect" (Matt. 5:48, NASB). Finally (although the Bible is filled with such passages), Revelation 3:21 makes the matter perfectly clear: "He who overcomes, I will grant to him to sit down with Me on My throne, as I also overcame and sat down with My Father on His throne" (NASB).

Trying Versus Doing

The last verse I cited doesn't say, "He who tries really, really hard to overcome . . . " Rather, it declares that we are to overcome just as Christ overcame! The meaning of the term *overcome* in this context is not left open to question. Christ is the standard of overcoming, and overcoming means the same thing for us that it did for Him.

Consider an illustration I have used when speaking on the topic. Crumbling a piece of paper into a small, tight ball and holding it in my open palm, I ask a small child in the audience to try to take the paper ball from my open hand. The child reaches out and picks up the paper. "No, no!" I protest. "I said to *try* to take it," and I retrieve the paper ball and once more hold it in my open hand, urging, "Now, *try* to take it." The child looks a bit confused, hesitates, then reaches out and removes the wad of paper from my hand. Again I reach for it, explaining, "No, you are confused. I understand. But I want you to *try* to take the ball, and you just keep on *taking* it." After assuring the child and sending him or her back to sit down again, I make this point: There is no *trying* to do that which is in your power to do. You either just do it, or you don't." When doing something is in your power, "trying" just is "doing." Too many Christians waste time praying for power that the Lord has already given them. And too many Christians are merely *trying* to overcome, and failing, because they do not use the power of the word of God to make the victory real.

Now, I know that many reading this are getting extremely nervous or even resistant right now. But please remember the principle of intellectual honesty from earlier and grant me a little charity, because I'm going to explain things as carefully as I can.

Let's think this matter through. Consider a particular temptation. Let's be innocuous for the moment. Suppose that you are tempted to eat a second piece of chocolate cake, and for dietary reasons you have been convicted that you should not. For you, eating that second piece would be gluttony. Now, I'm assuming for the purposes of this example that you *know* that eating that second piece of cake would be sin for you. So I'm taking the process of conviction for granted here. You recognize, for example, that murder or adultery is sin, but we're not ready to consider those implications yet. For the moment, just bear with me and grant me that you regard eating that second piece of cake as wrong.

Now, you're tempted to eat it. Not only do you want to eat it—you *feel* the force of what James 1:14 says: "But each one is tempted when he is carried away and enticed by his own lust" (NASB). The drawing power of your gluttony manifests itself by focusing on that second piece of cake.

Here, then, is the big question. Consider your answer carefully. Is God's power available to you *right then* to overcome that temptation? The correlative question is: when you are tempted in this one instance, must you give in?

If you say that God's power is not available to you to resist right then that very temptation, then you have never read or understood all that the Bible says about victory over sin. (See 1 Cor. 10:13; Heb. 2:17, 18; 4:15, 16; 10:26; 12:4; James 4:7, 8; and many others. Just use your concordance to find passages speaking about "temptation," "sin," and "victory.") But most Christians will admit that in this *particular* temptation God has power available to give them victory. They agree that in the power of God they can win over this one particular temptation. However, they also see that the implication I'm driving for is that they can have victory over all sin, and to them that smacks of *legalism* or *perfectionism,* terms with extremely negative connotations. Thus the problem most Christians have is with the idea of victory over sinning in the general sense.

OK, again, just stay with me step by step.

So far you have agreed that God can grant you victory over this particular temptation. You accept this because you believe that God wants you to triumph over this specific issue, and you do so because you believe that Jesus told the truth when He said that He is the "way, the truth, and the life" (John 14:6), and that the truth would set you free (John 8:32). Furthermore, you understand that "everyone who commits sin is the slave of sin" (John 8:34, NASB), and that the very mission of Christ is summarized two verses later: "If the Son therefore shall make you free, ye shall be free indeed" (verse 36). Thus you know that Jesus wants to set you free from this particular sin and to enable you to overcome this specific temptation.

Now, how is the power of God to give you victory implemented in this particular case? The Word of God tells you to "let this mind be in you, which was also in Christ Jesus" (Phil. 2:5), and that passage signifies "partaking of the divine nature." You see, it is our lower nature that cries out for and lusts after sin. But, as Revelation 3:21 signifies, we are to overcome exactly in the same way that Jesus did, and we know that He overcame totally! He was able to say, "The ruler of the world is coming, and he has nothing in Me" (John 14:30, NASB). The divine nature (the "mind of Christ" Paul refers to in Philippians) overcame each particular temptation. And we have read that we partake of the divine nature through the promises and Word of God. It is *by* reading ("hearing") and believing the Word of God that He puts within us His divine nature, which is the power of victory over particular temptations.

The next step is the clincher. If you agree that the Word of God has made you a partaker of the divine nature, and you accept that the divine nature in you is powerful and able to supersede each *particular* temptation (just as it did in the life of Christ), then you must acknowledge that victory over all sin (victory in the general sense) is just a function of getting victory over each and every *particular* temptation. If I'm tempted to do sin x, yet the power of the Word of God makes me victorious over temptation x, and I'm then tempted to commit sin y, but the power of the word of God gives me victory over temptation y, and so on, then at the point of each temptation, the Word of God gives me victory. I move from victory to victory. This is exactly what John meant when he wrote: "My little children, I am writing these things to you so that you many not sin" (1 John 2:1, NASB).

Faith, then, is the victory. A person of faith is a person of victory. Just as the little child has the power to take the paper ball, not just try to take it, the person of faith has the power to take the victory, not just try to take it!

Then why do we find so much trying and so little victory in the battle against temptation? First, it is because people love their sins, and they choose to keep committing them. But they cannot stand the thought that their sins actually separate them from God and nullify the sacrifice of Jesus for them. Such people become susceptible to any theology that tells them that they are saved (or are being saved) even while they intentionally and willfully continue sinning. Some theologians have generated "denying the power thereof" types of theologies to make excuses for our ongoing, willful sinning because that is the only way they can account for all the trying and failing. Thus certain popular theologies make much of trying, and "victory" becomes synonymous with forgiveness.

Now, I am not denying the power or need of forgiveness, because it is impossible to partake of the divine nature (the power for ongoing victory) without first having it. But I am saying that forgiveness for a sin is not the same thing as not committing that sin in the first place. Let us not overemphasize the second part of the passage in 1 John 2:1. Yes, we do have an Advocate with the Father *if* we sin. But just offering repeated forgiveness again and again is *not* God's goal for us. His intent for us is just as John said: that we "may not sin." We may triumph over each and every temptation as it comes to us, just as Jesus did.

At this point I know that many are squirming and thinking that I've gone too far. The more educated are reasoning, "Jensen has conflated perfection with perfectionism," and they conclude that I have moved fallaciously from discussion of victory over particular sins to talk of victory over sin in the general sense. Furthermore, most people read much more into the term *sin* than the Bible does, and so they look at their character defects as though they are the same thing as willful, intentional sins. Thus they conclude that *perfection,* meaning "victory over all sin," is not possible. (I will address such issues in the following chapters.)

However, I know that many, weary of being slaves to known sin, honestly seek the means by which the Son shall set them free. In the next chapter we will look very carefully at what the Bible actually says about sin, perfection, and victory. The Word of God *is* the power for victory, and we simply need to understand it correctly in order to internalize that amazing power.

---

* When I talk about "theism" and "theists" in this chapter, I am referring particularly to Judeo/Christian/Islamic theists who share the biblical account of Creation. These three groups combined make up more than three fifths of the world's population. However, there are "nonbiblical" theists for whom my biblical references here will have no weight. What I am explicitly contrasting in this section is a biblical account of origins with an evolutionary one. Other theistic but nonbiblical Creation accounts might square nicely with evolutionary theory, but I argue here that a biblical account cannot.

Chapter 9

THE CONDITIONS OF VICTORTY, PART 1

A s the previous chapter has revealed, perhaps the most profound implication of what I have been presenting about faith is also the most troubling to many people. Indeed, such confusion abounds about the subject of victory that the remaining chapters of this book can only provide an overview of the sort of detailed response ultimately needed. However, such an overview is itself useful. Let us consider the way genuine faith relates to victory in the Christian life.

The widespread debates about *victory* and *perfection* take many forms and employ many labels. *Perfectionism, legalism, works, grace, the fight of faith, the fight of sin,* and many other terms are more or less misunderstood, given the host of competing theological contexts in which people use them. Even the question "What does the Bible say?" is not very helpful, since the debates are fundamentally about biblical interpretation.

Indeed, Satan has so muddied the waters that many people despair of really understanding the issues. Driven by a sense of theological futility, they look for the simplest explanation possible. I can't count the number of times I have heard an exasperated person exclaim, "It's just too complicated! I'm not a theologian, and I can't believe that God intended the most important subject in the Bible to be so devious. To me, it's very simple: God loves me. He wants to save me. I'm not a legalist, so I believe that He has done everything required to save me. I accept that salvation. So I am saved—plain and simple."

I agree that God has made the plan of salvation the clearest thing in the Bible. But is it really as "simple" as summarized in the previous quotation? In fact, even the "simple" version quoted above employs some very loaded terms: *legalist, required, save,* and *accept.* Such terms are not "simple," and they have many different meanings depending upon the underlying theological context.

Another common refrain among frustrated saints is: "Doctrine, doctrine! There is too much talk about doctrine. I want to hear about the love of God. That's all that really matters. When you understand how much God loves you, then all this talk of doctrine becomes almost meaningless."

The problem with this, again, "simple" idea is that it also depends upon loaded terms: *doctrine, God, love,* and *meaningless.* Exactly what is a doctrine? What is this "God" we're talking about in the absence of all doctrine? What distinguishes "our God" from a Hindu deity? What does *love* even mean in the absence of doctrine? No, instead of *doctrine becoming meaningless* when you understand *love,* the opposite is the case: doctrine defines love. In the absence of doctrine the term becomes meaningless.

I do understand the frustration with the endless competing theological theories about salvation, and I well recognize that people don't have the time to become theologians in order to sort the mess out. However, there is no more important topic of study than that of salvation, and we must get clear about faith and its implications, because those implications are how we define and accept salvation. The Bible says that the way to damnation is wide and the way to salvation is narrow (see Matt. 7:13, 14). Being one of the "few" that find the way to salvation is a function of studying to show yourself approved (see 2 Tim. 2:15).

The matter of studying is not so simple anymore either. It has become increasingly popular in the church to think of the Bible as such a wholly socially contextualized collection of disparate writings that people are downright timid to proclaim what the Bible actually says. Theologians have led the charge to relativize every apparent doctrine or principle in the Bible, until the untrained person so doubts their own capacity to understand what the Bible teaches that they wonder whether it really says much of anything at all. Thus Bible study gets reduced to a superficial reading of "stories" in which we hope to find a "moral," or a vague hunt for "principles" to guide our lives, while we don't take specific passages very specifically at all. Some have reduced even the Ten Commandments to just some guidelines among many others, in which the real "principle" is only "love," whatever in the world that means.

In this book I have had the temerity to advocate that the Word of God is the power in our lives. And I have argued that the more closely we understand the Word of God, both in principle and in specific detail, the more directly and particularly He will work in our lives. But the debate about the type of inspiration that God employed in giving us the Bible goes on and on, which undermines taking the Bible at its word.

In the next chapter I intend to analyze the biblical principles of salvation, faith, and righteousness very specifically and closely. So it behooves me to clarify how I can justify such a close scrutiny of the actual phrasing and content of the various biblical passages. It is beyond the scope of this book to debate the various types of inspiration suggested as God's means of giving us the Bible. However, I can clarify exactly how I see various passages of Scripture.

I am not a "fundamentalist" in the sense of believing in word-for-word inspiration. Nor am I an "idea inspirationist" in the sense that God only supplied the most vague and general ideas and principles, while the Bible writers basically said whatever they themselves thought, under the almost opaque "guidance" of such inspired "impressions."

Instead, I believe that the propositional content of the Bible was inspired. In this chapter I carefully explain what a proposition is. For the moment, though, let me say that the "propositional content" of various passages consists of the specific idea that God sought to convey via that passage—what the passage is about. If a passage is explaining the nature of faith, for example, then I take that passage to be conveying the specific (not vague) ideas and relationships about faith that God actually intends to present on that very subject.

I find it unacceptable to hear suggested relativizations of contentious passages, such as: "That was Paul's logic, not God's." People advocating that we relativize even the logic employed in the Bible don't (I hope) realize that that sword cuts all ways. Such a response to a clear biblical argument ignores other passages in which Paul distinguishes between when he presents his own thinking "by permission" and when he switches back into writing *for* God. Treating anything in the Bible we have a problem with, willy-nilly, as "the writer's logic" absolutely guts the Word of God of its profound power to address me specifically and directly on the very particular points its passages are about.

Thus in what follows I treat the Word of God as though it is filled with specific and reliable propositional content, and that we can, with the power of the Holy Spirit, see that content for what it is. Furthermore, I treat the logic employed in the Bible as utterly reliable and as conveying the logical relations exactly as God intended them to be conveyed. For example, when a text is written as a conditional statement, I treat the order of the propositions in that conditional as not arbitrary or just "the writer's logic" as it happened to come out that day. Instead I approach the propositional order as reflecting exactly what God designed, because if we are to take the Bible seriously at all, then we really have no option.

This is not word-for-word inspiration. Instead, it is proposition by proposition inspiration, in which I must presume that the logic underlying those propositions is itself reliable. I believe that any approach to Scripture that so relativizes them that they will not endure this level of scrutiny simply reduces the Bible to a collection of stories conveying vague morals and indeterminate principles that will be forever subject to misunderstanding and fruitless debate. Satan would love to have the Word of God so gutted of its power because he well knows that, properly understood and assimilated into the life, it is the power of God for us. The Lord has very specific and well-defined things to say about His dealings with us. There are "rules to the game," so to speak, and we ignore or are unaware of those rules only at our peril. Conversely, understanding God's perspectives as the Bible carefully and specifically reveals them to us is the basis of power and victory in our lives.

Of course, the biggest problem facing people studying to understand faith, victory, and salvation is that they are not intellectually honest. I know that claim sounds harsh, so let me explain.

When polled, the vast majority of people call themselves "better than average" drivers. But by definition all of them cannot be accurately assessing their driving prowess. Many who think of themselves as better-than-average drivers are actually (at best) just average. Now, such people don't intend to be in error. They are sincerely reporting how they perceive their own motoring skill. But they are in error nevertheless, and as Clifford says, "The sincerity of [their] conviction can in no wise help [them]."

What does this have to do with intellectual honesty, particularly as that relates to Bible study about faith, victory, and salvation? Most Christians think of themselves as pretty decent people. I don't mean it as ridicule—they honestly believe that God has been working in their lives and that their lives are "better than before" as a result of His grace. Many probably share some version of "trend of the life" theology, by which God grants salvation to people who have lived a basically good life (as a result of His grace, of course), and the occasional sins or "downturns" do not threaten their salvation. Indeed, such things are to be expected. The vast majority of Christians believe that they *are* saved (and will remain saved), and because they hold that viewpoint so deeply and thoroughly, any "true" theology simply must correlate with that "fact." The (apparent to them) work of God's grace in their lives, producing a "basically good life," is the most fundamental data point with which all theologies must harmonize. Just as most polled drivers (in error) see themselves as better-

than-average drivers (and any discussion of driving simply must acknowledge the accuracy of their self-perception), most Christians
view themselves as basically good people because of the grace of God
(and any discussion of theology simply must recognize the legitimacy
of their self-understanding). This self-perspective, along with its supporting theology, is so fundamental that people find it nearly impossible to step back to see "if they are in the faith."

Remember the "worldly theistic" perspective discussed in chapter 6? There is another aspect to that search for worldly security that
is wrapped up in this perspective: spiritual security. Most Christians
believe that their relationship with God is fundamentally about pro-
viding them with spiritual security: God loves them so much that He
views their "good lives" as enough evidence of their relationship
with Him that He will save them. Their ongoing sinning really does-
n't matter, because that's what the blood of Christ is for. For them
"victory" just means accepting Christ's sacrifice and thereby being
"covered" even though they still knowingly sin. They live "basically
good lives," so it is clear that God's grace has been working in them
(slowly but surely), and thus they enjoy the security that comes from
knowing they are saved.

The problem is that we cannot completely shake that deep intuition that "spiritual victory" is supposed to mean victory over intentional sinning, too. So a deep tension arises in us. On the one hand,
we feel that we should have more success over intentional sinning
than we do. On the other hand, we so strongly feel the yearnings of
our lower natures that we really don't think that we can triumph
over all of our sins all the time. As a result, we find ourselves drawn
toward theologies that seem to resolve this tension and promise salvation in spite of our ongoing willful sinning. We naturally want the
security of salvation, even though we haven't a clue about how we
are supposed to stop sinning.

Indeed, one of the most widespread versions of "trend of the
life" theology urges us to "fight the fight of faith, not the fight of

sin" (as though there is actually a dichotomy between these struggles). According to the "fight of faith, not sin" model we maintain a relationship with God through the spiritual disciplines of Bible study, prayer, and witnessing. Everything else is His problem and His responsibility.

Our "fight" is to continue this "relationship" by engaging in these spiritual disciplines, and the "fight of sin" is then up to God as He sees fit at any given moment. This theory explicitly states that we are not to "fight the fight of sin," in which that means anything like active resistance against temptation, because struggling against temptation means that you have already lost that battle (God didn't "win the battle for you," because if He had, there would have been no difficulty on your part). And if we are letting God do the fighting, this theory asserts that we will often have to struggle to "maintain the relationship" even as Satan is constantly calling our attention to our ongoing willful sins. But we are not even to look at our deliberate sinning, because "that is not where the fight is" and "your behavior has no effect upon God's attitude toward you."

According to this model we are not to pay any attention to the ongoing, willful sins we commit, because God will take care of them whenever He is good and ready. Meanwhile, our sole role in our own salvation is to "maintain the relationship" by Bible study, prayer, and witnessing. And if we are doing those things, we are saved, regardless of our continuous sinning. Moreover, if we find that our ongoing sinning troubles us, that very fact shows that we are legalists rather than Christians—so we had better get over it and get back to "fighting the fight of faith, not sin" or we will be lost, because we can't fight both the fight of faith and the fight of sin.

This version of "trend of the life" theology has proved so appealing and become so pervasive in certain circles because it resolves the fundamental tensions between our intuitions of what "victory" is about. Such a theology provides a basis for the assurance of salvation (the "relationship," defined as Bible study, prayer, and witnessing) that even the willful sinner can enjoy a sense of peace.

And most insidious is its claim that if our willful sinning troubles us, that is itself evidence that we are not saved, because we have not been willing to give that fight to Jesus. Thus the clearest evidence that we are not genuine Christians is that we ever actively resist temptation because we find our sins to be troubling. This theology asserts that we are to ignore our sinning, because it has no relationship whatsoever to our salvation. And anyone that claims that sinning in any way affects our salvation is a legalist. Such a perspective is intuitively very appealing, because it explains why we keep sinning yet assures us of salvation during the time that God is "fighting the fight of sin" for us.

By making the "faith relationship" utterly independent of the fruit of the Spirit in the life, good works, and any ongoing and willful sinning, it provides a theory whereby sinners can be saved *in their sins*.

Now, it is simply impossible for a person immersed in this or any other "trend of the life" theology to read "everyone who commits sin is the slave to sin" (John 8:34, NASB) and understand it just as it appears there. They are forced to read Romans 7 with the interpretation that our "flesh" is a "slave to sin," even though we are "in Christ." Furthermore, they must then ignore the profound import of Jesus' claim "If the Son sets you free, you will be free indeed" (John 8:36, NIV), in which the *context* of that claim must mean freedom *from* sin. And they must ignore what Paul says in Romans 8, in which he talks about the complete victory available to all who are in Christ, because Christ came to condemn "sin in the flesh" (verse 3).

People who insist on believing that they are saved even while they are in fact slaves to sin simply cannot be intellectually honest about their Bible "study," because they prioritize their spiritual security over the Bible's condemnation of their ongoing, willful sinning. Let me be plain: if we are engaged in known, willful sin, then we are a slave to sin, and we have not been set free, regardless of what pretensions our "relationship" might have. Whatever else our "relationship" is doing, it is not what God intends. God wants us to have victory over our sins, and He wants that we have it now.

I am writing like this, directly and forcefully, because confusion abounds, and, sadly, in the judgment most "Christians" will find that they actually were not. I point you again to Clifford's provocatively correct statement: "Nor is it truly a belief at all which has not some influence upon the actions of him who holds it. He who truly believes that which prompts him to an action has looked upon the action to lust after it, he has committed it already in his heart. If a belief is not realized immediately in open deeds, it is stored up for the guidance of the future." What you believe about spiritual victory invariably affects your actions and perspectives.

The urgency of correctly understanding and believing the truth about spiritual victory demands that we stop for a moment right now and ask ourselves if we really can be intellectually honest about this subject. Are we prepared to seriously consider that our past "good life" or "trend of the life" theology has been in error, and that we have actually not been experiencing faith and victory as it is the privilege of Christians to experience them? Are we willing to seriously consider the evidence, and to go where the evidence leads, even if it threatens what we have been calling spiritual security so far in our lives? Genuine faith is far more than an intellectual understanding of the truth, but it is never less than that.

So if we are prepared to put our spiritual security on the line and honestly consider and internalize what the Bible actually does say about the requirements for salvation and victory, then I guarantee that by the end of this book each of us can choose to be a genuine Christian experiencing genuine faith and victory. People want "simplicity," and it really is that simple.

Before we can evaluate what the Bible really says, though, we must begin by addressing a fundamental logical misunderstanding that is the root of all the confusion about spiritual victory. Perhaps it seems shocking to hear that all the varied and divergent views about victory depend upon a fundamental and quite simple logical confusion, but nevertheless I believe that clearing up the matter depends foremost upon grasping some simple logical concepts: necessary and sufficient conditions.

In the rest of this chapter I will describe some of the logical relations and inferences[1] that we use all the time in everyday life, ones that form the basis for understanding some key biblical passages about salvation, faith, and victory. If you already have a background in formal logic, you may wish to skip the rest of this chapter, or you might skim it as a review.

The next chapter then takes our knowledge of these logical relations and analyzes a number of biblical passages to see what God is really telling us about salvation, faith, and victory.

Fair warning: these two chapters are the most philosophically rigorous in this book. Unfortunately, being crystal clear and systematic usually has the side effect of being somewhat dry and even difficult. I do my best to minimize your pain, but the material is still not easy to read, and I definitely emphasize being systematic over being appealing. If you choose to just believe in my analysis, without seeing it demonstrated, you can just jump straight to chapter 11, "All Victory," and benefit from my conclusions. However, for those who want to view the careful and rigorous demonstration of those conclusions, here we go.

Logical Conditionals

Arguably the most fundamental logical concept we have is that of "if, then." We use this logical relation constantly as we think and communicate. The most common use of the conditional is called the *material conditional,* and countless examples fill every aspect of life: "If it's raining, then the streets are wet." "If there's smoke, then there's fire." And so on. Often the "then" gets dropped, although it is always implied. Other forms of the conditional exist, such as the subjunctive form: "If it had been raining, then the streets would have been wet."

And there are others (for a thoroughgoing treatment of conditionals, see Michael Woods, Dorothy Edgington, and David Wiggins, *Conditionals* [New York: Oxford University Press, 2003]). But for our purposes the material conditional is the only form needed, and we will see that the scriptural passages I quote belong to this form.

Now, when we talk about logical relations, we must begin by clarifying what it is that is being related. Logical relations don't relate material things, like arranging groups of wooden blocks into patterns. Instead, logical relations relate *propositions*. A proposition is just a declarative statement, and we can use two criteria to distinguish propositions from other forms of speech: (1) all propositions have a truth value, while not all sentences do; (2) sentences can vary in phrasing or language, while the proposition conveyed remains the same.

Let's begin by understanding the first criterion of a proposition. All propositions have a truth value. It means that propositions are either true or false.[2] If I say, "The door is open," that statement is either true or false. If the door is cracked open even a *little,* then the statement is true,[3] and if the door is fully closed, then the statement is false.

Sentences don't *all* have truth values. For example, it makes no sense to say that commands have a truth value. If I order you to open the door, you cannot sensibly reply "True" or "False." You might instead say "I will" or "I won't," but "True" is a confused response. Similarly, questions don't have truth values. The typical response to a question is itself a proposition that has a truth value, but the question is a request for a proposition.

Next, let's consider the second criterion. Sentences can vary in phrasing, while the proposition conveyed remains the same. This principle is central to our hope of accurately translating ideas between languages; thus the basis of our belief that the Bible in English is fundamentally "the same thing" as the Bible in Greek or Hebrew. Even within the same language we find many ways of saying the same thing. For example, I might report, "For lunch I had a grilled-cheese sandwich." I might also say, "For my midday meal, I had two slices of grain-based baked product with a slab of solidified, fermented, bovine milk between them, and I had heated the conglomeration in a frying pan until the solidified, fermented, bovine milk had begun to melt." Though we certainly recognize the first expression of the proposition as the more straightforward of the two, they both have the same propositional content.

The key point to distinguishing between sentences and propositions in this way is that intellectual honesty demands that we get clear about what proposition(s) is/are being conveyed by natural languages. For example, sometimes questions are rhetorical, and the "questioning" sentence seeks to convey a proposition. The point is that we not get so caught up in the verbiage that we don't look for what is really being stated.

Let's take the proposition: "It's raining." Again, I might convey that thought in many different languages and using all sorts of phraseology. But there is an underlying idea,[4] the proposition, and *that* is what we want to get clear about. Where I am right now, as I write this, that proposition has a truth value of false. That is one *scenario*, or, in other words, one state of affairs. The forecast in my locality calls for rain tonight, so if it proves accurate, then in tonight's scenario that proposition will be true. The notion of a *scenario* is critical, because when we evaluate logical relations, we must hold scenarios constant, as I will further explain.

From the point of view of logic, which will concern us in this chapter, logicians have developed some convenient shorthand notation, something that I believe actually clarifies logical relations. The shorthand plays on the fact that propositions have truth values, and consequently, we want to start dealing with the truth values themselves as quickly as possible, without getting bogged down in the linguistic content. So we want to see beneath the linguistic content to the proposition, then symbolize the proposition so that we can evaluate just the formal relations in which that proposition appears.

The shorthand we will use is to convert all propositions to uppercase letters. For example, I can represent "it is raining" with the sentence letter "P." Within a particular inference, once I have assigned "it is raining" to "P" I must hold that assignment constant. I might also assign "it is raining" to "Q," but I cannot put *some* other proposition into "P." Assignments, once they are made in an inference, must remain constant.

A final point is that we try to put the content of propositions in present perfect tense. This is part of what distinguishes the material conditional from other forms. In evaluating the propositional content of a sentence, we must be very sensitive to whether or not tense is crucial to the proposition.

For example, "If it's raining, then the streets will get wet" seemingly makes a forward-looking prediction. However, when most people say such a sentence, they are not making a claim about the future. Their use of "will" is just a way of implying the apparent certainty with which wet streets follow rain. We will lose nothing of the meaning if we convert such a sentence into the material conditional form: "If it rains, then the streets are wet."

Of course, the propositional content of other sentences is about tense. Subjunctive tenses in particular are not open to tenseless reinterpretation. When I say, "If I had gotten into that accident, I would have died," that sentence does not apparently convey the same proposition as "If I get into that accident, then I am dead." In the first case, I am speaking counterfactually (since I did not wind up in the accident), and I well recognize that my being dead is only a most-likely outcome of the accident. But the material conditional guarantees my death in the accident scenario, which is a much stronger claim than my subjunctive claim was probably making. Furthermore, in the material conditional, my being dead from any cause in the accident scenario follows from the claim. For example, if I got into the accident but actually died from the cancer that I already had, that is consistent with the claim of the material conditional. Yet death by any other cause in the context of the accident is quite apparently not what I meant by the original subjunctive conditional claim.

So we must be very sensitive to tense when we evaluate propositions. We can convert conditional claims into material conditionals only when it is truly the case that the propositional content is not about tense. This is actually the case with the vast majority of conditional claims that people make. And, fortunately for our purposes, all of the Bible passages we will evaluate can be cast as material conditionals.

Using what we know so far, let's start looking at some logical relations. Here is our example conditional sentence: "If it's raining, then the streets are wet." Notice that it explicitly uses the "if, then" construction, which makes the sentence an obvious conditional. The conditional is a binary relation, which means that the conditional always relates two and only two propositions. What are the two propositions in this conditional sentence? The first is "It's raining" while the second is "The streets are wet." The entire conditional sentence is itself a proposition: it has a truth value, and it can be conveyed entirely independently of any particular phraseology or language.

We can symbolize conditional sentences in our shorthand by converting the propositions into sentence letters, and then using a symbol to show the relation between them. "If it's raining, then the streets are wet," can be symbolized as "P ⊃ Q." We will use the "⊃" symbol to signify the conditional relation.

Notice that the "P" is to the left of the "⊃" symbol and the "Q" is to the right. We call the left side the *antecedent* and the right side the *consequent*. Such terms just mean "before" and "after," which makes sense when you look at the symbolization.

One thing you might have already noticed is that our symbolization has lost all of the content of the original conditional sentence. "P ⊃ Q" does not say anything like "If it's raining, then the streets are wet." No indeed. The symbolized sentence shows us the logical structure rather than the content. So we distinguish between the form and content of sentences. We need the content to tell us what a proposition's truth value is in the present real-world scenario. But in logic we care only about the relations between propositions, and for that purpose, the present real-world scenario is just one of many possibilities.

To illustrate what I mean, our example conditional sentence has four possible scenarios that define how the two propositions could relate to each other: (1) it is raining, and the streets are wet; (2) it is raining, and the streets are not wet; (3) it not raining, and the streets are wet; and (4) it is not raining, and the streets are not wet. Whatever the real-world scenario is for you right now, it is just one of those four possibilities.

Do you remember that we said our example conditional sentence is itself a proposition? What determines its truth value, since it actually *relates* propositions? The proposition "It's raining" is easy to evaluate: just stand outside and see what's happening. The same thing is true of "The streets are wet." However, the conditional proposition requires that I relate two propositions in a particular way, and the truth value of the conditional is always determined by the potential truth values of its antecedent and consequent propositions. While simple propositions have truth values according to the real-world scenario, logical relations such as the conditional have truth values defined by all the possible combinations of truth values their component propositions could have. This is a complex notion, but for the conditional we can summarize it this way: a conditional sentence is true if there is no scenario in which the antecedent is true and the consequent false. But a conditional sentence is false if such a scenario does exist.

An example will help. Let's suppose that I tell you, "If I go to the store, I bring home some bread." Later we evaluate what actually happened to see if my conditional sentence proved to be true. In the first scenario I went to the store and then returned home with the bread. According to the second scenario I did go to the store, but when I arrived home we see that I had forgotten to pick up any bread. The third scenario would have me never making it to the store, but I happened to get some bread from a street vendor. And in the fourth scenario, I became sick, didn't go out at all, and so didn't get any bread.

When evaluating the truth value of a conditional sentence, we must consider all four possible combinations of antecedent and consequent truth values, and see if there are any possible scenarios in which the antecedent could be true in the same scenario as the consequent is false. In our example above, we see that there is such a scenario: the second one. So my example conditional sentence is false. It is simply *not* the case that my going to the store guarantees that I will arrive back home with bread. We have discovered that it is certainly possible that I can go to the store and do not return with bread.

Let's consider a true conditional statement and see how its scenarios preclude having a true antecedent along with a false consequent. "If the Earth is a planet, then the Earth orbits the sun." Since orbiting the sun is what we mean by being a planet, it should be immediately obvious that there can be no scenario in which the antecedent is true while the consequent is false.

So, to repeat, conditional sentences evaluate as true if there exists no scenario in which the antecedent is true and the consequent is false. If there can be any scenario in which the antecedent is true while the consequent is false, then the conditional sentence evaluates as false.

While there are many ways of explaining how the conditional works logically, perhaps the most useful for our purposes is to talk about the antecedents and consequents of the conditional in terms of necessary and sufficient conditions. We can discuss the logic of the material conditional by considering which of the two propositions counts as a *necessary* and which counts as a *sufficient* condition for the other.

Here is an example: "If I love my wife, then I am faithful to her." In this example we see that the antecedent ("I love my wife") acts as a sufficient condition for the consequent ("I am faithful to my wife"). In other words, this conditional sentence is saying that in any scenario that I love my wife, in that same scenario I am faithful to her. Thus we call the antecedent of any material conditional the sufficient condition for the consequent. For any true conditional statement, the antecedent being true guarantees that the consequent is true.

Conversely, in our example sentence, if I actually do love my wife, then a necessary result of that fact is that I am faithful to her. After all, as we just noted above, the antecedent being true guarantees that the consequent is true, which is just another way of saying that the consequent being true is necessary to the antecedent being true. As a result, the consequent of any material conditional is the *necessary condition* of the antecedent. Since it is necessary for me to be faithful to my wife if I actually do love her, then if I really do love her, it *must* be the case that I am faithful to her.

We often perform powerful inferences using conditionals. Conditional inferences are so common and useful that logicians have named many of them. Because three of the named inferences will prove most useful to us, I will explain them.

The most common form of conditional inference works like this (remembering our use of sentence letters to stand for propositions): "If P, then Q. It is the case that P. Therefore, it is the case that Q." This form of inference is called *modus ponens*. We will call it MP for short. MP depends upon the fact that the antecedent of every true material conditional is a sufficient condition for the consequent. So whenever the antecedent is true, we know that the consequent is true.

The second most common form of conditional inference goes: "If P, then Q. It is not the case that Q. Therefore, it is not the case that P." The example about loving my wife illustrates this form of inference. Since being faithful is a necessary condition for loving my wife, if I'm being unfaithful to her, then I don't love her. Philosophers term this form of inference *modus tollens,* and we will label it MT. MT depends upon the fact that the consequent of every true material conditional is a necessary condition for the antecedent. Thus if the consequent is not the case, then the antecedent cannot be the case either.

The third form of inference we will use goes by the label hypothetical syllogism, abbreviated to HS. HS works by putting two conditional claims together to draw a third conditional as a conclusion. However, the form of all the conditionals must follow the rules: "If P, then Q. If Q, then R. Therefore, if P, then R." Notice that the antecedent of the first conditional must be the antecedent of the conclusion conditional, and the consequent of the second conditional must be the consequent of the conclusion conditional. The second conditional acts like a bridge between the first and the second. As a result, the consequent of the first conditional must be its antecedent, and its consequent must be the consequent of the conclusion. An example of this form of inference is: "If it's raining, then the streets are wet. If the streets are wet, then the streets are slippery. Therefore, if it's raining, then the streets are slippery." HS allows us to quickly follow a chain of conditionals and then connect the sufficient condition of the first one to the necessary condition of the last one.

Notice that one of the powers of the conditional is that it can help us get clear about the proper use of terms—conditionals can help us define terms. For example, if I want to know what "love" means I can look to true conditional statements about it, just as we did with our earlier conditional about love and faithfulness. "Love" means not committing adultery: "If I love my wife, I am faithful to her." According to Jesus, this is a true conditional. Here "love" is defined in terms of faithfulness, which is a necessary condition of love. Thus if I claim to love my wife, yet I am unfaithful to her, then I am confused about love—I might have some sort of sentiment or feeling, but I do not treat her with actual love. To truly love her, I must be faithful, because faithfulness is a necessary condition for love.

The order of the propositions in conditionals matters very much. In our example about love and faithfulness, we could not reverse the order, saying, "If I am faithful to my wife, then I love her." Faithfulness cannot be the sufficient condition for love, because love involves just too many other things. Perhaps I am faithful to her, but I murder her. Then according to Christ's definition of love, I do not love her. When used to define terms, we see that the term being defined is the antecedent of the defining conditionals, while the definitions, thought of as necessary conditions, are the consequents. Usually it takes more than one conditional to define a term, because most states of affairs or terms require a number of necessary conditions to specify them. The point for the moment is: beware of proposition order. "P ⊃ Q" is not the same conditional as "Q ⊃ P."

Finally, let's look at what happens when we put two conditionals together to form a very powerful configuration called a *biconditional*. Biconditionals can be formed (by an inference sometimes called *biconditional introduction*) whenever the antecedent of one conditional is the consequent of another conditional, and vice versa: "If P, then Q; and if Q, then P." This relationship is very, very powerful because it tells us that the truth conditions of P and of Q are exactly the same. In any scenario in which P is true, Q is also true. And in any scenario in which P is false, Q must also be false. The proposition order does not matter in biconditionals, because we can say that the propositions are logically equivalent. Thus in any inference following a biconditional, whenever we can derive either side of a biconditional, we are entitled to put the other side in its place, because we know that the two propositions are logically equivalent.[5]

Biconditionals are the most powerful form of definition, because they are effectively saying that the term being defined *just is* the definition. We could recast our earlier example about the Earth being a planet into a definition of a planet: "If an object orbits the sun, then that object is a planet; and if an object is a planet, then that object orbits the sun."[6] Such a claim can be symbolized as (P ⊃ Q) & (Q ⊃ P), and our shorthand for the biconditional is: P ≡ Q. The triple bar stands for "logically equals." Another way of explaining the biconditional relation is to say that the antecedent is both a necessary and sufficient condition for the antecedent, and vice versa.

Now for the final part of our discussion about how conditionals work: how do we symbolize a conditional from a normal sentence? In our examples so far, it's been pretty easy and intuitive. All we have done is call whatever follows the "if" the antecedent and whatever appears after the "then" the consequent. Things can get confusing in the case of linguistic variations. For example, words such as "because" and "only if" make things more interesting. "Because" indicates that something results from something else, and so we say that whatever follows the "because" in a sentence is the antecedent, and whatever precedes the "because" is the consequent. "The streets are wet because it is raining" is just another way of stating "If it's raining, then the streets are wet."

In the case of the difference between "if" and "only if," there is a simple rule: "Whatever follows the 'if' is the antecedent, unless the 'if' is preceded by 'only,' in which case whatever follows the 'if' is the consequent." "If P, then Q" is just another way of saying "P only if Q." The phrase "only if" signifies what is necessary. P is the case only if Q is the case, and that must be because Q is necessary to P. The necessary condition in a conditional statement is always its consequent. Thus whatever follows "only if," being necessary, is the consequent.

Most of the time when we use logic in real life, we are evaluating the truth of conditional and biconditional claims by examining the scenarios affecting the antecedent and consequent propositions. Intuitively we are applying the truth conditions for the conditional claims to see if there can be any scenario in which the antecedent can be true while the consequent is false. If we then accept the conditional or biconditional claim as true, we employ it to perform inferences. We do this so intuitively that, unless we are trained in logic, we never think about the process in the terms I have outlined above. Nevertheless, such terms do describe what we are instinctively doing.

However, in the next chapter, we will employ the exact opposite process that we usually do in everyday life. Instead of evaluating the truth conditions of propositions in order to see if a conditional claim is true, we will assume that the Bible's conditional claims are true. This means that we know what the necessary and sufficient conditions are, and that we recognize that there can be no scenario in which the antecedent of a biblical conditional is true while its consequent is false. This knowledge will allow us to perform very revealing inferences using those conditionals, and we can see how the Bible defines some of its most important terms.

---

[1] Inferences are logical moves. An inference takes at least one proposition as a premise and then draws a conclusion from that premise. Such inferences can conform to correct logical rules or they can violate logical rules. We call inferences that violate logical rules "bad inferences" or "faulty logic." "If it's raining, then the streets are wet; and it is raining, so the streets are wet" is a valid inference, while "If it's raining, then the streets are wet; and the streets are wet, so it's raining" is faulty logic. Many forms of inference (both good and bad) are so common that they have received specific names.

[2] Of course there are "nonclassical" logics in which a "null" value is also used, and there are "multvalent" logics that employ up to an infinite number of truth values. However, such logics are (if they are taken seriously) consistent with classical bivalent logic. So we will stick with classical logic, which is certainly sufficient for our purposes in this book.

[3] I'm not going to get bogged down in the logic of ambiguous terms here. Along with the majority of philosophers, I believe that classical logic is sufficient to deal with ambiguous terms, and I'm not going to get pushed into multivalent logics in order to cash them out.

[4] I call this an "idea" for simplicity. Along with most philosophers, I believe that propositions are actually objective abstract objects, such as numbers and geometric objects, but it sounds too strange to the uninitiated to say, ". . . the underlying object."

[5] Each system of logical notation uses different names for the inference rule(s) that allow such substitutions.

[6] Of course, some astronomers utterly revamped this intuitive but contentious definition of a planet in recent years. The revamped and expanded definition of a planet disallowed calling Pluto a planet, so those astronomers began to recognize only eight planets in our solar system.

Chapter 10

THE CONDITIONS OF VICTORY, PART 2

Now, this is arguably the most important chapter of the entire book. As I said, you can just grant me my conclusions and jump to the next chapter if you like. But in this one I actually demonstrate how I arrive at my conclusions. So it is crucial that I start by addressing a preliminary and fundamental point about my methodology of evaluating biblical conditionals. Because I have not presumed that you have any particular educational background, I have made efforts to explain the philosophical underpinnings of my thinking as I have gone along. In this section I will be demonstrating the underlying logical relations of a number of passages of Scripture, and the results will certainly disquiet or even shock some. Perhaps some will find my conclusions utterly unacceptable.

In most of my logic courses I would always have at least one student who would try to play hard to get by denying the undeniable. For example, I would use "1 + 1 = 2" as an example of an undeniable truth, and the reticent student would argue something like "No, 'always' isn't the case. It's possible that in some other world somewhere 1 + 1 equals something other than 2. Maybe on this other world '2' means something completely different." Or I would offer "If the door is open, then the door is open," thereby showing an example of the logical axiom: "P ⊃ P." But the student wouldn't have it. He would say, "Not always! What if the door is partly opened and partly closed?"

Now, I'm the first to encourage questioning, but in this case the student's reluctance indicates confusion. I would then have to explain that he or she was failing to recognize the formal relations—that is, the student was getting confused by the content, while the form of the statements is what matters. Sure, another world, or even another society here on Earth, might use different labels to signify "1" and "2." But those labels would pick out the same abstract objects as our "1" and "2," namely, the numbers 1 and 2. And the principle of addition signified by the statement that 1 plus 1 equals 2 is absolutely, universally true, regardless of what *labels* you employ to refer to the terms of that statement. Similarly, regardless of what statement you put into the label "P," it is absolutely, universally true that $P \supset P$. If the moon is made of green cheese, then the moon is made of green cheese. If I love to smash my finger with a hammer, then I love to smash my finger with a hammer. If ferrets can fly, then ferrets can fly. These are all examples of the same form of statement, and every statement of this form is true, regardless of its content. The last statement is not saying that ferrets *can* fly but merely that that *if* ferrets can fly, then certainly they *can* fly.

The underlying problem that this discussion reveals is that some people treat logic as though it can be employed like magic—that is, as though a person trained in logic can use it to make things that are not true appear to be true. People not versed in logic are also suspicious that its rules are somehow relative or arbitrary and that they don't apply to everybody at all times. So when somebody such as me uses logic to prove a point they disagree with, a common response can be: "Well, I don't agree, but I don't know how to argue with you. I know you are wrong, but I just don't know how to show it." And such a person typically goes away feeling secure in their beliefs, untouched by the logic, and unwilling even to investigate. Such individuals believe that they have thereby saved themselves from the results of some sort of hand-waving attempt to use logic to make something appear true that really isn't.

Let me clarify a few points right here and now. Whether or not you are trained in mathematics, its truths are still absolutely and universally true. The same point holds for logic. Valid inferences remain valid whether or not you recognize that fact, and the formal relations of logic hold whether or not you are trained to recognize them. We have focused upon the material conditional and the inferences that can be drawn from it. The conditional relation works just the way I have said it does, as do the inferences, regardless of whether or not you believe these facts. (For a more developed account of the model of knowledge I am employing, which emphasizes the absolute nature of logic, please turn to the back of this book and read the epilogue: "Lockean Model of Knowledge.")

It is true that I *could* try to play on the ignorance of some readers by using fallacious arguments and invalid inferences to draw unwarranted conclusions. But that would make me a sophist rather than a philosopher, and one could detect such tactics. Furthermore, I know that some of my readers will have had some training in logic, so I can be confident that some of my readers will recognize whether or not I am trying to pull a fast one. Consequently, I have at least two good reasons to be completely honest and careful in my employment of logic in what follows. First, I am a truth seeker—a philosopher. Second, I know that there are readers who can recognize if I'm making logical mistakes, whether intentionally or inadvertently. I might also mention that I believe that God holds me accountable for what I write here, but I assume that we all take that for granted.

Thus whether or not you have had training in logic, I assure you that I am being careful and honest to employ it correctly to draw valid conclusions. If you have any doubt of this, given the conclusions I draw, it is your responsibility, in the spirit of intellectual honesty, to get the needed education to verify that what I am saying here is correct.

With that out of the way, let's look at what the Bible really says about the relationships between grace, forgiveness, salvation, righteousness, victory, and other critically important topics.

Biblical Conditionals

To begin with, let me clarify my method. I will quote Scripture, analyze the propositional content and logical relations expressed in each cited passage, and then perform inferences based upon those logical relations. As we proceed, I will refer back to earlier statements (which I have numbered for clarity of reference), and I will use only earlier numbered statements in my inferences. For those having some familiarity with formal deductive approaches, you can view the remainder of the present chapter as one long top-down derivation. If you have no idea what I just said, don't worry—the point is that as I proceed, I am entitled to employ only earlier-numbered statements in my inferences. So you will never see me referring to a later-numbered statement in an earlier-numbered inference. This is important, because as we proceed we must prove each point systematically, and valid logical inferences do not allow us to appeal to statements that we have not yet demonstrated. Therefore we must first prove something before we can use it later. We are now ready to proceed.

Remembering that tradition has identified John as the "beloved disciple" of John 13:23, I think it is appropriate to start with John's letters to see what a loving God tells us about salvation and victory. In the spirit of God's grace and love, let us begin with the topic of forgiveness.

"If we confess our sins, He is faithful and righteous to forgive us our sins and to cleanse us from all unrighteousness" (1 John 1:9, NASB). "And if anyone sins, we have an Advocate with the Father, Jesus Christ the righteous" (1 John 2:1, NASB). So if we sin, then we have an Advocate. And if we confess our sin, then our Advocate will forgive our sin and cleanse us. Notice that God loved us so much that our sinning was the sufficient condition for there being an Advocate. Our sin made an Advocate necessary, because God loved us so much that He determined to give us another chance. That is why our confession is a sufficient condition for Jesus to forgive us.

Such a conditional relation is a powerful promise. If we confess our sin, it is necessary that Jesus forgive us. "Necessary" means that it could be no other way. So God hands us a promise of forgiveness that is as certain and valid as the truths of logic themselves. If we confess our sins, then *it could be no other way* than that Jesus forgives our sins. Such is the power of this conditional. Here, then, is our first numbered premise:

1. I confess my sin ⊃ Jesus forgives my sin

Confession, of course, implies repentance, because we cannot honestly confess our sins until we have repented of them. "Repent" just means "turn away from," as we see in Ezekiel 18:30: "Repent and turn away from all your transgressions, so that iniquity may not become a stumbling block to you" (NASB). Just mouthing some words without a genuine heart change is not sufficient for forgiveness, as Peter declared in Acts 3:19: "Therefore repent and return, so that your sins may be wiped away" (NASB). "Repent ye therefore, and be converted, that your sins may be blotted out." Paul amplifies the necessity of repentance by adding that repentance must include evidence of a changed heart. His entire sermon to King Agrippa is well worth contemplating, but let us look at Acts 26:20: "That they should repent and turn to God, performing deeds appropriate to repentance" (NASB). The very first deed required by repentance is confession, which leads to forgiveness. Thus there is a conditional relation between confession and repentance. If I confess, then I repent. In order to confess my sin, it is necessary that I repent of it. No confession without repentance is real or legitimate.

2. I confess my sin ⊃ I repent of my sin

Again and again in the Bible we see the same question: "What must I do to be saved?" And it repeatedly receives the same answer: "Repent!" A conditional relation exists between repentance and forgiveness: If I repent, then I am forgiven. Notice the sequence now: If I confess, necessarily I repent; and if I repent, necessarily I am forgiven. Thus repentance is the sufficient condition of forgiveness.

3. I repent of my sin ⊃ Jesus forgives my sin

We can immediately see that (2) and (3) get us (1) by HS, which is how confession can be a sufficient condition for forgiveness, because confession implies repentance, which is itself a sufficient condition for forgiveness.

But what enables and empowers me even to repent? I can confess and repent because of the grace of God, which is a free gift. Romans 5:15 tells us: "But the free gift is not like the transgression. For if by the transgression of the one the many died, much more did the grace of God and the gift by the grace of the one Man, Jesus Christ, abound to the many" (NASB). And Ephesians 2:8 makes the point abundantly clear: "For by grace you have been saved through faith; and that not of yourselves, it is the gift of God" (NASB). What is the first thing God's grace does in our lives? It calls us to repentance: "I have not come to call the righteous but sinners to repentance" (Luke 5:32, NASB). We still have to choose, but the grace of God enables us to make that choice, which is how we can call repentance a gift. We have no possibility of choosing to repent without the grace of God. And Acts 5:31 denotes that the very first work of Christ in our lives is to give us repentance: "He [Christ] is the one whom God exalted to His right hand as a Prince and a Savior, to grant repentance to Israel, and forgiveness of sins" (NASB). Finally, 2 Timothy 2:25, 26 clarifies the relationship between the gift of grace, which is repentance, and the acknowledgment of truth, which sets one free from the entrapment of Satan: "... with gentleness correcting those who are in opposition, if perhaps God may grant them repentance leading to the knowledge of the truth, and they may come to their senses and escape from the snare of the devil, having been held captive by him to do his will" (NASB).

Here we see yet another level of conditional before forgiveness and repentance. I cannot choose the gift of repentance until I first accept God's gift of grace. But once I choose God's grace, it is all-powerful to give me repentance:

4. I have the grace of God ⊃ I repent of my sin

Using (4) and (3), again by HS, we can now derive this new conditional:

5. I have the grace of God ⊃ Jesus forgives my sin

Keep in mind here that we are not talking about timing. The temporal order is not a part of the propositional content. It's not that the first thing (in time) I do is confess, and then (at a subsequent point) I repent, and then still later (after still more time has passed) I am forgiven, all of this presupposing some activity of God's grace at a much earlier period of time. We are talking about logical relations here. On the Bible model, the grace of God in my life produces confession, which necessarily includes repentance, which necessarily involves God's forgiveness. When we choose God's grace in my life, we are necessarily also accepting all of its implications. It all "starts," speaking within the perspective of logic, with the grace of God. The grace of God is always the sufficient condition for every good thing that enters our lives. It is always and only the antecedent of conditionals that include it. Thus it is always God's grace that establishes us in a saving relationship with Him.

Now, let us examine the chain of relations between our saving relationship with Jesus and spiritual victory.

"No one who abides in Him sins; no one who sins has seen Him or knows Him" (1 John 3:6, NASB). Taken at face value, the two statements do not seem as conditionals. However, actually they are conditionals, and those familiar with quantificational logic will recognize them as such. I won't subject you to even a brief course in quantificational logic, but the "no one" in both of these statements acts as a universal quantifier, and that means that the relations between the parts of the two statements are actually conditionals.[1] You don't need to understand how this works, but I mention it so that you will realize that I am not pulling a "fast one" when I treat these two statements as conditionals, because that is what they really are. The first statement is actually saying:

6. I abide in Jesus ⊃ I do not sin

The second statement includes two concepts: seeing and knowing. We immediately understand the notion of "knows." But "seen" can mean many things. Here "seen" comes from the Greek word *horao,* which means "to stare at, to discern clearly, to attend to, and to take heed to." Remember our commitment to be sensitive to the propositional content of sentences—and perhaps the most straightforward way to grasp this proposition is to say "pay attention to." So the second statement actually means:

7. I sin ⊃ I do not pay attention to Jesus

8. I sin ⊃ I do not know Jesus

Here is more information about sinning. "No one who is born of God practices sin, because His seed abides in him; and he cannot sin, because he is born of God" (1 John 3:9, NASB). Again we see the phrase "no one," which is a universal quantifier, denoting that the statements are conditionals. This verse actually contains a string of conditionals, revealing to us the mechanism of victory.

Because the verse is complex, let's consider it a step at a time. First, "no one who is born of God practices sin, because His seed abides in him." The end of this section actually contains the overarching "because," which is: "Because His seed abides in him." The "because" here signifies the reason, or method, a person is "born of God." As we noted in the previous chapter, "because" signifies an antecedent of a conditional. Thus the very first part of the chained conditional appears at the end of the first part of this verse.

Now, in the spirit of getting the propositional content correct, what is this "seed" all about? The Greek word is *sperma,* which literally means something sown. We see the same word in verses such as Matthew 13:37, which talks about the "good seed" of the gospel, and Luke 8:11, which uses the variation *sporos* (a scattered or sown seed). In both cases, made clear by Luke 8:11, this "seed" is the Word of God. Finally, the connection between "seed" and the Word of God become clear beyond doubt in 1 Peter 1:23-25, which announces, "For you have been born again not of seed which is perishable but imperishable, that is, through the living and enduring word of God" (NASB). We can now interpret this section of 1 John 3:9 as:

9. Jesus' word is in me ⊃ I am born of God

The next part tells us:

10. I am born of God ⊃ I do not sin

The HS move from (9) and (10) is begging to be made, so let's do it:

11. Jesus' Word is in me ⊃ I do not sin

(11) explicitly denotes the sufficient power of God's Word to cleanse us from sinning, as John 15:3 reminds us: "You are already clean because of the word which I have spoken to you" (NASB). Here "clean" means much more than just forgiveness—it indicates being empowered not to sin.

Now let's look at the second part of 1 John 3:9: "He cannot sin, because he is born of God" (NASB). Again we encounter "because," signifying an antecedent, and again the antecedent is "I am born of God." However, in this second part the statement has become even stronger than before, lest we have any doubt about what "practices sin" might mean. "Cannot" translates the Greek *dunamai,* which literally means "impossible." This part of the verse literally declares:

12. I am born of God ⊃ I cannot sin

To remove any doubt about the tightness of the relationship specified here between conversion and active sinning, let us remember the definition of the conditional relation and keep in mind that this is a true conditional: it is impossible for the antecedent to be true and the consequent false in any scenario. By MT, this means that at any time I am able to sin, I am not converted. For me to actually succeed in willfully sinning, I must have given up my conversion. (10), (11), and (12) all make the same point in slightly different ways: for me to sin is to have given up conversion and the Word of God in me.

First John 3:8 also gives us the corollary statement: "The one

who practices sin is of the devil" (NASB). Again, using quantificational logic, the statement declares:

13. I sin ⊃ I am of the devil

And this verse continues to claim that Jesus entered the world to
destroy the works of the devil. And what are they? The passage explains that "the devil has sinned from the beginning" (NASB). As a
result, my sin makes me a child of the devil, because I do the same
kind of things he does. But Jesus came to set me free from the works
of the devil—from sin—by putting His word in me. It is the point
of the conditional form of Galatians 5:16: if you walk by the Spirit,
you will not carry out the desire of the flesh.

There can be no clearer dichotomy between Jesus and Satan in
our lives than this. We are either "born of God," with His "seed"
(gospel, Word) in us, or we are "of Satan," with his works (sin) in
us. What distinguishes which of the two is the case for us at any
given moment? It is simply this: whether or not we sin. Again, (9),
(10), (11), and (12), by MT, if I sin, I do not have the Word of God
abiding in me, and I am not converted. That makes sense, because
God's Word cannot abide (or have any active power) in me while I
choose to be "of the devil" by sinning. Thus God's Word in me is
sufficient for me to have victory over sin, while my victory over sin
is a necessary condition for having the Word of God in me.

First John 3:24 presses the point home further when it declares
that "the one who keeps His commandments abides in Him, and He
in him" (NASB). When we examine it with quantificational logic,
we find that the verse says the following two things:

14. I keep Jesus' commandments ⊃ I abide in Jesus

15. I keep Jesus' commandments ⊃ Jesus abides in me

But we can now put (14) together with (6) (from 1 John 3:6),
which indicates: I abide in Jesus ⊃ I do not sin. As I will demonstrate in a moment, this is the same as saying: I abide in Jesus ⊃ I
keep Jesus' commandments.

To put (14) and (6) together properly, we need to know what

the relationship is between "keeping" Jesus' commandments and sin. First John 3:4 tells us that "everyone who practices sin also practices lawlessness; and sin is lawlessness" (NASB). The King James Version renders it even more clearly: "Whosoever committed sin transgresseth also the law: for sin is the transgression of the law." Sin, therefore, is not keeping the commandments. When (6) says, I abide in Jesus ⊃ I do not sin, that is the same thing as declaring, I abide in Jesus ⊃ I do not not keep Jesus' commandments.[2] But, logically, a double negative is a positive, giving us:

16. I abide in Jesus ⊃ I keep Jesus' commandments

Together (14) and (16) form a biconditional relation. Remember that when the antecedent of one conditional is the same as the consequent of another conditional, and vice versa, we can combine the two conditionals into a biconditional:

17. I abide in Jesus ≡ I keep Jesus' commandments

As we saw earlier, a biconditional establishes logical equivalency. It is the strongest form of definition because it says that any inference derived from the one side also emerges from the other side. Thus we know something for certain about "abiding in Jesus"—that abiding in Jesus just is keeping His commandments. And keeping His commandments just is abiding in Jesus. In any scenario in which we keep Jesus' commandments we are abiding in Him, and in any scenario in which we are not keeping Jesus' commandments (sinning) we are not abiding in Him.

Don't forget that 1 John 3:24 has two parts. The second part of the verse talks about Jesus abiding in us, and, again, that relates to keeping the commandments, as we see in (15): I keep Jesus' commandments ⊃ Jesus abides in me. Also, (16) tells us: I abide in Jesus ⊃ I keep Jesus' commandments. Putting (16) together with (15) using HS, we get:

18. I abide in Jesus ⊃ Jesus abides in me

A most important verse about "abiding" is John 14:20, because it explains what Jesus wants us to understand about it: "In that day you will know that I am in My Father, and you in Me, and I in you" (NASB). The passage refers to three "abiding" relationships:

19. Jesus abides in the Father

20. I abide in Jesus

21. Jesus abides in me

Of course, Jesus is here speaking to His disciples in the same conversation and context in which He tells them that they are "clean" because of His Word in them (except, of course, for Judas). Therefore, just as our abiding in Him implies not sinning (keeping His commandments), His abiding in us implies not sinning (that is, we keep His commandments). To make that implication crystal clear, we will cast (21) in an even weaker form than it appears here, because that more properly captures the propositional content, given the context of the statement. The following rendering is much more true to the intent of Christ's abiding in us as it appears in John 15:5: "I am the vine, you are the branches; he who abides in Me and I in him, he bears much fruit, for apart from Me you can do nothing" (NASB). We recast 21 as:

22. Jesus abides in me ⊃ I keep Jesus' commandments

With (22) we can now derive the other conditional that will form a biconditional about abiding. Using (22) together with (14), we employ HS, giving us:

23. Jesus abides in me ⊃ I abide in Jesus

Putting (18) together with (23) entitles us to that biconditional about abiding:

24. I abide in Jesus ≡ Jesus abides in me

These verses tell us that this "abiding" relationship is a sort of deep unity in which we are in Him and He is in us. Notice that (24) reveals that my abiding in Jesus and His abiding in me are logically equivalent, and (17) indicates that my abiding in Jesus is logically equivalent to my keeping His commandments. As a result, any place in which I would say, "I abide in Jesus," I can logically also say, "Jesus abides in me." And any place I would say, "I abide in Jesus,"

I can logically say, "I keep Jesus' commandments." Therefore, "abiding" is logically equivalent to keeping Jesus' commandments.

Next, let's look at the meaning of "love" as it applies to our relationship with God. Earlier I mentioned that conditionals can serve as definitions, because they show the necessary conditions of antecedent propositions. Well, here is the definition of "love," as John explains: "And this is love, that we walk according to His commandments" (2 John 6, NASB) (echoed in 1 John 5:3). This statement is in its logic comparable to "If I love my wife, then I am faithful to her." John means:

25. I love Jesus ⊃ I keep Jesus' commandments

Jesus makes this exact same statement explicitly in John 14:15: "If you love Me, you will keep My commandments" (NASB). And John 15:10 makes a correlative claim: "If you keep My commandments, you will abide in my love; just as I have kept My Father's commandments and abide in His love." When we simplify[3] the verse, the first part says:

26. I keep Jesus' commandments ⊃ I love Jesus

But now we see that the antecedent of (25) is the consequent of (26), and vice versa. Again we have a biconditional:

27. I love Jesus ≡ I keep Jesus' commandments

Jesus declares here that loving Him is logically equivalent to keeping His commandments. That is why love is the fulfillment of the law. Christ never states that being loving stands in place of keeping the Ten Commandments, as though you could keep the commandments *or* you could just be loving. Jesus teaches us that being loving is keeping the commandments, and genuinely keeping the commandments is what God means by being loving. He defines love in terms of commandment keeping. (A point specified explicitly regarding love to others is found in Romans 13:10: "Love does no wrong to a neighbor; love therefore is the fulfillment of the law" [NASB]).

Of course this makes sense, given what we have seen about the "abiding" relationship, as stated in John 14:21: "He who has My commandments and keeps them is the one who loves me; and he who loves Me will be loved by my Father, and I will love him and will disclose Myself to him" (NASB). But now we can look at the conditional arising from the last part of this verse:

28. I keep Jesus' commandments ⊃ Jesus reveals Himself to me

Compare (28) with (7) and (8), repeated here for convenience:

7. I sin ⊃ I do not pay attention to Jesus

8. I sin ⊃ I do not know Jesus

Keeping Jesus' commandments is the means by which we come to pay attention to and know Him. Although the concept seems strange on the face of it, it becomes crystal clear when we contemplate some additional texts. David sings: "But his [the blessed man's] delight is in the law of the Lord, and in His law he meditates day and night" (Ps. 1:2, NASB). "I will meditate on Your precepts and regard Your ways. I shall delight in Your statutes; I shall not forget Your word" (Ps. 119:15, 16, NASB). "If any one is willing to do His will, he will know of the teaching [of Jesus] whether it is of God or whether I speak from Myself" (John 7:17, NASB). And the conditional relations in this text are worthy of particular note: "By this we know that we have come to know Him, if we keep His commandments. The one who says, 'I have come to know Him,' and does not keep His commandments, is a liar, and the truth is not in him" (1 John 2:3, 4, NASB). If we know that we have come to know Him, then certainly that must be the case. So we can cash out the first part of this text as:

29. I keep Jesus' commandments ⊃ I know Jesus

And John makes the corollary clear in the second part of the verse. He is actually using MT in this next principle:

30. I know Jesus ⊃ I keep Jesus' commandments

From that principle, John imagines someone who does not keep Jesus' commandments, and he then concludes that such a person is a liar in the sense that the individual does not know Jesus.

Notice another biconditional relation here. Putting (29) together with (30), we get:

31. I know Jesus ≡ I keep Jesus' commandments

And, as if there could be any doubt, given the definition of sin the Bible explicitly states in 1 John 3:4, it bears noting at this point that the definition is in biconditional form: "Everyone who practices sin also practices lawlessness; and sin is lawlessness" (NASB). Sin is lawlessness (not keeping Jesus' commandments). If we sin, we also don't keep Jesus' commandments, which is saying that when the one is true, so is the other. It is impossible to do the one and not the other, and that is logical equivalency:

32. I sin ≡ I do not keep Jesus' commandments

But this means that if I sin, then I do not know Jesus (8). We recognize this from (32) and (31), performing HS on the conditionals contained in those biconditionals—and that is just what (8) actually says (repeated here for convenience):

8. I sin ⊃ I do not know Jesus

And, by (32) and (17), again performing HS on the embedded conditionals, we recognize that if we sin, then we do not abide in Jesus, and, adding (24) to our inferences, He does not abide in us.

Now we can see that the "fight of faith, not sin" theory completely confuses what the saving relationship with Jesus is. It claims that "sin is not about behavior. We sin only by severing the saving relationship with Jesus," and by that "severing" this theology means neglecting Bible study, prayer, or witnessing. [4] Thus the theology tries to establish a new concept of sin, one defined by the neglect of Bible study, prayer, or witnessing. But Scripture equates the saving relationship with Jesus with commandment keeping. From a theological point of view, Scripture does not define that relationship by anything touchy-feely or ambiguous. Rather, the Bible makes it crystal clear: if I have a saving relationship with Jesus, then I don't sin, and if I sin, then I don't have a saving relationship with Him. The Bible declares that I sever the saving relationship with Jesus by sinning, because the saving relationship with Jesus is logically equivalent to commandment keeping. You cannot have one without the other!

So the "fight of faith, not sin" claim is utterly confused when it states, "Christianity and salvation are based not on what you do, but on whom you know." That makes a dichotomy between commandment keeping and knowing Jesus, as though you could know Jesus and still continue to sin willfully. But as we have found so far, not sinning and having a saving relationship with Jesus are not two separate things. Thus it is completely accurate to say that Christianity and salvation are based upon our behavior, *because* Christianity and salvation rest upon whom we know!

Now that we have observed the connection between the relationship with Jesus and victory over known, willful sin, let us look at the relations the Bible clarifies between faith and victory, an analysis that will also reveal where salvation fits into the grand scheme of things.

Habakkuk 2:4 tells us: "Behold, as for the proud one, His soul is not right within him; but the righteous will live by his faith" (NASB). We also know this passage from the familiar paraphrase of the King James Version of it: "The just shall live by his faith" (as we also see in Romans 1:17). The conditional form of this statement is:

33. I am just (justified) ⊃ I live by faith

Romans 1:17 clarifies the point when it states: "For in it [the gospel] the righteousness of God is revealed from faith to faith; as it is written, 'But the righteous [justified] man shall live by faith'" (NASB). How is the righteousness of God revealed? According to Scripture, God displays His righteousness by justifying us. But faith is the necessary condition for justification, as we see in (33) above. Christ's righteousness (which is the sufficient condition) justifies us, as we will further develop below.

The idea of Christ's righteousness justifying (saving) us becomes even clearer in some other passages. The book of Psalms in particular has some wonderful statements about the relationship between the Lord's righteousness and salvation. In Psalm 71:1, 2, we read the plea: "In You, O Lord, I have taken refuge; let me never be ashamed. In Your righteousness deliver me and rescue me; incline

Your ear to me and save me" (NASB). Psalms 89:16 states: "In Your name they rejoice all the day, and by Your righteousness they are exalted" (NASB). And in a grammatical construction that virtually equates the Lord's salvation and His righteousness, Psalm 98:2 announces: "The Lord has made known His salvation; He has revealed His righteousness in the sight of the nations" (NASB). Psalm 143:11 adds: "In Your righteousness bring my soul out of trouble" (NASB).

A simply amazing passage appears in Isaiah 41:10: "Do not fear, for I am with you; do not anxiously look about you, for I am your God. I will strengthen you, surely I will help you, surely I will uphold you with My righteous right hand" (NASB). "I will uphold thee with the right hand of my righteousness" (KJV).

Perhaps the clearest passage in the Bible relating salvation to the Lord's righteousness is Jeremiah 23:6: "In His [the Messiah's] days Judah will be saved, and Israel will dwell securely; and this is His name by which He will be called, 'The Lord our righteousness'" (NASB). When Jesus, as the Messiah, comes to save Israel, the name that Scripture calls Him as He performs that work is "The Lord our righteousness."

And the name correlates beautifully with what we read in Romans 3:25, 26: "whom God [Jesus] displayed publicly as a propitiation in His blood through faith. This was to demonstrate His righteousness, because in the forbearance of God He passed over the sins previously committed; for the demonstration, I say, of His righteousness at the present time, so that He would be just and the justifier of the one who has faith in Jesus" (NASB).

We can sum the matter up with one more passage: "so that, as sin reigned in death, even so grace might reign through righteousness to eternal life through Jesus Christ our Lord" (Rom. 5:21, NASB). We will see in (36) below that God's grace is sufficient to justify us, which is what this verse also states. But it also reveals the means by which God's grace provides justification/salvation to us: God's righteousness. The righteousness of Christ is the channel through which God justifies us. Thus our justification is the result of God's righteousness, revealed and demonstrated in Jesus Christ, which is the sufficient condition of our justification/salvation, as we see here:

34. I have Jesus' righteousness ⊃ I am justified

I spent some time developing (34) because it bears some weight in what follows. To begin with, (34) along with (33) and HS give us:

35. I have Jesus' righteousness ⊃ I live by faith

And this makes sense, as we have seen, because I have the righteousness of Christ and justification "by faith." Romans 3:24 indicates that God's grace is a sufficient condition for our justification: "being justified as a gift by His grace through the redemption which is in Christ Jesus" (NASB).

36. I have God's grace ⊃ I am justified

Of course, this correlates with (5) above: I have the grace of God ⊃ Jesus forgives my sin. And it makes sense that God's grace is sufficient to justify us, even though, as (34) says, it is also the case that Christ's righteousness is sufficient to justify us, because, as we saw earlier in Romans 3:21-25, God's grace demonstrates His righteousness: "But now apart from the Law the righteousness of God has been manifested. . . . for all have sinned and fall short of the glory of God, being justified as a gift by His grace through the redemption which is in Christ Jesus. . . . This was to demonstrate His righteousness." So God's grace manifests His righteousness, and we can rightly say that either justifies us.

What is the necessary condition for receiving God's grace? Putting (36) together with (33) by HS, we see:

37. I have God's grace ⊃ I live by faith

Ephesians 2:8 emphasizes this point: "For by grace you have been saved through faith; and that not of yourselves, it is the gift of God" (NASB). And Romans 5:1, 2, adds: "Therefore, having been justified by faith, we have peace with God through our Lord Jesus Christ, through whom also we have obtained our introduction by faith into this grace in which we stand; and we exult in hope of the glory of God" (NASB). The grace of God is the sufficient condition of our salvation, and it is a gift. But it is also the necessary condition of our salvation that we accept this gift by faith.

Thus Romans 3:28 can declare: "For we maintain that a man is justified by faith apart from works of the Law" (NASB). The righteousness of Christ, which, as we have seen, is demonstrated by God's grace, is always the sufficient condition for our justification/salvation (34)—not our own works or righteousness alone. Our faith is the necessary condition for our salvation, but by saying "apart from works of the Law," Paul cannot mean that works have *no* relation to our salvation, as we will see (and as Paul himself is quick to point out in verse 31). The apostle is instead here focusing upon establishing that Christ's righteousness is put in its proper place as the antecedent of the conditional, with our faith as the consequent of the conditional, just as we observe in (35). While our faith and our works do have connections, as we shall examine, Christ's righteousness alone, thought of as God's grace, is the sufficient condition for our salvation, and Paul emphasizes this point here.

We see an even more developed explanation of "living by faith" in Galatians 2:20: "I have been crucified with Christ; and it is no longer I who live, but Christ lives in me; and the life which I now live in the flesh I live by faith in the Son of God, who loved me and gave Himself up for me" (NASB). We know from (24) above that the "abiding" relation is biconditional. As a result, wherever we see the proposition "Jesus abides in me," we can substitute that with "I abide in Jesus." We know that in this verse the phrase "Christ lives in me" is very important, because as we discovered earlier (17) and (24) the phrase is logically equivalent with victory over sin and keeping Jesus' commandments.

Here Paul declares that he has died (that is, his lower nature, symbolized by the flesh, has been crucified), which means that he abides in Christ and Christ abides in him. That, in turn, indicates that he does not sin: he keeps the commandments. Finally, he claims that his living in crucified flesh—living in Christ—is actually living by faith:

38. I abide in Jesus ≡ I live by faith

But if "abiding in Jesus" and "living by faith" are logically interchangeable, then "living by faith" is also equivalent with "keeping the commandments" (17) and "not sinning" (32).

We know from previous paragraphs that "I live by faith" appears as the consequent of the salvation conditionals, as we see in (33) and (35), because, after all, being justified is being made right with God. Thus all of the terms logically equivalent with "living by faith" must also be consequents of any salvation conditionals (conditionals that have the sufficient conditions for justification, or justification itself, as their antecedents).

The overarching salvation conditional as we understand it so far says this: If I am justified/saved by the grace of God (also thought of as the righteousness of Christ), then I abide in Christ and Christ abides in me; I keep the commandments; I do not sin; and I live by faith. This list of consequents of the salvation conditional are logically equivalent to each other, as they all serve as different ways of saying the same thing, and they all describe the necessary condition of our salvation. We are saved by grace "apart from the works of the Law," which is to say that there is nothing but God's grace (His righteousness) as the antecedent of the salvation conditional. We must accept this grace by faith, which is the necessary condition of our salvation, and which means that we abide in Christ; Christ abides in us; we keep the commandments; and we do not sin.

The relation between righteousness and faith becomes explicit in several other passages. Consider Philippians 3:9: "[I] may be found in Him, not having a righteousness of my own derived from the Law, but that which is through faith in Christ, the righteousness which comes from God on the basis of faith" (NASB). The phrase "on the basis" tells us how Paul intends the conditional. His "not . . . derived from the Law" makes it clear that he is talking about the antecedent of the conditional, because he never wants to have the law or the works of the law as the antecedent of the conditional.

Although different Greek words lie behind "derived from" and "on the basis of" in this verse, both words signify the origin or channel by which a thing comes to be. Paul is saying that he wants to have righteousness, but he doesn't want it from (as antecedent) the works of the law. Rather, he desires righteousness from (as antecedent) faith in Christ. Thus the conditional for the correct way to live righteously should read: I live by faith ⊃ I live righteously.

But we can clarify what "living righteously" is in this context, while revealing a stronger biconditional relation between living by faith and living righteously, by putting together what we already know. Consider the logical equivalencies (17) and (38) from above:

17. I abide in Jesus ≡ I keep Jesus' commandments
38. I abide in Jesus ≡ I live by faith

Since (38) tells me that I can substitute "I live by faith" any place I find "I abide in Jesus," I can convert (17) into the following biconditional. Not only does it capture Paul's intention from Philippians 3:9, it also reveals that living righteously is the same thing as keeping Jesus' commandments.

39. I live by faith ≡ I keep Jesus' commandments

And we know that keeping Jesus' commandments is logically equivalent to not sinning and enjoying the "abiding" relationship with Jesus.

It is to say that Paul wants that relationship with God, and the righteousness that results from it, entirely on the basis of faith. On the apostle's model, then, faith in Christ produces the righteousness *in* the believer. Faith is logically equivalent to living a Christlike life of righteousness, what Paul means by the "work of faith" in 2 Thessalonians 1:11: "To this end also we pray for you always, that our God will count you worthy of your calling, and fulfill every desire for goodness and the work of faith with power" (NASB). The "work of faith" is righteousness—it is "keeping Jesus' commandments," just as (39) above states.

Hebrews 11:1-31 uses the exact same conditional construction again and again: "By faith . . . [some great deed was accomplished]." Faith is the sufficient condition for accomplishing great things, and all the deeds of righteousness are accomplished "by faith." Again: if faith, then deeds of righteousness. It is the obvious point of James 2:18-22: "I will show you my faith by my works. . . . But are you willing to recognize, you foolish fellow, that faith without works is useless? Was not Abraham our father justified by works when he offered up Isaac his son on the altar? You see that faith was working with his works, and as a result of the works, faith was perfected" (NASB). And verse 24 continues: "You see that a man is justified by works and not by faith alone" (NASB). But this seems to be saying that our works can act as the antecedent of salvation conditionals:

40. I keep Jesus' commandments ⊃ I am justified

How, then, is this not legalism? Because putting (39), read left to right, and (40) together with HS, we get:

41. I live by faith ⊃ I am justified

Living by faith is the sufficient condition for righteous works, which in turn is the sufficient condition for salvation. But now, putting (41) together with (33) establishes another biconditional relation:

42. I am justified ≡ I live by faith

Paul says that works alone can never act as the antecedent of a salvation conditional. Rather, we are saved by grace alone, by which Paul is contrasting the "works of the law" alone. However, James is noting the fact that genuine grace and living by faith never really exist in isolation. As we have been seeing, capped off by James, faith results in righteous works. In fact, faith *necessarily* produces righteous works, as righteous works are a necessary condition of saving faith. This is how James can make the seemingly outrageous statement: "You see that a man is justified by works." James is simply recognizing the truth of (42) and noting that "living by faith" is logically equivalent with keeping Jesus' commandments. Anyone who claims that they are justified while they do not live by faith is a liar, just as anyone who claims that they live by faith while they willfully sin is also a liar. The grace of God produces justification *by* producing a life of faith, which results in righteous works and victory. And the point to all of this logic so far is to show that faith, righteous works, commandment keeping, victory, and salvation are all logically equivalent. They are all so inseparably tied together that it is impossible to have any one of them without possessing them all.

Now we can clearly understand the relationship of salvation to faith and victory as summed up in 1 John 5:4: "For whatever is born of God overcomes the world; and this is the victory that has overcome the world—our faith" (NASB). The song says, "Faith is the victory . . . that overcomes the world," and it is in a biconditional sense that faith is the victory:

43. I live by faith $\equiv$ I have victory (and that victory overcomes the world)

And this notion of victory makes perfect sense, as we have seen that living by faith is logically equivalent with abiding in Jesus, keeping Jesus' commandments, not sinning, and being justified. The life of genuine faith is one of power, victory, union with Jesus, and salvation.

So, then, what is legalism? It is the effort to pick and choose between the various logical relations (and their supporting Bible texts) until you have selected *only* those ones that will put your own righteousness as the antecedent of a salvation conditional, while you deny, ignore, or live in violation of the whole train of logical equivalencies that are the real story of faith, victory, and salvation. Your own righteousness alone can never act as the antecedent of a salvation conditional. Genuine righteousness always comes inseparably tied to a whole train of other relations, and this whole package is what God offers us as the life of faith.

To sum up, here is a list of the logical equivalencies we have established in this chapter. As you contemplate them, you will realize the extent to which God honors our faith in Him by supplying everything to make an entire change in our lives and give us power and victory. There are certainly many additional ways to combine what we know now, to show additional logical relationships or to arrive at them in slightly different ways. But these biconditional relations are what the Bible says about our relationship with Jesus, faith, commandment keeping, righteousness, and victory. To recap:

17. I abide in Jesus ≡ I keep Jesus' commandments
24. I abide in Jesus ≡ Jesus abides in me
27. I love Jesus ≡ I keep Jesus' commandments
31. I know Jesus ≡ I keep Jesus' commandments
32. I sin ≡ I do not keep Jesus' commandments
38. I abide in Jesus ≡ I live by faith
39. I live by faith ≡ I keep Jesus' commandments
42. I am justified ≡ I live by faith
43. I live by faith ≡ I have victory (and that victory overcomes the world)

From these, it is worth quickly deriving a few more that make the relations even more clear:

44. I keep Jesus' commandments ≡ I live by faith ([17] and [38])
45. I keep Jesus' commandments ≡ I have victory ([43] and [44])
46. I keep Jesus' commandments ≡ I am justified ([42] and [44])

Lest there remain any doubt, (44) through (46) make abundantly clear that living by faith, having victory, keeping Jesus' commandments, and justification are all just different ways of denoting the all-encompassing power of God in our lives. When we choose to let His power reign in us, He does not employ any halfway measures. Once we are ready to give up our sins, God's grace sweeps into our lives like a flood to provide everything sufficient for salvation and victory, just as Paul prays in Ephesians 3:16-19: "that He would grant you, according to the riches of His glory, to be strengthened with power through His Spirit in the inner man; so that Christ may dwell in your hearts through faith; and that you, being rooted and grounded in love, may be able to comprehend with all the saints what is the breadth and length and height and depth, and to know the love of Christ which surpasses knowledge, that you may be filled up to all the fullness of God" (NASB).

---

[1] For the interested reader, in this one case I will demonstrate the quantificational inferences involved, which will serve as a basis for further investigation if desired. I won't repeat this sort of demonstration for each of my quantificational inferential claims, and I'm not going to explain the symbolization, but it might prove helpful to see such a thing at least once. Those with any introduction to quantificational logic will immediately see what's going on here, as this is pretty basic stuff.

Let's start by assigning two predicates: A and C, in which A means "x abides in Jesus," and C means "x sins." Now, the most obvious way to cast the "no one" claim of this verse is to treat it as: "it is not the case that there is someone…," and we can symbolize it like this: ~Vx (Ax ∧ Cx). This symbolization is the "on the face of it" way to represent the verse, but the conditional form of it is still there to be had. Using quantifier negation, we can produce this: ∧x~ (Ax ∧ Cx). The quantifier is universal rather than existential, which better captures the actual text anyway. But now we can push the negation inside the parentheses using DeMorgan's theorem, producing: ∧x (~Ax v ~Cx). And by implication, we can convert the internal disjunction to a conditional: ∧x (Ax ⊃ ~Cx), and this form actually most clearly captures what the verse is saying: "It is universally the case that if a person abides in Jesus, then that person does not sin." As I said, this verse really is in conditional form, even though it is not apparent on the face of it. Since we are using sentential (elementary) logic (rather than quantificational logic) in this book, I simply perform the universal instantiation from all such sentences, which entitles me to use "I" or "me" in place of "the one" or "anyone" or other such universal constructions.

[2] The only way to avoid this inference is to try to float the claim that "the law" and "Jesus' commandments" are two entirely different things. That's going to be a hard point to sustain, however, given that Jesus was the "I Am" of Sinai and was the lawgiver (as the Word of God) down through all of human history.

[3] I realize that the passage has more in it than my simplified version, but it certainly does not have less. So I am certainly entitled to state that this verse says at least as much as I am noting here.

[4] I was never able to understand how this definition of sin was not about behavior. Bible study, prayer, and witnessing are all "works," that is, human behaviors or activities. The "fight of faith, not sin" theology always struck me as just another sort of legalism, but with Bible study, prayer, and witnessing standing in place of commandment keeping in the typical legalistic conditionals (with the "works" as the antecedent of the salvation conditional).

Chapter 11

ALL VICTORY

The previous chapter established some powerful relations, telling us the exact rules that God employs to make an entire change in our lives. Yet even hearing that "faith is the victory" doesn't seem to explain exactly *how* faith gives us victory when we find ourselves confronted by temptation. In this chapter I intend to employ the logical relations of the previous chapter to get practical and down-to-earth about spiritual victory.

We must talk about perfection, which, believe it or not, is the central concept to victory. The problem is that we cannot have the divine nature, which is what enables victory over particular sins, as long as we are not committed to victory in a general sense. Many people want victory over this or that particular sin, yet they are not prepared to (they don't even believe that they can) stop sinning in the general sense. Deep in their perspective, they believe that they must and will keep on sinning until the day they die or Christ returns. While they want this or that particular victory, they cling to this or that other cherished sin, and they feel the force of the lower nature so thoroughly that they simply cannot believe that the Word of God has enough power to actually create in them a new heart as it has promised. But this is a "denying the power thereof" perspective, and such "Christianity" can have no victory (genuine victory). As James 1:7, 8 says: "For that man ought not to expect that he will receive anything from the Lord, being a double-minded man, unstable in all his ways" (NASB).

Notice carefully what precipitated the failure of the Israelites as they stood on the brink of entering the Promised Land for the first time (see Num. 13; 14). God tells them to send spies into the land, and He assures them of complete victory in taking the land. The spies go out, traverse the land for 40 days, and then return. Ten of them have a baleful message: "So they gave out to the sons of Israel a bad report of the land which they had spied out, saying, 'The land through which we have gone, in spying it out, is a land that devours its inhabitants; and all the people whom we saw in it are men of great size. There also we saw the Nephilim (the sons of Anak are part of the Nephilim); and we became like grasshoppers in our own sight, and so we were in their sight' " (Num. 13:32, 33, NASB).

Contrast this report with the report given by Caleb and Joshua: "And they spoke to all the congregation of the sons of Israel, saying, 'The land which we passed through to spy out is an exceedingly good land. If the Lord is pleased with us, then He will bring us into this land and give it to us—a land which flows with milk and honey. Only do not rebel against the Lord; and do not fear the people of the land, for they shall be our prey. Their protection has been removed from them, and the Lord is with us; do not fear them' " (Num. 14:7-9, NASB).

We know which report the Israelites believed, and we remember that the Lord punished that generation by causing each and every member of it (except Caleb and Joshua) to die during the 40-year wilderness wandering. The Lord viewed the fear of the people, and their subsequent refusal to go in and overcome the inhabitants of the land, as rebellion. Why rebellion? Surely He could understand their fear? No! He viewed their reaction as rebellion because He had promised the land to them, had assured them of victory, and had told them about the inhabitants, that "their protection" had been "removed from them" (see verse 9, NASB). Given the power of the Word of God, which the Israelites had seen again and again, He justly expected His people to move forward from victory to victory in the power of that Word.

Eventually the people did cross the Jordan, and they did inhabit the land. But, after early victories, they grew comfortable and disinclined to continue the battle. While the Lord told them to subdue the inhabitants of the land, instead the people stopped fighting. They formed alliances with their enemies. Intermarrying with the Canaanites, they began to worship the false gods of their enemies. Eventually what had started out as a campaign of victory turned into such utter apostasy and defeat that the Lord punished Israel with repeated captivities.

How is it in your life? Is there a particular sin (or sins) that appears to you as a giant, and you are a grasshopper in your own sight? Have you decided that the best course is no longer to think about overcoming this mighty sin, but instead to form some sort of alliance with it? Have you developed or adopted some theology that tells you that the Lord actually doesn't demand that you get the victory over this sin, but instead that He is satisfied with just your "trying," whatever that means?

Whatever fake "victories" Satan lets you experience as he withdraws his temptations in other areas, you must know that his studied goal is to keep you from having complete, Christlike victory over all your sins. He does not want you to fully "inhabit the land," because he well knows that he will bring your utter downfall and ruin through any sins you fail to overcome.

How many sins did it take to bring about the ruin of our first parents? How evil did that first temptation seem to them? How big of a deal was just eating a piece of fruit? Consider the train of woe that has followed that first sinful act, and how each and every act of known sin now "crucifies Christ afresh" (see Heb. 6:6; 10:26-32).

We tend to make sin a light thing. Many view the sacrifice of Christ as so allencompassing and complete that they inadvertently treat it as a license for willful sinning, even if they adopt a theology that claims that it endorses no such concept. If we honestly believe that we cannot cease from willful sin, then whatever theology we adopt will have excuses for such deliberate sin as at least an implicit component. Very few are intellectually honest enough to recognize that they are lost in their willful sins.

Even though the Bible is crystal clear that each and every act of known sin is rebellion against God and a slighting of His sacrifice and His power, we tend to minimize the import of our sinning and the power of God to "keep [us] from stumbling, and to make [us] stand in the presence of His glory blameless with great joy" (Jude 24, NASB). But bear in mind that repentance must precede forgiveness, and repentance implies reformation of life. Willful sinning is no light thing.

However, I honestly believe that most Christians want victory, and they long to be free from sin's slavery. Even desiring freedom from sin, though, most people find the idea of sinless living utterly overwhelming, and they cannot imagine how even the power of God could make it a reality in their lives. As they look at all the things they know they should be doing, all the duties they know they have, it seems impossible to juggle things perfectly enough to keep all the balls in the air without ever dropping any of them.

One simple ethical distinction can make things seem dramatically less overwhelming: that between negative and positive duties. Kant was the first to really explain this distinction, and it is ingeniously perceptive.

You can satisfy all your negative duties by doing nothing. They are "negative" because they require nothing of you. Examples are: don't commit adultery, don't lie, don't take the name of God in vain, and so forth. If you did absolutely nothing, you would satisfy these demands.

In contrast, there are positive duties. As you have probably already figured out, we call them "positive" because you must actually *do* something in order to fulfill them. Examples are: feed the hungry, take care of the poor, spread the gospel, and so on.

Negative duties are also called "perfect duties" because you have an infinite capacity to satisfy them. You can never have conflict between perfect duties, because at the same time that you are *not* lying, you are *not* murdering and *not* committing adultery. It requires no additional resources from you not to murder and not to commit adultery. You can always *not do,* and thereby satisfy your negative duties.

Positive duties, however, are "imperfect," because your resources are finite. You cannot feed all the hungry people in the world and care for all the sick and take the gospel to all who need to hear it. And while you are feeding someone, you are neglecting someone else who is sick. Or when you turn your attention to an ill person, you ignore someone who is hungry. It is impossible for you to be everywhere at once, and your time, money, and energy are all limited. Thus you can only "imperfectly" satisfy your positive duties.

One significant problem that people have with the idea of perfection is that they conflate negative and positive duties. They think that no matter how hard they try, no matter how much they accomplish, they will always leave things undone that they should have done. Faced with the overwhelming prospect of unsatisfied positive duties, thinking that every unsatisfied positive duty is actually a sin, they become discouraged about the obvious impossibility of "overcoming sin."

The best way to offset the sense of impossibility is to realize that the realm of right is huge, while that of wrong is extremely small, a principle illustrated by the very first ethical confrontation in human history. Remember how Eve recounted to the serpent what God had said: "We can eat of any tree except this one," in effect saying, "We have a vast range of 'right' things we can eat and only one 'wrong' one." As she herself recounted it, the realm of right was huge, while what God had told the first couple not to do consisted of just one thing in particular. Nothing has really changed through time. Of all the things we might choose to do at any given moment, the vast majority of them are within the realm of right. The list of what we must not do is a fairly short list, and we have a "perfect" capacity not to do any of those things. While not doing any of those things, we are free and right to engage in an almost unlimited array of other things. The latter include such positive duties as feeding hungry people, helping sick people, and other such deeds.

Now, we know we cannot feed all the hungry people. Does that mean we give up and serve nobody? Of course not. We do what we can. At the same time, we realize that it is impossible for us to "perfectly" satisfy the duty to feed the hungry. The question that arises about positive duties is: When have we done enough?

It has no simple answer. At one end of the spectrum, we know that we are not right if we are doing *nothing* toward satisfying our positive duties. If we are living utterly selfish, uncaring lives in complete disregard for the needs of others, we can be confident that we are in sin. However, beyond that, it is between each person and God how much they really can do in satisfaction of positive duties. The more resources we have, the more He expects us to accomplish. But there is no automatic formula for this. Let all work out their salvation with fear and trembling, while being very sensitive to the Lord's convicting power.

However, while we are conscientiously seeking to serve, and thereby satisfy our positive duties, there is a clear, bright line surrounding negative duties: don't ever do the things marked off-limits by our negative duties.

Thus one way to cast the idea of victory is to advocate that it involves perfectly satisfying our negative duties while conscientiously fulfilling our positive ones. With this idea in mind, let's talk about exactly how to implement in a practical way what the Bible says about spiritual victory.

Legalism

The first thing we need to understand is that genuine faith (with its attendant victory over sin) is not a form of legalism. *Legalism* and *righteousness by works* are terms that have come to include any effort or desire on the part of a believer to keep God's law and not sin against Him. But as we saw in the previous chapter, this is a huge mistake. The Bible demands that we cease from sinning, and it offers all the grace and power of heaven to make that a reality. Salvation and faith come to a believer inseparably coupled with victory. *Legalism* is a term that properly means one and only one thing: appealing to one's own "righteousness" and "good works" as though they had merit by which to obtain salvation, making "works" alone the antecedent of any salvation conditional. Such is the bubble-gum-machine God idea again: we put in enough "righteousness" and "good works," and the Lord then says, "Good job! Yes, that will be enough to atone for your past sins (and even your ongoing, willful sinning), so now you are saved."

Of course, this is not the biblical model. From the Fall in Eden to Christ's struggle in Gethsemane, one point has been emphasized again and again. Even *one* single sin is so offensive to God that it must cost the life of the sinner—forever. No amount of "good works" can ever "make up for" the offense of that one sin. Thus even *one* sin is enough to ensure that the sinner must eternally die: "The person who sins will die" (Eze. 18:20, NASB). And we know that "all have sinned," which means that all of us are in the same boat: no amount of ongoing good works can atone for our past sins or save us.

Thus legalism is a lie and an affront to the plan of salvation. The Bible teaches that only the sacrifice of the perfect, sinless Son of God *on our behalf* can atone for our sins. As we have seen, the Bible teaches a very different conditional from that of legalism, and it goes like this: "If Christ's righteousness covers me, then I have salvation." Only His righteousness on my behalf is the sufficient condition for my salvation. My own righteousness can never be sufficient for my salvation, no matter how perfect it is from now on. Having sinned even once in my life (as we all have), my own righteousness after that (no matter how perfect it is) can never act as the antecedent of the conditional. As people who have sinned (at least once), we must now always keep Christ's righteousness the antecedent of all salvation conditionals. Only it can ever be sufficient for our salvation, and

MFAUP-7

even our most perfect righteous works must always be immersed in His righteousness to be acceptable to God.

With Christ's righteousness in its proper perspective, our past sins can be separated from us, and we can stand before God as though we had never sinned. What will we do with this freedom from sin? Well, unfortunately, in their quest to avoid legalism, many Christians then act as though they believe, "So that God doesn't think I am trying to earn my way to heaven, I'd better give Him lots of ongoing sins to atone for. This way it will be crystal clear that I'm relying only on the merits of Jesus to save me, because I obviously have none of my own." Such reasoning is as confused as that of medieval painters who would intentionally create an "imperfection" in their paintings, because to produce a "perfect" painting would be to aspire to Godlike status. But intentional imperfection does not glorify God. He wants us to be perfectly righteous, and we can avoid legalism simply by placing the right person's righteousness as the antecedent of the salvation conditional. And the only righteousness for that job belongs to Jesus.

Legalism finds its cure in recognizing the breadth and depth of the sacrifice of Christ, forcing legalists to recognize how vastly short their own "righteousness" falls in comparison. Then they grasp the sinfulness of sin and the utter inability of any future good works to atone for it. Even one past sin forever disqualifies me from using my own ongoing and even perfect righteousness as the sufficient condition for my salvation. I am forever dependent upon the righteousness and merits of Christ.

But this fact says nothing whatsoever about the supposed "need" to keep sinning in order to avoid legalism. Having set believers free from past sins, God also empowers them to have ongoing future victories: "For we are His workmanship, created in Christ Jesus for good works, which God prepared beforehand so that we would walk in them" (Eph. 2:10, NASB). As people of faith walk forward from that very first act of repentance and forgiveness, they enter a new life of victory and good works that God prepared for them. As we have already noted above, for the Christian righteous behavior and, ultimately, perfection are consequents of the salvation conditional: "If I have salvation, then I behave righteously."

Now that we are crystal clear that the desire for complete victory in Christ is not legalism, and thus it is not "perfectionism" in any sort of negative sense, we can recognize that our ongoing and future good works are the *necessary result of* Christ dwelling in us, and that we are thereby living out the good works that God prepared for us to walk in.

Confronting a Bus

Everything I have said so far leads me to the inevitable confrontation with a bus. Well, actually I must confront a theory about a bus. One of the most intuitively compelling arguments in favor of "trend of the life" theologies uses a bus (or something like it) to argue this way: "Let's say that a person has lived a perfect life. God's grace covers all past sinning, and the person has been demonstrating a beautiful, Christlike existence. However, the individual is tempted, say, to eat the second piece of chocolate cake, and this time he or she succumbs to temptation and willfully sins by consuming the cake. One tiny little sin! Even before this person has a chance to repent, he or she starts across the street, and *Wham!* A bus hits and kills him or her. Now, Jensen, are you *really* saying that our God is so heartless and cruel that He is going to eternally damn this person over this one little sin, in the face of a lifetime of perfect service?"

So the "trend of the life" theology argues that God would have to be cruel and unreasonable to rescind an individual's salvation under such a scenario, and a theology that suggests that God is really so cruel and unreasonable must be in error.

Let's think very carefully about what this argument is actually urging upon us. It has a lot more hidden baggage than meets the intuitive eye.

First, let us remember how many "little" sins it took to doom the whole human race. One single intentional act of willful defiance destroyed humanity and doomed us to death. How many sins did it take to keep Moses out of the Promised Land? After a lifetime of perfect service, one act of impatience and pride was sufficient to demand his death. It is true that he repented and God later resurrected and took him to heaven, but that one act cost him the fulfillment of his life's mission. So before we continue, let's be very clear that using loaded phrases such as "one tiny little act of sin" belittles God's sovereignty and minimizes His absolute intolerance of willful sin.

Because Jesus interposed Himself to act as our substitute just as soon as we first sinned, and because we like to emphasize that we live in the "dispensation of grace," we tend to think very little about the price of sin—the cost of even one willful and rebellious act.

Sin is not "free" just because Jesus died. It's not as if we can take our willful sinning lightly just because we don't see people instantly struck down whenever they sin. Even one sin cost the life of God, and, as the apostle put it, we "put Him to open shame" and crucify Him afresh each and every time we willfully sin (Heb. 6:6, NASB).

Is God any less fair and just now to wipe us out for one act of willful sin than He was when He destroyed Jesus for our sins on the cross? Do we affront Him any less by our deliberate sins now than when our first parents affronted Him by their one sin? No indeed. If anything, in the "dispensation of grace," when we know full well as we do what it cost God to set us free from sin, our guilt is the greater when we disparage God's grace and mercy by willfully sinning against Him now.

Now let's think about how this "trend of the life" theology supposedly works. Can it be anything but a cleverly disguised legalism?

Here is a theology stating that if the trend of my life is good enough, it crosses some threshold beyond which God is no longer fair and just to destroy me for my premeditated sins. It must involve some sort of adding and subtracting of my good works and bad works to see if at my death the net assessment was more "positive than negative." But how does this work out, exactly? We don't know how long Adam and Eve lived in perfection prior to their first sin. Yet however much "perfection" they could put on their side of the balance sheet, it wasn't enough to offset the offense of their sin. How much "good work" does it take to counterbalance one willful sin?

Let's say that the amount of good works it takes to offset the offense to God of a single egregious sin is X. Thus X amount of good works can offset the most egregious single sin. Then, on the "trend of the life" model, as long as the number of my willful sins does not exceed however many multiples of X I have accumulated by the time I encounter the lethal bus, I can be assured of salvation. Although the Bible constantly warns me against treating good works as sufficient for salvation, on this model what those warnings really mean is that I should not consider anything less than the requisite number times X good works as sufficient for salvation. And, since I can never be entirely sure what X is from God's point of view, I had better be really careful to err on the good side and keep a huge volume of good works in store against those times when I do willfully sin. That is why I should "try" not to sin rather than just to sin willy-nilly, because I should have "victory" much more than I have willful sin, in order to keep my ratio safe.

Of course, sincere and honest believers in "trend of the life" theologies are uncomfortable with such an analysis. They have never consciously thought to quantify their good works in this way, and it is offensive even to consider such a thing.

Honest "trend of the life" believers have emphasized God's mercy. They have stressed God's grace, given the death of Jesus, and surely I am somehow distorting this whole matter to cast it as a form of legalism.

Let's get down to it. Honestly, now, where is God's grace in the "trend of the life" theology? Is it grace that allows or enables Him to count our good works as "enough" to purchase our salvation?

How is this not the old legalistic notion of indulgences? Is it not making Him a bubble-gum-machine God? "Trend of the life" theologies make a mockery of the sacrifice of Jesus by asserting that some quantity of "good works" will justify a person. The sacrifice of Christ is not our sole justification—"good works" have merit too!

Here we have the real issue, don't we? The issue is about merit, about deserving salvation. Of whether or not our "good works" can contribute any merit. We find really only two options here: either the grace of God alone justifies us, or our "good works" alone justify us. If the grace of God is truly sufficient for our salvation, then, as Paul so often puts it, such justification is entirely "apart from works of the law" (Rom. 3:28, NASB). Conversely, if our good works in any measure contribute to our salvation, then it is possible in principle for us to "have enough" of them piled up to offset our sins.

Romans 11:6 makes the dichotomy between grace and works crystal clear: "But if it [salvation] is by grace, it is no longer on the basis of works, otherwise grace is no longer grace" (NASB). Grace is, by its very nature, entirely sufficient; so any supposed addition to it actually nullifies it. (See also Rom. 3:24-28; 4:4, 5; 2 Cor. 9:8; Gal. 2:21; 5:4; and Eph. 2:8.)

Legalism in all its versions says that our "good works" *do* contribute to our salvation—our "good works" *are* the coins we put into the bubble-gum machine. Sure, maybe on some legalistic theologies Christ has to turn the crank of the machine, and maybe sometimes we even come up a bit short so that He contributes some of His good works too, but some amount of our good works has to contribute to our deserving salvation, and thus it is possible in principle for us to provide enough of our own. But if we need to contribute *any* good works toward meriting our salvation, then "grace is no longer grace."

So salvation is either merited solely by grace, and works count nothing toward earning it or offsetting our sins; or it is solely merited by works, and grace is unneeded in the face of enough good works to offset our sins. People who think that salvation and justification require grace and works in some mixture simply do not realize the all-sufficiency of grace or the force of the bus scenario. When it comes to the merit for salvation, a true dichotomy exists between grace and works. Either Christ crucified merits our salvation, or our own good works lead to it.

Some may be saying, "Jensen, you are truly confused! You have just spent the whole last chapter arguing that perfect obedience to the commandments is inseparably related to salvation and justification. How can you now claim that our good works contribute nothing toward our salvation? You can't have it both ways."

The Bible teaches that our righteousness is logically inseparable from our salvation—you can't have one without the other in any scenario at any time. But this is not because our righteousness causes us to be saved or contributes to our being saved. Remember that I earlier warned against treating logical relations as though they are causal—that the one produces the other? The accurate way to say it is that the relation between God's grace for salvation is so intimately tied to His grace to give us victory over sin that the power of grace for one just is the power of grace for the other. God's grace that saves us is not some other thing from God than that which sets us free from sin. His grace enables us both to be saved and to be free from sin. It is absolutely sufficient to accomplish *both* salvation and freedom from sin in our lives.

This means that at any moment that we refuse the grace of God for victory we are also at the same time choosing to live apart from His saving grace. We can repent, and God will forgive us if we truly repent. However, people have come to treat willful sinning so lightly that they think nothing of jumping out of (and then, they think, quickly back into) the realm of God's grace. But it is a fearful and terrible thing to live even a moment apart from divine grace.

"Trend of the life" theologies rest upon the following confusion:

all such theologies teach that God's grace for justification is something completely different and separable from the power and process
that He employs to give us victory against sin. Thus such theologies
assert that we can be living in justification even during the times we
are willfully sinning. They imagine that we can live apart from God's
sanctifying power at any given moment, and in that moment our
"good trend of life" will still motivate God to employ His grace to
justify us in any lethal bus encounter. While they may claim that we
are "saved by grace," it is really our "good trend of life" that merits
us that saving grace in the face of our willful sins.* Thus our "good
trend of life," not grace, is the logically primary antecedent to the
salvation conditional.

But this is works—*legalism*—not salvation by the grace of God.
The Bible teaches that legalism is a lie, because no amount of "good
works," even as an ultimate result of "grace," can nullify even one
single sin. Only the grace of God, and that alone, can atone for a single sin, and it brings both salvation and victory over sin at each moment that His grace is in our lives. Thus living apart from victory just
is living apart from salvation, as I have demonstrated in the previous
chapter, and willfully sinning just is living apart from God's grace.
No amount of "good works" can buy us salvation apart from God's
utterly saving grace, so no amount of "good works" can provide us
salvation while we choose to sin willfully.

Should you be killed by a bus while living apart from God's saving grace, then you *are* lost, as Ezekiel 18:24 makes clear: "But when
a righteous man turns away from his righteousness, commits iniquity
and does according to all the abominations that a wicked man does,
will he live? All his righteous deeds which he has done will not be remembered for his treachery which he has committed and his sin
which he has committed; for them he will die" (NASB). No amount
of past righteousness can offset deliberate sinning—the past righteousness will not even be remembered! Ezekiel 33:13 makes the same
point even more straightforwardly: "When I say to the righteous he

200

will surely live, and he so trusts in his righteousness that he commits iniquity, none of his righteous deeds will be remembered; but in that same iniquity of his which he has committed he will die" (NASB).

Yet nothing about these facts reveals God to be unfair or unreasonable. The Lord has stated clearly that even one sin makes one forever worthy of death. He does not give His grace to us to save us in our ongoing deliberate sinning. Rather, He offered it to provide both justification and victory over our sins. And should we have the audacity to reject His saving grace at any time, then we make His grace, the price He paid to offer it to us, and our own salvation a light thing.

Even in the face of such willfulness God never looks for that one instant we have sinned so that He can send a lethal bus hurtling our direction. Instead, He is so merciful toward us that He saves us from death, protecting us from bus scenarios again and again, giving us chance after chance to return to Him and be saved. "I take no pleasure in the death of the wicked, but rather that the wicked turn from his way and live" (verse 11, NASB). And 2 Peter 3:9 adds: "not wishing for any to perish but for all to come to repentance" (NASB). The Lord has not reserved a bus for you, waiting for that moment He can strike you down in your sin. Instead, He wants your repentance and for you to have spiritual victory.

The Reality of Victory

Daily we confront real temptations, and at times we choose defeat. How can the ongoing victory I have theorized about be an actual reality in our lives? How can we overcome each and every temptation that comes to us, so that we honor our Savior and not "put Him to open shame" (Heb. 6:6, NASB)? First, let us not belittle the theorizing and doctrine. If you honestly do not believe that complete victory is possible, then it is indeed impossible for you to have it. In all intellectual honesty, you must first genuinely internalize what the Word of God says about the overwhelming power of

God's grace: "Where sin abounded, grace did much more abound" (Rom. 5:20). It is no mere formal judicial act in heaven that justifies us. No, instead, where sin abounds in us, grace does much more abound to save us from it! In order to experience complete victory over sin, we must first accept that such righteousness was "prepared beforehand that we should walk in [it]" (Eph. 2:10, NKJV), realizing that our ongoing righteousness is logically equivalent to our salvation.

Now, the method for obtaining complete victory is simple though not always easy. When confronted with temptation and everything in us cries out to sin, it is then that we must decide what side we are on.

You see, at the moment of temptation most Christians (if they are even attempting to gain victory) begin praying for power. If they don't feel the power, they pray some more. The lower nature still wants the sin, though, and instead of feeling the power of God, they instead sense the clamoring of the lower nature. Eventually, they grow tired of "trying" to "resist that feeling" without feeling any of God's power, so they capitulate and knowingly, willfully sin. Afterward, filled with guilt, they attempt to figure out why they did not experience God's power. "Where was God when I was crying out to Him to save me? Why didn't He give me victory?" But their reaction is all a huge mistake—one that throughout this book I have been setting up to gun down.

The "fight of faith, not sin" theology tells us that such "trying" and then failing is the very problem with waging the "fight of sin," which must always result in failure. It claims that the reason we fail in all such struggles is that we are engaged in the wrong battle, and that we are "fighting against sin in our own power," which must always result in failure.

I agree that "trying" while waiting for a feeling of power to overcome is doomed to failure. However, there is another alternative to the claim that our failure is because we are engaged in the wrong spiritual warfare. We *are* to resist temptation, and at times temptations seem to come from the very cores of our beings, which makes them a hard struggle. But when we wage the *true* fight of faith, which will produce victory out of the struggle, we will successfully resist.

Faith is not feeling! It has nothing to do with how circumstances appear to us, how consequences seem as if they will turn out, or how things feel to us. Instead, faith is nothing more than acting on the belief that the Word of God has in itself the power to do the very thing it says. The Word of God declares that each one of us is a new creation and that God has granted all power in heaven and earth to us. According to the Word of God we can be overcomers in the face of each and every temptation.

Too many Christians pray for the power that the Word of God has already given us. Assuming that they are "struggling against temptation" as they pray for the power to overcome, they go down to defeat, because they do not choose to stand on the Word of God and simply employ His power to stand. Everything depends upon our will. If we will not decisively choose to be free and have victory, then we will not have it.

The Lord bids us to experience the miracle of victory, to in effect "take up our bed and walk," as He offered the man at the Pool of Bethesda. So how long will we continue to lie there waiting for a feeling? If we will simply choose to do what the word of the Lord says, we will find what it says to be true in our life. We wait for a miracle, praying for it, and we want some "sign" to assure us that it is true. But the miracle of salvation is that it is *already* true! As a result we don't have to wait for it or ask for some additional signs and wonders (or feelings) before we will believe in it. It is our privilege to believe in our salvation and act upon it right now and forevermore.

When we turn our heart toward God and honestly desire spiritual victory with a single mind, with all our will focused upon the victory as Jacob's was focused upon clinging to God, then we will have victory each and every time. If we commit ourselves to the victory that God has promised us, then He will ensure by His mighty power that we can never be *forced* to sin. Our lower nature is powerless to resist temptation, but when we partake of Christ's divine nature, and when He abides in us, He empowers our wills. And when our wills are empowered by the nature of Christ, they cannot be overcome.

Here are the defining conditionals of victory: if Christ abides in us, He does not allow sin in us. If Christ does not allow sin in us, then His power ensures that we do not sin. And if His power ensures that we do not sin, then we do not sin. From these conditionals, we may use the inference called hypothetical syllogism to draw this powerful conclusion: If Christ is in us, we do not sin. This is the promise of God to us—it is the promise of spiritual victory whenever and for as long as we are in Christ and Christ is in us! The corollary, using MT, is, of course: If we sin, then Christ is not in us.

Of course, I am fully aware of the fact that many Christians will reject what I am saying here. Many do not believe that God offers them complete victory over sin right now, and so they think that the plan of salvation is God's mechanism to "save" them even while they continue to be slaves to their sins. Such people will always reject the concept that they have to choose victory. They want to claim that "Christ did it all at the cross" or that "faith is entirely about relationship," and thereby ignore the vast array of verses that assert that it is our privilege to also crucify ourselves in Christ, deny our lower natures, and overcome and gain victory just as Christ did. To put it bluntly, all such will find the "broad" way that leads to destruction.

But the narrow way is for those who have committed their lives to be God's warriors. They love their Savior and Commander so much that they find it their highest honor to do whatever He asks and to be used and used up in any way He sees fit. As a result, they find that faith is the victory, as it provides in their lives *all* the power of the Word of God. Each will experience the most amazing miracle of all: that God's righteousness can utterly subdue sinful flesh. Just as creation was an unfathomable miracle, so is our re-creation. Yet faith grasps these realities and acts as though they are true!

It is now clear how distorted theistic evolution is. It denies God's creative power, mixing in large parts of naturalistic theory. In a parallel way certain forms of theology combine the "facts" of our tendency to sin as though the divine nature simply isn't powerful enough to overcome it. In a sense most Christians are "evolutionary theists" when it comes to the process of sanctification. They believe that as they keep "trying," slowly, eventually, they might get a little better and then a little better, but they will never really be any good, because then they wouldn't need Jesus anymore. How tragically confused. In place of this evolutionary process, the plan of salvation actually offers us power and freedom beyond our wildest imaginations. The Bible tells us that if we would *choose* to be free, then we *are* free. And if we would *choose* to employ the power of God, then we *have* that power. But let us not fail so to choose and then blame our subsequent failures on God, as though He didn't give us the power when we asked for it.

Perfection

Now I must clear up one final point about "perfectionism." Even people excited by what they have read so far have a lingering fear: "If I start thinking that I'm always victorious, won't I become proud and haughty and start concluding that I don't need Jesus anymore? If I become a 'perfectionist,' how do I ensure that I don't slip into legalism, thinking that my works in some way help earn my salvation?"

Because it is the crucial question for "perfectionists," let's clearly think it through. But to do that correctly, we need to employ two philosophical terms we used earlier: metaphysics and epistemology. In case you don't remember, metaphysics is the study of the way things actually are—the realities of existence, the "furniture of reality," if you will. Epistemology is the study of knowledge, what we know and can know, and how we come to know (and believe) things. We can quickly distinguish them by saying that metaphysical facts concern the way things *really are,* while epistemological facts concern what people *know or believe.* Many often conflate these two. For example, in our discussion of perfectionism, most people would say that I would not actually want to be perfect (the metaphysical fact of being perfect), because if I was perfect (by which they really mean "if I knew I was perfect"), then I would be proud and not need Jesus anymore. So they conflate *being* sinless with *knowing* that they are sinless.

The basic problem that we have while we live with our lower natures is that we can be deceived about our true condition. The Bible constantly reminds us that we tend to be mistaken about what we are truly like. Many people believe they are saved (epistemological fact) when they actually are not (metaphysical fact). Since we well know this tendency in ourselves, we have no hope whatsoever except to depend constantly upon the mercy and atonement of Jesus. Another point is that we can never be certain that we have properly satisfied all of our positive duties. Even if from God's perspective we have, we cannot know that. Even as the most conscientious of Christians, therefore, we are never in a position to assume that we are sinless, so we are never justified to have spiritual pride or assurance in ourselves. However, what we would never dream to claim for ourselves or imagine about somebody else (epistemology) might in fact be reality (metaphysics).

Despite that, we *can* know the particular cases of whether or not we have willfully decided to sin. We can recognize when we have intentionally chosen to sin, and this we can always knowingly avoid in the power of God. Otherwise we have no chance to become what God designs for us to be, and we have no opportunity to obtain complete victory as long as we deliberately choose to sin. However, it is also the case that just because we get this or that victory over this or that particular temptation, that fact alone never entitles us to believe that we are perfect. The epistemological principle here is this:

we can know about our particular responses to particular temptations, but we cannot reliably extrapolate from them to the general knowledge of our spiritual state or condition.

At first glance the principle might seem a bit odd, so let me explain it. I am distinguishing between known sins and unknown sins. Now, known sins are apparent to us, which is why we can know whether or not we are gaining victory over them. However, we also commit unknown sins—we do things that we have no idea until later that God finds them offensive. Perhaps we respond to a situation in the wrong way, or perhaps He expects us to do more to satisfy one of our positive duties. Such unknown sins result from defects in our characters, which are those ways in which our perspectives are out of harmony with God's. It is only with the conviction of the Holy Spirit (and the guidance of ongoing Bible study) that we come to recognize that we have unwittingly sinned, and such conviction reveals character defects to us, just as Jesus said to James and John, "Ye know not what manner of spirit ye are of" (Luke 9:55). As the Holy Spirit discloses to us additional ways in which we have been out of harmony with God's will for us, we can then intentionally choose to bring more and more aspects of our lives into conformity with the divine will.

But throughout this process of God's pointing out and correcting our character defects, we can always choose not to sin knowingly. So, as I say, there is a distinction between our response to ongoing, known temptations and the fact that we may be out of harmony with God in ways completely unknown to us. Thus we can know about particular temptations and our responses to them without being aware of our general condition compared to Christlike perfection of character. We realize that regarding all those unknown sins we must have a Savior to cover us with His blood. Even if we realize that we are gaining victory over each and every sin that we are aware of, we clearly recognize that we still need our Savior to cover all our past sins and those present sins that we are not aware of. This sort of perfectionism is clearly not legalism or a recipe for spiritual pride.

Well, if we are constantly engaging in unknown sins, then how can we ever have perfect characters?

The process of sanctification leads us from victory to victory regarding known sins, as the Holy Spirit reveals those things we didn't previously know about. However, we can never be confident that we have no more things for the Holy Spirit to bring to our attention. Thus we can never be in an epistemically privileged position such that we can *know* when we have overcome the last thing that has kept us from perfection. But here again, let us be very careful not to conflate epistemology with metaphysics.

Here is the exciting fact of the matter. When you look at your own life and the vast array of evil in the world, it seems as though evil is infinite. But it is not. Each of us has a finite number of ways in which we are out of harmony with God's will for us. For example, of all the sins that might be a problem for me, it turns out that, for example, alcoholism is one that doesn't tempt me in any way. While others will have to overcome alcoholism, it is not a sin I will have to deal with. On the other hand, things I have grappled with will not be temptations for others. So out of the large (but finite) array of potential depravities, each of us suffers from a relatively tiny subset of them. God must work with each of us to erase our particular depravities from our characters, to bring us back into a condition of perfection like that of our first parents before the Fall. But the fact is that this is a finite work for each of us. It is not an endless process. The day can come for each of us in which we gain victory over the last sin in our lives. We can then stand before God completely recovered from the Fall. But even when that happens, we will not know that it has taken place.

The point will come (metaphysical fact) that every believer who will stand before God when Christ returns will perfectly reflect Jesus' character. That is God's plan and promise. However, they will not know (epistemological fact) that they have attained such close harmony with Him. As they look at their past lives, all they see is a train of sinning (most of the sins unknown at the time they were committed). Yes, they recognize victories over known sins, but that seems overwhelmed by the seemingly endless string of previously unknown sins the Holy Spirit has convicted them of during the course of their lives. They cannot yet know that there are no more to come, and their past experience gives them no reason to think otherwise. Even a Christian who would never knowingly sin would also never make a claim of perfection.

Another epistemological claim commonly used to denigrate perfectionism is: "Well, I have never yet met a perfect person!" But would we *know* a perfect person if we met him or her? Remember that the mob, along with the religious leaders, were so confused that they did not recognize in Jesus the *perfect* Son of God. Although we cannot recognize (epistemological fact) perfection in ourselves or someone else, that does not mean that we or someone else has not attained perfection (metaphysical fact).

Thus we see that perfectionism, properly understood, has none of the negative connotations that typically keep people from being energized and excited by the prospect of complete spiritual victory. And, let's face it, you really cannot strive toward something that you honestly believe is impossible in principle to attain. So the whole notion of "trying hard," while you are really committed to defeat, is a contradiction in terms. The Christian life has no "trying"—only victory or defeat.

God offers complete spiritual victory, and genuine faith reaches out and grasps all His power to make it a metaphysical fact, regardless of circumstances, appearances, or feelings (all those epistemological factors). It is our privilege to experience that power, to see particular victories, and thereby to know that we have committed ourselves to fighting on the Lord's side.

But this is just the beginning! When we have genuine faith, are committed to the Lord, and are prepared to be warriors in His cause, then He will live within us and empower us to accomplish things that we cannot now imagine. Will you be one who raises a lame man to walk? Will you be one who leads another person to commit himself or herself to serve the God of the universe? In His service miracles will often happen, yet our genuine faith will place them in proper perspective.

The profound faith that God wishes for us to enjoy gains victory over temptations, and it transcends all appearances and feelings. It lays hold of the mighty arm of Jesus Christ and experiences the reality that His arm is mighty to save to the uttermost!

Do you want victory and power in your life? Then read and rely upon the Word of God, just as it is. Study it to understand the propositions and relations it conveys, for they are the very keys of the kingdom. There in the Word of God is all of His power for you. Believe it and act as though it is filled with metaphysical facts about how the universe really works and about God's real relationship to you. *Choose* to believe that what the Word of God says is true in your life, and then *act* upon it. If you will exercise genuine faith, you will immediately find that heavenly power and victory attend it. This is God's plan and ultimate will for you. May all the power and victory of God be yours is my prayer.

★ Anybody who thinks I am being uncharitable, that I am emphasizing works in a way that such theologies would not, is just not aware of their inherent implications. After all, not everybody is going to be saved. The lost will die in their sins. What, then, distinguishes those who perish in their sins from those "saved" in their sins? Supposedly, it is faith in Jesus. "We are saved by faith, not works," so the "trend of the life" theologies insist. But we must ask: what distinguishes "true believers" who are "saved" from "false believers" who are not saved, given that both classes continue willfully sinning? And, we are told, as defines these theologies: "The trend of your life reveals which side you have been on." "Trend of your life" must mean the net volume of your good works compared against your willful sinning. So if your "trend" has been "good," then you are saved, while if your "trend" has been bad, then you are lost. But this is legalism in which "grace" itself is purchased by "enough" good works!

The difference between works in the biblical gospel compared to works in "trend of the life" theologies is revealed by bus scenarios. According to the Bible, works merit nothing for saving us. If we die in willful sin, we are lost. But "trend of the life" theologies assert that we are still under grace even during our willful sinning. Thus should something happen to us then, we are still saved. We ask: Why will God save some who perish while willfully sinning, but damn others who die willfully sinning? "Some have faith even though they are willfully sinning, while most don't have faith" is the response. "Thus some are under grace, even in their willful sinning, while most aren't." But we note that many who will be lost think that they have saving faith, think that they are under grace, when actually they are not. Again we ask: What distinguishes the "faith" of the saved and the "faith" of the lost when both classes are willfully sinning? And the answer is: "The trend of the life reveals 'faith' as genuine or false." Thus the positive balance of good works is sufficient to keep one "under grace" and offset willful sins, while the biblical gospel states that no amount of either "faith" or "good works" can compensate for even one willful sin. The biblical gospel presents us with an all-or-nothing package of salvation and victory, whereas "trend of the life" theologies offer a vague continuum of "good works" that are more or less sufficient to offset our willful sinning.

The most blatantly legalistic of the "trend of the life" theologies is the "fight of faith, not sin" version. In this model the "good works" that count are nothing more than Bible study, prayer, and witnessing. Do these, they assert, and you are "fighting the fight of faith," regardless of your willful sinning. Such a viewpoint elevates such "good works" as sufficient to keep you in a "saving relationship," which in turn is your justification, in spite of your willful sinning.

Legalism (by a variety of mechanisms) offsets willful sins by "good works." However, the biblical gospel proclaims that nothing in heaven or on earth can offset willful sinning. The grace of God alone covers repented sins, but repentance and grace are inseparable from spiritual victory. Repentance and grace are incompatible with deliberate sinning. While legalism offers various ways to save you in your sins, the biblical gospel seeks only to deliver you from your sins!

GLOSSARY

Antecedent: Literally, before. For our purposes, we are talking about the left side of a conditional statement, the sufficient condition. In the symbolized statement, $P \supset Q$, the P is the antecedent. In the sentence "If it's raining, then the streets are wet" the claim "it's raining" is the antecedent.

Argument: A set of propositions, one of which counts as the conclusion, with the others being reasons offered in support of the conclusion. While most people think of an argument as a verbal confrontation between two or more people ("Joe and Mary had another argument"), a philosophical argument is simply a presentation (verbally or in writing) of the reason(s) supporting a particular conclusion.

Charity: In philosophy charity is the principle of ensuring that a position is fully and most strongly understood. Being charitable to a viewpoint is the opposite of treating it as a "straw figure" that is easily knocked down. A common sophistic (see Sophism) practice is to make a weak caricature of a viewpoint and then shoot down that caricature, claiming to demolish the viewpoint itself (the "straw figure" fallacy). Thus charity requires that we seek to evaluate a viewpoint in its most coherent, strongest light. Perhaps we even help an opponent recast or develop the viewpoint and articulate it in clearer fashion. Only once we are confident that we fully understand a viewpoint can we evaluate the reasons we disagree (or perhaps come to agree) with it. Charity, then, is central to intellectual honesty and stands in contrast to sophism.

Conditional: For our purposes, the material conditional, as opposed to a variety of other forms of conditional (such as counterfactual conditionals). The material conditional is "tenseless," and is defined according to the logical relation between its antecedent (sufficient condition) proposition and its consequent (necessary condition) proposition. (See Logical Relation.) A material conditional is true if it is impossible for there to be any scenario in which its antecedent is true while its consequent is false.

Consequent: Literally, after. For our purposes, we are talking about the right side of a conditional statement, the necessary condition. In the symbolized statement, $P \supset Q$, the Q is the consequent. In the sentence "If it's raining, then the streets are wet" the claim "the streets are wet" is the consequent.

Consequentialism: Ethical theorizing that asserts that the rightness of an act is determined by whether or not that act produced good consequences. (See also Utilitarianism.)

Dichotomy: A division of things or statements into two different mutually exclusive or contradictory groups.

Empirical: Literally, "from experience," which can also be called a posteriori. Typically modifying such terms as *proposition, knowledge,* or *theory,* it is to be contrasted with a priori, which means "prior to experience." In the case of science, the "experience" is that of the senses, although many philosophical theories include some form of "inner experience," which signifies awareness of our own inner states. Both empirical knowledge and a priori knowledge have distinguishing attributes. For example, empirical knowledge is uncertain, while a priori knowledge is certain. Empirical knowledge is relative, while a priori knowledge is universal. The principle of addition is an example of a priori knowledge, while my count of the number of chairs in a particular room illustrates empirical knowledge. Notice that if I get two different counts of chairs on two different occasions, I never think to say, "Wow, sometimes 27 plus 1 equals 28 and sometimes 27 plus 1 equals 30," thereby calling the principle of addition into question. Instead, I question my experience: "H'mm . . . I thought there were 28 chairs in this room, but now there appear to be 30. I must have miscounted, or somebody brought in two chairs since I first counted."

Epistemology: The philosophical study of knowledge, justification, and belief. Epistemological inquiry concerns itself with the nature of evidence and truth, and with theories of how we come to have evidence to know and believe anything.

Existentialism: Many variants exist, but the common thread is an emphasis upon human individuality and a de-emphasis upon essence. The de-emphasis of essence provides the basis for a claim of radical freedom in which human beings literally define (on some readings: make) themselves by their choices and actions. "Nihilistic existentialism" emerged as the dominant strain of existentialism (and its proponents are perhaps most well known and identified with existentialism), so this is the version of existentialism to which I refer in this book. It takes "radical freedom" to imply further claims about the subjectivity of all values and the absence of objective meaning in the universe.

Fallacy: An attempt to draw a conclusion using faulty reasoning. Informal fallacies seek to utilize the content of statements (such as ambiguities of meaning and claims about relations between groups and group members, among other issues) to draw unwarranted conclusions. Formal fallacies are actual logical errors in which illogical inferences are drawn, having to do with the formal structure of the relations between statements.

False Dichotomy: A fallacy that asserts two and only two options, when in fact there exists at least one more option. This fallacy attempts to limit options so as to force a conclusion out of one or the other of the options. However, an alternate conclusion is actually possible, because of the existence of other options. An example of such a fallacy is: "You either love me or you hate me. I know you don't hate me. So you must love me." Perhaps the person to whom this argument is directed is indifferent, in which case, he or she would correctly respond: "Despite what you say, I do not love you. In fact, I couldn't care less."

Hypothetical Syllogism (HS): A valid form of conditional inference using two conditional statements to draw a third conditional statement as a conclusion. The form is this: $P \supset Q$; $Q \supset R$; therefore $P \supset R$. A content-laden example is: if it's raining, then the streets are wet; if the streets are wet, then the streets are slippery; therefore if it's raining, then the streets are slippery.

Inference: An inference takes at least one proposition as a premise and then draws a conclusion from that/those premise(s). Inferences can either conform to correct logical rules or violate them. We call inferences that violate logical rules "invalid," "bad inferences," or "faulty logic." "If it's raining, then the streets are wet; and it is raining, so the streets are wet," is a valid inference, while "If it's raining, then the streets are wet; the streets are wet, so it's raining" is faulty logic. Many forms of inference (both good and bad) are so common that they have received specific names.

Logical Relation: The formal way in which propositions combine their truth values to produce a single truth value. For example, for the material conditional $P \supset Q$, in every scenario in which P is false, regardless of the truth value of Q, in that scenario the conditional statement is true; and in any scenario in which P is true and Q is true, in that scenario the conditional statement is true; and in any scenario in which P is true and Q is false, in that scenario the conditional statement false. Considering all of the possible scenarios defines the relation between the component propositions in this way: for any true material conditional, it is impossible for there to be any scenario in which the antecedent is true while the consequent is false.

Two types of logical relations exist: unary and binary. The unary relation is negation, which means that the relation contains a single proposition. Negation simply reverses the truth value of its proposition: "It's raining" becomes "it's not raining." The other commonly used logical relations are binary: conditional, biconditional, disjunction, and conjunction. All binary relations relate two propositions, and each relation has its own defining rules.

Material Conditional: See Conditional.

Metaphysics: The philosophical study of existence and the nature of reality. Metaphysical inquiry concerns itself with the components and relations of reality and its appearances. (See also Ontology.) Metaphysics is more fundamental than science because it deals with questions that science cannot approach, yet science often presupposes the answers to such questions.

Modus Ponens (MP): A valid form of inference that moves from a conditional premise and a restatement of the antecedent of the conditional to a conclusion of the consequent of the conditional. The form is: $P \supset Q$; P; therefore Q. A content-laden example is: if it's raining, then the streets are wet; it is raining; therefore the streets are wet.

Modus Tollens (MT): A valid form of inference that moves from a conditional premise and a denial of the consequent of the conditional to a conclusion that denies the antecedent of the conditional. The form is: $P \supset Q$; not Q; therefore not P. A content-laden example is: if it's raining, then the streets are wet; the streets are not wet; therefore it is not raining.

Negative Duty: From Kantian ethics—a negative duty is a duty that you can fulfill by doing nothing. Since you can never be placed in a position of a conflict between doing-nothings, and you have an unlimited capacity to do nothing (it does not take resources from you to do nothing), negative duties are called "perfect." Nothing in principle precludes you from satisfying all of your negative duties perfectly. Examples include: never lie, never steal, and never murder.

Nihilism: The many versions of nihilism all share a common doctrine of denying objectivity. Nihilism can be of a metaphysical or epistemological sort, denying the objectivity of the external world or our knowledge of it (see also Solipsism). Or nihilism can be of an ethical sort, denying the objectivity of values.

Ontology: The set of entities and relations of reality entailed by a particular metaphysical theory. For example, a Christian's ontology includes God, Christ, the Holy Spirit, angels, and other spiritual/supernatural entities. A naturalist's ontology would not include such entities.

Philosophy: From the Greek, literally, "love of wisdom." A philosopher, then, is a "wisdom lover," which has come to mean a "truth seeker." But a philosopher is not a truth seeker at random. He or she does not wander around waiting for random impressions that "feel true," with such wandering counting as "seeking." Instead, the practice of philosophy is a very directed, methodological approach to truth seeking. Fundamental to philosophy's methods is a reliance upon deductive logic and carefully reasoned argumentation. Philosophy advances via the process of "dialectic," which just means a chain of argumentation. Someone presents his conclusion on a particular subject and outlines his reasons that support it. Another person, who usually disagrees, notes mistakes that might have been made in reasoning, points out additional information that pertains, disputes with the truth of some of the reasons cited, or provides counterexamples to the conclusion (among many other methods of disputing a conclusion). The original person (or someone else taking up that cause) then responds, and that response generates a new response, and so on. As time passes, the philosophical community comes to reject certain positions and to accept others on the basis of the weight of the dialectic surrounding them. Truth seeking is not a "quick and dirty" affair. Instead it is a careful, thoughtful, and reasoned assessment of as much evidence as can be accumulated.

Even people who rely on the "Bible and the Bible only" actually employ or benefit from philosophical methods. The very study of legitimate biblical interpretation, which we Christians all rely upon, has produced principles we use now almost without thinking about them. Yet these principles of what counts as "legitimate" interpretational approaches to Bible study are the product of the very kind of process I am here describing (see the appendix: "Lockean Model of Knowledge").

Around the turn of the twentieth century, Christians tended to become especially suspicious of philosophy because of the appearance and growing popularity of a type of philosophy of science, "logical positivism," that had as its goal to elevate empirical evidence to such an extent that statements without empirical truth conditions could not even count as meaningful. Since much of Christianity relies upon claims about the nature and attributes of spiritual entities, rather than necessarily empirical entities, philosophy appeared to be disallowing theism and Christianity by definition. By the middle of the century, however, positivism was falling on hard times, as philosophers had a growing awareness of its inadequacy, and they even recognized that positivism's most strident and defining claims could not satisfy its own criterion of meaningfulness.

We should note, however, that the radical evidentiary claims of positivism have never been widely adopted in the whole history of philosophy. And today one is hard pressed to find a truly positivist philosopher. Meanwhile, even as Christianity became suspicious of the practice of philosophy, it itself continued to employ philosophical methods—it really has no alternative. It is important to distinguish between philosophical methods and whatever particular view happens to be popular among some subset of philosophers at any given moment.

Positive Duty: From Kantian ethics—a positive duty can be satisfied or fulfilled only by doing something. Positive duties require that you expend your (limited) resources of time, energy, money, etc. Consequently, conflicts between your positive duties can arise, making them "imperfect" insofar as you can never perfectly satisfy all your positive duties. Examples include: help those in need, keep your promises, and tell the truth. Notice that positive duties can often conflict. Keeping a promise to be home at a certain time might get overridden by a more pressing duty to help an accident victim.

Telling the truth might be overridden by a more pressing duty to protect a person in danger. Notice also that the negative duty never to lie cannot be placed in conflict with the positive duty to tell the truth. You may not lie to protect a person in danger, but nothing requires that you tell the whole truth when that endangers the person. Sometimes silence is golden.

Proposition: The underlying idea (abstract object) that is the meaning of declarative sentences. Propositions have truth values (true or false), while not all sentences do (for example, questions and commands). Also sentences can vary in phrasing and language, while the propositions they convey remain the same. Propositions can be simple or complex. Simple propositions convey a single thought sufficient to have a truth value, such as "It's raining." Complex propositions are composed of simple propositions along with logical relations, such as "If it's raining, then the streets are wet." In sentential logic (which is what we employ in this book), a simple proposition is the smallest truth-functional unit.

Solipsism: Many varieties of solipsism share a few common features, which I will emphasize here. A first-person, subjective viewpoint is taken to imply empathetic, epistemological, ontological, and psychological facts to the effect that a person's own mental states are prioritized to the exclusion or minimization of "external" states. For example, epistemological solipsism can take the form of skepticism about the external world, which can be cast as "being alone with one's mental states as the only reality."

Sophism: Early in the development of Western philosophy the persuasive power of philosophy's methods became an end unto itself. In ancient Greece men originally trained as philosophers hired themselves out as professional arguers, with their goal being to endorse whatever case they were paid to make. Entire schools formed to train individuals how to become professional arguers, and very quickly tactics of persuasion took the place of methods of seeking truth. The "tactics of persuasion" became some of the earliest intentional fallacies, as slight and subtle divergences from legitimate argumentation were employed to mislead the unwitting into thinking that a weak position was strong or that a false position was true. We see such tactics from time to time in our modern courtrooms, in which some clever lawyers employ persuasive tactics to win rather than use solely legitimate inferences to seek and reveal the truth. Those not carefully trained in both legitimate and illegitimate tactics of argumentation and persuasion (most jurors, for example) find themselves easily misled by clever persuasive tactics. Sophism is the use of tactics (often illegitimate) to win arguments rather than to seek the truth honestly.

Utilitarianism: A type of consequentialistic ethical theorizing that asserts that the rightness of an act is a function of maximizing some highest good. We can classify types of utilitarianism according to the good each prioritizes and the means by which that good is to be maximized.

Valid: In logic the term means that a formal inference is legitimate and that the following formal relation holds: it is impossible for all the premises to be true and the conclusion false, which is another way of saying: if the premises are all true, then the conclusion must be true. This is not to be confused with the more ambiguous uses of "valid" in everyday contexts, such as "I have a valid driver's license." For the field of logic "valid" always means that an inference has "followed the rules" such that the truth of the conclusion is guaranteed by the truth of the premises.

APPENDIX
LOCKEAN MODEL OF KNOWLEDGE

I have said so much about evidence in this book that I owe you at least a brief account of a model of knowledge.[1] I believe this model to be intellectually responsible and consistent with Christian principles. Although it derives from the seventeenth-century philosopher John Locke, I have modified it enough that I present it "with apologies" to Locke. We'll call it "neo-Lockean," if you like.

One could surely write, debate, then rewrite a whole book on this subject alone, so perhaps my nutshell presentation here is irresponsible. However, presenting nothing at all is irresponsible as well. So I briefly present the model here and leave the ongoing thinking and debating to the readers. I believe this to be the most responsible approach.

Below I have produced a helpful diagram picturing relationships between types of knowledge. The first thing to notice is that all forms of human knowledge are bounded by circles. The circles overlap in various ways, but in principle all that a human being can know is contained within one or more of the circles. Outside of the circles are all the things that can possibly be known, but not by human beings. This is to say that they can only come to know a subset of all the facts that actually exist. God, of course, knows everything that can be known. Other beings (such as angels), having perhaps other modes of knowledge from us, might know things that we cannot with our modes of knowledge. But even such other beings cannot know all there is to know. Only God can.

As you can immediately see, one thing that distinguishes this neo-Lockean model from other models of human knowledge, such

as, say, that of Hegel or various Eastern religions, is that this model
signifies at the outset that human knowledge can never reach out to
encompass all that can be known.

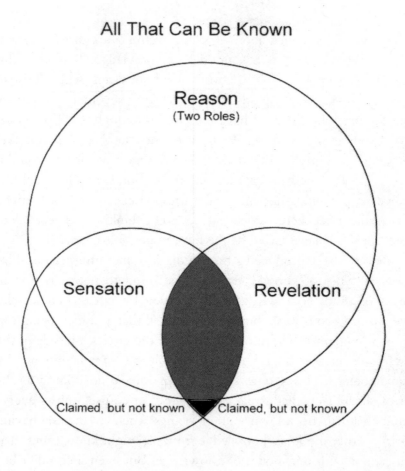

Since the modes of knowledge are themselves what limit the scope of knowledge on this model, let's get clear about each of the three modes.

Locke was an empiricist, which means that he prioritized knowledge by sensation, that is, knowledge derived from the senses. I do not emphasize that mode of knowledge in this model, but we will start there. By "sensation" I include not only the five senses but "inner sense" as well.

Knowledge from sensation has countless examples: ice is cold and will cool other things; fire is hot and will heat other things; a clear glass of pure water is transparent; rocks are hard and can break less-hard things; and a kilometer takes longer to walk than 10 meters. I also include inner sense, such as: I feel a pain in my finger; I am aware that exactly one minute has elapsed since I started paying attention to the passage of time; I remember the last occasion I had a cold drink; and I am suddenly aware right now that I am writing this very sentence, just as you are that you are reading it.

Revelation is a more contentious mode of knowledge. Many people would claim that it is not a mode of knowledge at all, because they deny that there is any supernatural (not obtainable from our senses or our reason) realm from which such knowledge could come to us. However, Christians (among others) assert that such a realm does exist, that it is the source of knowledge not available by other modes, and that the source of such knowledge is God. Other religions of the world might also accept this exact model, but they would deny that the Judeo-Christian God is the source of such knowledge. Some Hindus, for example, might accept this model but would substitute a very different version of God for the Judeo-Christian Deity. And the means by which "God" chooses to engage in the process of revelation will vary from religion to religion. However, any revelation fitting a model such as mine will have to share the same characteristics that I will describe in what follows later. Examples of Christian revelation (which are also propositions not derivable from sensation or reason) include: a resurrection of the dead will occur; God will judge and reward/punish according to the moral law as He has defined it; and Jesus existed as God prior to His appearance on earth as a man.

Reason plays two roles in this model, and, as we will see, it is a critical point.

First, reason is the source of some knowledge. By "reason" I mean deductive reason. "Inductive reason," as it is sometimes called (and better referred to as "induction"), is properly a form of knowledge by sensation. See David Hume, particularly *An Enquiry Concerning Human Understanding,* for a thorough analysis of the link between induction and sensation—it is something that I believe that he gets exactly right. By "reason" as a mode of knowledge, I mean knowledge derived from deductive processes. Examples include: the Pythagorean theorem and other geometrical truths; the principle of addition and other mathematical truths; "P ⊃ P" and other logical truths; and the conclusions of valid arguments that have true premises.

But reason also plays a second role in this model. Deductive reason acts as the adjudicator of all three modes of knowledge. This is to say, propositions claimed as true from the three modes of knowledge cannot violate deductive logic. However, it is also a contentious claim, and again, one could write a whole book about it. But let me explain further, and you will see what I mean. The basic idea here is consistency, and what Locke most cared about was the logical law of noncontradiction. We too emphasize the law of noncontradiction, although all the laws of logic come into play. For the Bible to claim inconsistent things would bring its value as a form of revelation into question. Of course, there might be ways to resolve apparent inconsistencies (as I believe that there are for the supposed "contradictions" people "find" in the Bible), but a genuine inconsistency ("Jesus will return to earth someday" and "Jesus is never coming back to earth"), if it existed, would be devastating. Revelation itself and/or Christianity itself might not suffer the pains of such an inconsistency, but certainly the Bible as an exemplar of Christian revelation would.

Knowledge gained by sensation must conform to the principle of noncontradiction as well. Consider two claims about the same pencil: "This pencil is straight" and "This pencil is bent." The second claim arises, of course, from viewing the pencil partially immersed in a clear glass of water. Sensation provides us with both propositions, yet because of the principle of noncontradiction we are convinced that both propositions cannot be true of the same pencil. As a result we appeal to other purported facts provided by sensation: in this case, refractive properties of light. But the propositions that make up our knowledge about the refractive properties of light must themselves be consistent, and they must not be inconsistent with other knowledge that we have.

Notice that both sensation and revelation have "claimed, but not known" regions that lie outside of the circle of reason. Such regions denote propositions that we believe, yet that also violate the law of noncontradiction. In both modes almost invariably such violations of reason occur as the result of not being aware of implications of other propositions. For example, many Christians hold two propositions to be clearly revealed in the Bible: "God's grace is all-sufficient" and "It is impossible for us to be perfectly sinless as long as we are in these bodies with their fallen natures." I have tried to show in this book that one cannot hold both of these propositions to be true. The implications of both result in an inconsistency. I argue that the second one of them is really in the "claimed, but not known" region of revelation, and that it is inconsistent with other propositions that we really do know from revelation. Thus I have argued that the second one is the one to discard, in order to maintain consistency in our set of knowledge by revelation.

People rarely are blatantly irrational or hold obviously inconsistent propositions to be both true. As I said, these two "claimed, but not known" regions almost invariably contain propositions the im-

MFAUP-8

plications of which we do not yet recognize.

Notice also the gray and black areas of overlap between modes of knowledge. For example, the Bible says that human beings die, and we do have sensible evidence to the effect that this proposition is true. Both revelation and sensation sustain it, and no violation of the law of noncontradiction seems immediately apparent. Furthermore, biblical literalists will claim that the earth has widespread sensible evidence of a worldwide flood, which is consistent with biblical revelation. Christians can justifiably believe the revelation of the Bible on this point as long as that flood proposition does not violate the principle of noncontradiction in some way.

This model does not claim that revelation must not contradict any of the propositions of sensation. What it does say is that revelation must not contradict knowledge by sensation. This is to say that if a proposition derived from revelation and one emerging from sensation contradict each other, then reason says that (at least) one or the other proposition is not knowledge. Just as the pencil example shows how a contradiction within the mode of sensation must be resolved by denying one of the propositions (in that case, rejecting the "bent" proposition by appeal to other propositions derived from sensation), a contradiction between propositions of revelation and sensation must be resolved by falsifying one of the propositions. Christians who believe in the biblical revelation of a flood must find ways of denying sensory evidence to the contrary.

The black area in which sensation and revelation overlap outside of the mode of reason is one in which sensation and revelation contradict each other, yet propositions are still believed in this region. As with the "claimed, but not known" regions of sensation and revelation, almost invariably this region gets defined by unrecognized implications of other propositions from sensation and revelation. As I have stated earlier in this book, I believe that theistic evolutionists have a number of propositions in this region. The implications of Christianity and their particular commitments to science produce an inconsistent set of propositions. While they claim to "know" each of the propositions in this set, not all of them can be true. Some of them must be false, despite the fact that theistic evolutionists claim to believe all of them.

Paying close attention to the overlaps between sensation and revelation is a crucial issue for Christians, and we should be especially careful to consider the implications of our beliefs so that we do not believe propositions in that black region. We must, in intellectual honesty, detect and resolve such inconsistencies. Perhaps we have misunderstood the Bible on one or more points, or perhaps our sensory evidence is not reliable. But it will not do to remain willfully ignorant or irrational about the implications of our beliefs, particularly in this crucial region.

Considering the "claimed, but not known" regions of this neo-Lockean model, it is worth briefly developing the point that it will not appeal to some Eastern religion believers. As one example, Zen Buddhism asserts that human knowledge is not bounded by reason as I have defined it. It would argue that the "claimed, but not known" regions of this model are precisely where to begin the journey to ultimate truth, and the human capacity to grasp ultimate truth is boundless. Zen koans are meditative exercises designed to effectively flagellate the reasoning mind into "giving up." Zen teaches that the violation of the law of noncontradiction (and other laws of logic) is a necessary condition to enlightenment. Of course, the laws of logic are central to our ability to think about and articulate propositions, which is why Zen claims that ultimate truth is ineffable and nonpropositional.

Back in the realm of propositions, since Christianity is decidedly a propositional religion, a few more points are worth considering.

To begin with, knowledge from sensation is uncertain. Only knowledge from reason is certain. As I noted in the glossary under Empirical, if I count 28 chairs in a room and later count 30, I never question the principle of addition—I cannot! Instead I question my count or what happened in the room between my counts. I will make this point stronger. The principles of reason—the laws of logic—are the necessary basis of thinking itself. Someone attempting to deny $P \supset P$ must employ that very principle in the attempt. It is impossible to think *at all,* much less *about* anything, apart from the principles of reason.[2] In this sense I can talk about the "primacy of reason."

Immediately many Christians get concerned that the "primacy of reason" threatens revelation. They regard revelation as primary. Indeed, some quote various authorities to the effect that anyone who elevates reason above revelation is placing human wisdom above divine wisdom.

Before I resolve that concern, let me add to it a little bit. On this neo-Lockean model of knowledge, revelation is uncertain, just as sensation is. While this might strike some as heretical on its face, it doesn't take much thinking about it to realize that the propositions of revelation *must* be uncertain. If they were certain, in the same manner as the principle of addition, then there would be no role for faith. Faith, thought of first as a matter of believing, is about interpreting and weighing evidence. Consider that the neo-Lockean model is one of human knowledge. It is a model of how we get in touch with some facts, not what the facts really are. The universe contains endless facts. We access some of them through the senses, some by reason, and some by revelation. Some we cannot in principle ever know. However, we also take as "facts" or "truths" many of our own interpretations of the data we get from the sensation and revelation modes of knowledge. Indeed, there is no such thing as a noninterpreted proposition from either sensation or revelation. Our "knowledge" is what is uncertain in the realms of sensation and revelation, and that is because our "knowledge" in these realms is subject to interpretation and to reason itself.

Now, let's get back to the primacy of reason over revelation. I have yet to hear the hermeneutical model that allows for inconsistencies in biblical interpretation. So before you state, "The Bible and the Bible only," as though you can know things from Scripture that literally violate the principles of reason, let me warn you that casting reason to the wind like that only invites responses such as "Of course you do . . . and don't." If our criteria for evaluating revelation includes violating the law of noncontradiction, then we elicit absurd responses to our own criteria.

Some will now say, "God has not placed Himself on trial in the Bible in words, logic, or rhetoric." And they may assume that such a statement means that God's revelations to us can be entirely inconsistent and yet are still true nevertheless. But at most such a statement can mean that God as He is in Himself (as He really is, entirely apart from how we think about Him and apart from how we perceive Him) is beyond our reason (just as this model states). Thus we should not presume that we are getting a picture from the Bible of God as He is in Himself. But note that such a statement about God not placing Himself on trial itself relies upon the principles of reason. The statement is a negation—it asserts that something is *not* the case about God. Without the logical principle of negation, I can have no clue what this statement supposedly declares about God, and the Bible is chock-full of negated statements.

Furthermore, the principle of disjunction is there as well: words, logic, or rhetoric are disjoined. God does not put Himself on trial to any of them. The Bible is full of statements about God in disjunctive form as well. It has conjunctions and conditionals too. Indeed, how can we think or say anything about God, including this "on trial" statement itself, without using words, logic, and rhetoric? Our "on trial" statement itself fails the supposed criteria, unless we realize that it is about how God is in Himself rather than about how we must think about Him. Paradoxes such as "Can God make a stone so heavy that He can't lift it?" are paradoxes about how we must think about God, given that our reason is and must have primacy. They do not threaten or address God as He is in Himself. The proper answer to such paradoxical questions is always "I can't know."

When I have been asked whether or not God can do or know things that violate our logic, I respond by saying, "I can say absolutely nothing about how God is in Himself. The revelations He has given us are necessarily couched in human language and logic, so that they can reach us where we are, but they do not constrain God in Himself. Any such paradoxes, then, involve our language and logic rather than God in Himself." Here is the sense in which God has not placed *Himself* on trial via our words, logic, or rhetoric.

The whole idea of the primacy of revelation over reason conflates the two roles reason plays in this model. As adjudicator of knowledge, reason is and must be primary—we cannot even think at all, including about the propositions of revelation, without reason fulfilling its proper role. However, as a mode of knowledge, reason is just one of the three, and it is not sufficient to provide us with all of the knowledge that God wants us to have. In fact, the most important knowledge we humans require *must* come to us via revelation. In that sense, revelation does have primacy over reason.

To sum up, sensation and revelation are on a par in terms of uncertainty. We must adjudicate both by reason, and only reason can determine possible solutions to inconsistencies between the two modes of knowledge. Faith and interpretation are necessary components of knowledge through the senses and revelation, and both components make propositions derived from sensation and revelation uncertain. Reason as adjudicator provides the very tools by which interpretation can take place and creates the fabric upon which faith can paint any picture. However, as a mode of knowledge, reason, with all its certainty, offers only a tiny subset of all the knowledge we can and do have. Revelation provides the most important knowledge. As adjudicator, reason has primacy over revelation. But when thought of as modes of knowledge, revelation has primacy over reason.

At this point, I well realize that for many people I have raised more questions than I have answered. Just a few include: How can this model address religions and philosophies that begin by denying this model? How do we properly weight evidence arising from the different modes of knowledge? And how can this model distinguish between putative revelations? But despite these and other questions, I believe that this model provides a solid basis for Christians to think about how they relate and prioritize the various sorts of knowledge they have. It allows much room for further thought, discussion, and study, and I enthusiastically urge you on to these activities. May the Lord bless you in all of them.

---

[1] I am using no particular definition of "knowledge" from epistemological theorizing. "Justified, true belief" is as good as any for my purposes, but here is not the place to defend a particular epistemological viewpoint. Thus I use the word "knowledge" loosely here, implying just enough to connect it with the law of noncontradiction: you cannot claim to "know" two inconsistent propositions.

[2] The Buddha is supposed to have said, "The no-mind no-thinks no-thoughts about no-things." Such is the intentional denial of the primacy of reason.

An INSPIRING STORY of COURAGE and HOPE

CAROLYN SUTTON

When nothing is left, you still have God

LEANING On GOD'S HEART

Foreword by E. Lonnie Melashenko

Leaning on God's Heart

Diagnosed with cancer, Carolyn Sutton faced her soul's darkest night. In the midst of that darkness, she placed her life in God's hands and discovered that when nothing was left, she still had God. Her story will inspire anyone facing a difficult time—a "cancer" in life—whether it is illness, abuse, grief, financial crisis, or divorce. Paperback, 128 pages. 978-0-8127-0433-4.

3 Ways to Shop
- Visit your local Adventist Book Center®
- Call 1-800-765-6955
- Order online at www.AdventistBookCenter.com

REVIEW AND HERALD®
PUBLISHING ASSOCIATION
Since 1861 www.reviewandherald.com

DISCOVER A LOVE THAT WILL CHANGE YOUR LIFE

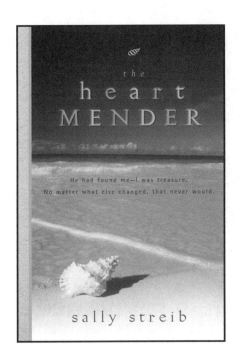

As a child and as a wife, Sally Streib was told that she was worthless, that she would never amount to anything. But her life journey proves how wrong humans can be. Now Sally shares her story of struggle and renewal—along with the biblical stories of other women restored by Jesus—and reveals how God's love can fill empty hearts with a sense of worth, purpose, and joy. 0-8280-1890-1. Paperback, 160 pages.

Can we trust in the ancient writings of the Bible to express the will of God for us?

Yes, when trusted as God's Word, the Bible has the power to energize and motivate us to live the kind of lives that will glorify God. As you read the pages of *God's Book of Wisdom,* you'll be convinced that the Bible is dependable, relevant, and life-changing. 978-0-8280-2017-6. Paperback.

Discover the Bible's relevance for your life today.

Thy word is a lamp unto my feet and a light unto my path.

—Psalms 119:105

Surprising Things Happen When You

Follow God

When God called Curt DeWitt to be a missionary in Africa, Curt found himself fighting off spitting cobras, helping capture criminals, and spiritually wrestling with the powers of darkness. In this hilarious account of his African adventures Curt proves that ending up where you least expected can be more exciting and satisfying than you ever imagined.

Paperback, 156 pages.
978-0-8280-1942-2.

WHY DO WE NEED GOD WHEN WE SEEM TO HAVE ALL WE NEED?

Seven Reasons Why Life Is Better With God

Nathan Brown

Christianity is often styled as an answer to our problems, particularly for those who have no options left. But what about those who seem to have everything going for them? who are well off, well fed, well educated, faced with many different opportunities, and apparently doing OK?

The truth is that we don't have to hit rock bottom to need God. This book ponders seven reasons life is better with God—when things are bad, God can make them better; when things are good, God makes them better still. 978-0-8127-0436-5. Paperback, 160 pages.

3 WAYS TO SHOP

- Visit your local ABC
- Call 1-800-765-6955
- www.AdventistBookCenter.com

REVIEW AND HERALD ®
PUBLISHING ASSOCIATION
Since 1861 | www.reviewandherald.com